Helion & Company Limited
Unit 8 Amherst Business Centre
Budbrooke Road
Warwick
CV34 5WE
England
Tel. 01926 499 619
Email: info@helion.co.uk
Website: www.helion.co.uk
Twitter: @helionbooks
Visit our blog http://blog.helion.co.uk/

Photographs: unless stated otherwise, all the photographs used in this volume have been obtained in form of prints from the Military Museum of Hanoi and the Vietnam News Agency, in the Socialist Republic of Vietnam, which in turn sourced them from multiple official sources and news agencies abroad.

Designed & typeset by Farr out Publications, Wokingham, Berkshire
Cover design by Paul Hewitt, Battlefield Design (www.battlefield-design.co.uk)

ISBN 978-1-913336-24-0

British Library Cataloguing-in-Publication Data
A catalogue record for this book is available from the British Library

Contents

Note: In order to simplify the use of this book, all names, locations and geographic designations are as provided in *The Times World Atlas*, or other traditionally accepted major sources of reference, as of the time of described events. Correspondingly, the term 'Congo' designates the area of the former Belgian colony of the Congo Free State, granted independence as the Democratic Republic of the Congo in June 1960 and in use until 1971 when the country was renamed Republic of Zaire, which, in turn, reverted to Democratic Republic of the Congo in 1997, and which remains in use today. As such, Congo is not to be mistaken for the former French colony of Middle Congo (Moyen Congo), officially named the Republic of the Congo on its independence in August 1960, also known as Congo-Brazzaville.

Dedication

For Brigade 2506 and the Makasi

Abbreviations

ACU	Agrupación Católica Universitaria
ACU	Advisory Committee on Uranium
AM	Agrupación Montecristi
ANC	Congolese National Army
AVG	American Volunteer Group
BAF	Belgian Air Force
BGCC	Banque Genevoise de Commerce et de Crédit
BMI	Bureau of Military Intelligence
BOI	Bureau of Investigation
BRAC	Bureau for the Repression of Communist Activities
BSIS	British Secret Intelligence Services
CAF	Chinese Air Force
CARAMAR	Caribbean Aeromarine Corporation
CAT	Chinese Air Transport
CAT	Civil Air Transport
CCT	Cuban Confederation of Workers
CCP	Chinese Communist Party
CDP	Christian Democratic Party
CGTG	Confederación General de Trabajadores de Guatemala
CNCG	Confederación Nacional Campesina de Guatemala
COI	Coordinator of Information
CIA	Central Intelligence Agency
CIDA	Comite Interamericano de Desarrollo Agricola
CIG	Central Intelligence Group
CINSTRIKE	Commander in Chief, Strike Command
CONACO	Congolese National Convention
CNL	Conseil National de Libération
CVP	Cuban Volunteer Program
DOD	Department of Defense
DRC	Democratic Republic of the Congo
DRE	Directorio Revolucionario Estudiantil
ERT	Emergency Response Team
FAC	Force Aérienne Congolaise
FAK	Force Aérienne Katangaise
FAR	Revolutionary Armed Forces
FATAC	Force Aérienne Tactique au Congo
FBI	Federal Bureau of Investigation
FEU	Federacion Estudiantil Universitaria
FHA	Federal Housing Administration
FNC	Force Navale Congolaise
FNL	National Liberation Front
FRD	Frente Revolucionario Democratico
GVC	Grupo Voluntario Cubano
HUAC	House Un-American Activities Committee
IGSS	Instituto Guatemalteco de Seguridad Social
INRA	National Institute for Agrarian Reform
KMT	Kuomintang
LCI	Landing Craft Infantry
LCS	Light Cargo Ship
MBSOG	Maritime Branch of the Special Operations Group
MDC	Movimento Demócrata Cristiano
MPLA	Popular Movement for the Liberation of Angola
MRR	Movimento de Recuperación Revolucionaria
NBCI	National Bureau of Criminal Identification
NIE	National Intelligence Estimate
NME	National Military Establishment
NSC	National Security Council
NSRB	National Security Resources Board
OAS	Organisation of American States
OAU	Organisation for African Unity
ONI	Office of Naval Intelligence
OPC	Office of Policy Coordination
OSP	Office of Special Projects
OSS	Office of Strategic Services
OWI	Office of War Information
PCF	French Communist Party
PGT	Partido Guatemalteco del Trabajo
PLR	Partido de Liberación Radical
PPC	Partido del Pueblo Cubano
PRC	Partido Revolucionaro Cubano
PRC	Peoples' Republic of China
PSB	Psychological Strategy Board
RAF	Royal Air Force
SAD	Special Activities Division
SFIO	French Section of the Workers' International
SOD	Special Operations Division
STEG	Sindicato de Trabajadores de Educacion de Guatemala
UAR	United Arab Republic
UFCO	United Fruit Company
UMHK	Union Minière de Haut-Katanga
UNOC	United Nations Operations Congo
UK	United Kingdom
UN	United Nations
USA	United States of America
USAF	United States Air Force
USSR	Union of Socialist Soviet Republics
USSS	United States Secret Service
VOA	Voice of America
WIGMO	Western International Ground Maintenance Organisation

1
The Development of the United States Covert War Apparatus

The fear that Communism in some way undermined the traditional social order in America was not a product of the aftermath of the Second World War and neither was it part of a phenomenon that appeared overnight. Indeed, some form of Socialism – the ideological roots of Communism – had made an appearance in the United States as early as the beginning of the nineteenth century: utopian socialists such as Frenchman Charles Fourier are known to have inspired the creation of intentional communities and to have promoted communal associations. Although utopian socialism was mainly adopted by religious movements, its tenets were later taken up by labour movements such as the Workingmen's Party, the forerunner of the Socialist Labor Party (SLP) created in the 1880s making it the oldest socialist party in the United States. Presided by Eugene Victor Debs, the SLP opposed US entry into the First World War and its opposition led the US government to repress many of the activities perceived as being linked to anarchism and, later, Bolshevism. Such was the influence of the SLP in the first decades of the twentieth century, President Woodrow Wilson had found it necessary to set up the Committee on Public Information in 1917 to convince the public that America was going to war for the right reasons. During this period known as the First Red Scare, Wilson's government also put in place legislative measures intended to halt the activities of organised labour movements seen as being behind the Seattle General Strike, and the Boston Police Strike of 1919. The Espionage Act (1917), the Sedition Act (1918), and the Immigration Act (1918) were all intended to root out seditionists and they made it possible for the US government to deport anyone suspected of being an agent of the Soviet Union or carrying out treasonable activities. One of these agents, an Italian activist called Luigi Galleani presented a particular interest. Though Galleani was deported in 1919, it was suspected that his followers, the Galleanists had carried out bombings on Wall Street that killed 38 people. Even more stringent legislation was voted through Congress in reaction to the bombings and it enabled the US Department of Justice to organise the so-called Palmer Raids. Taking their name from Attorney General Alexander Mitchell Palmer, the objective of the raids was to root out, arrest and deport leftists. Identifying Italians and Jews as those most susceptible to initiate subversive activities against the United States, the Immigration or Johnson-Reed Act of 1924 banned all immigration from Asia and prevented Southern and Eastern Europeans from emigrating to America in large numbers. More legislation intended to limit seditious activities followed in the 1930s. Indeed, both the Fish Committee set up in 1930, and the McCormack-Dickstein Committee (1934-1937) sought to examine suspicious anti-American sentiment running through US institutions.

The impression that anti-American activists were operating inside some of the most sensitive areas of US policymaking was not without a certain degree of foundation. In 1941, it was discovered that the Nazi-sponsored Duquesne Spy Ring had been operating in the US since the early 1930s and, furthermore, that its leader, Frederick Duquesne was an employee of the US government's Works Progress Administration. Duquesne's association with the enemy only served to heighten public fears of enemy infiltration and they seemed validated when Operation Pastorius was uncovered in 1942. Involving eight Germans resident in the US who were plotting attacks on US soil, Operation Pastorius occurred two years before the FBI uncovered Operation Elster. This was an attempt by Hitler to gather intelligence on America's technological capabilities by landing two agents off the coast of Maine by submarine. Public intrigue surrounding Operation Elster was so great that it inspired Alfred Hitchcock to direct the 1942 film *Saboteur*, and Hollywood also took advantage of public interest to produce *They Came to Blow Up America* in 1943. The US film industry was itself accused of harbouring communist agents and of spreading Soviet propaganda. In order to root out seditionists supposedly hiding in the shadows in Tinseltown, the House Un-American Activities Committee (HUAC) hauled actors, producers or screenwriters before its public tribunals. Around 300 of them were subsequently blacklisted by studios and were no longer deemed as being employable in the film industry. They included Charlie Chaplin, Orson Welles, Paul Robeson and Yip Harburg, the composer of all of the songs in the Wizard of Oz.

Captain Claire Chennault was the founder of the Flying Tigers and later created Air America. (Louisiana Digital Library)

Throughout the modern history of the United States, the task of unearthing domestic and foreign threats to America and its institutions was handled by a number of government agencies each with its own mandate and each with its own operational areas. As is the case with anti-American movements, these agencies were products of their time and responded to the requirements of whichever administration dictated US domestic and foreign policies. Nevertheless, these agencies were not monolithic entities, and as requirements needed to be adapted to suit the time and circumstances so did their activities. Domestically, the

FBI was a development of the Bureau of Investigation (BOI), the National Bureau of Criminal Identification (NBCI) and the United States Secret Service (USSS) whereas an early version of the Central Intelligence Agency (CIA) can be found within George Washington's Continental Army and a further development in intelligence gathering was the creation of the Contingent Fund of Foreign Intercourse in 1790.[1] This fund enabled Washington to conceal the purposes of intelligence activities and in doing so set the precedent for the president to finance covert actions without first seeking approval from the US Congress. Structures put in place to obtain intelligence on military matters also developed throughout the nineteenth century. The Bureau of Military Intelligence (BMI) was created in 1863, the Office of Naval Intelligence (ONI) was created in 1882, and the Military Intelligence Division was created in 1885. These were the first professional intelligence gathering services devoted entirely to supporting military operations. Their operatives were used to incite revolution in Panama and to justify the annexation of the Panama Canal in 1907.[2]

Though the need for intelligence services remained throughout the First World War and during the interwar period, the first efforts to provide coordination between the different entities did not come about until 1941 when President Roosevelt dispatched General William Donovan to London to assess Great Britain's ability to defend itself after the capitulation of France. Inspired by what the head of the British Secret Intelligence Services (BSIS), Colonel Stewart Menzies, had to say on intelligence management and covert operations, Donovan returned to the US to report back to Roosevelt. It was not long after that Roosevelt ordered that Donovan create a new civilian service that would complement the military in much the same way as the BSIS. Establishing the Office of the Coordinator of Information (COI) on 11 July 1941, its role was to "collect and analyze all information and data which may bear upon the national security". Despite its promise the COI was a short-lived entity and differences of opinion on how best to spread propaganda and provide the government with information led to a splitting of the COI's functions in June 1942. From now on, activities would be divided between the Office of Strategic Services (OSS) and the Office of War Information (OWI).[3]

Assigned to conduct espionage, sabotage and morale operations against the Axis powers and to carry out research and analysis on the enemy capabilities, at its peak the OSS was to employ almost 13,000 men and women with around 7,500 of its agents serving overseas and operating in China, Burma, North Africa, India or Europe.[4] However, just as previous wars had changed America's perspective on the gathering of intelligence, the Cold War also brought about the realisation that the OSS was not adapted to the changing requirements and the fear that a new war could break out at any moment. After the disbanding of the OSS in September 1945, high-level discussions now focused on how to deal with the threat posed by the Soviet Union. As had been the case with Nazi Germany, US Joint Chiefs of Staff began to fear that the Soviet Union would also seek to expand its influence throughout Europe and, then, seek to gain influence in the Mediterranean, the Persian Gulf, northern China, and Korea. It was also concluded that any open attempt to stop this expansion could lead to war.[5]

The first attempt at setting up an agency whose principal role was to deal with the new Communist threat occurred in January 1946 with the creation of the Central Intelligence Group (CIG). Given the mission of correlating "all relevant information available to the US government on any given issue of national security", it was developments in the Mediterranean that would have a resounding impact on US foreign affairs and on the need for an intelligence gathering service endowed with specific missions.[6] In effect, in February 1947 British authorities informed their American counterparts that in view of its commitment to the rebuilding of the United Kingdom following the Second World War it was withdrawing financial support to Greece and Italy. With fears having already been aired on possible Soviet expansion into southern Europe, and with a second Red Scare in full swing on the domestic front – Senator Joseph McCarthy's activities coming into the mix – on 12 March 1947 President Harry S. Truman made a speech to a joint session of Congress giving warning of the danger now faced by the United States. As well as the Soviet threat in Greece and Turkey, expounded Truman, the Soviet Union had failed to withdraw its troops from northern Iran in respect of the 1943 Tehran Declaration, it had made 'frequent attempts "to coerce and intimidate Poland, Rumania and Bulgaria", and it had rejected the 1946 Baruch Plan which called for international control over nuclear weapons.[7] Becoming known as the Truman Doctrine, this speech outlined Truman's promise "to support free peoples who [were] resisting attempted subjugation by armed minorities or by outside pressures".[8] In late June 1947, it was reinforced by the signing of the National Security Act 4-A, and this piece of legislation laid the foundations for the creation of four new services: the CIA, the National Security Council (NSC), the National Security Resources Board (NSRB), and the National Military Establishment (NME).[9]

Headed by Rear Admiral Roscoe H. Hillenkoetter of the US Navy, the role of the CIA was to advise "the National Security Council in matters concerning such intelligence activities of the Government departments and agencies as relate to national security" and to make "recommendations to the National Security Council for the coordination of such intelligence activities of the departments and agencies of the Government as relate to the national security". Moreover, and in addition to its role of correlating and evaluating intelligence, in what is an acknowledgement of the perceived need to take a more proactive approach towards intelligence gathering, the CIA was authorised "to perform such additional services of common concern" and to "perform such other functions and duties related to intelligence".[10] The "additional services" and "other functions and duties" are, of course, an implicit reference to types of activity: covert and clandestine.[11]

One of the first opportunities to test the effectiveness of covert operations came shortly after the CIA was created. In France, a country with a strong socialist tradition, the interwar years had seen the growth of an alliance of left-wing movements which included the French Communist Party (PCF), the French Section of the Workers' International (SFIO) and the Radical Party led to the creation of the Popular Front. Holding wide public support for its ideals such as democratic socialism, social democracy, social liberalism and communism, in 1936 the Popular Front won legislative elections which saw Léon Blum elected Prime Minister. Ceasing to exist in 1938, the Popular Front had nevertheless managed to proceed with many social reforms during its short time in office and, while this ensured a political legacy evident in French society today, it was its stance against the rise of Nazi Germany and Vichy regime collaborators which meant that its influence over French politics continued in the post-war years.[12] With a highly unstable political and military situation developing in France, the left and right-wing spectrums of French politics fought to decide who would carry the Fourth French Republic through the ordeals of having to fight a colonial war in Indochina, and reuniting a French people deeply divided along political lines. Resistance to the type of pre-war social

The Curtiss P-40 Warhawk was used by the Flying Tigers in operations over Burma and China. (Airplane Geeks)

reforms advocated by the Popular Front came from business leaders in the post-war years.

Strong popular support for socialist ideals expressed in elections held in 1946, led contemporary US intelligence to believe that the PCF could seize power whenever it wanted. Worried by the potential of seeing a communist regime on its doorstep, UK intelligence services also started to devise plans to counter the communist threat. Working in conjunction, US and UK authorities, therefore, created the Blue Plan which was a project intended to stop the PCF from coming to power through the possible use of a surrogate army. Blue Plan agents secretly contacted wealthy industrialists with the aim of funding a secret war, and they included the Peugeot brothers and the heads of other leading car manufacturers who had been affected by a long series of strikes initiated by powerful unions. Later, in June 1947, and in the face of continued communist-backed industrial action, the CIA, MI6 and French paramilitaries had even gone to the point of planning a coup d'état.[13] While this drastic measure was never put into force, a further CIA plan given the name 'Paix et Liberté' (peace and freedom) provided funds and propaganda to anti-communist elements in order to stop communist parties from gaining a foothold through further industrial strife.[14] With the number of geographical areas open to possible Soviet infiltration on the increase, US authorities came to the conclusion that devising the means to counter communist expansion required greater organisation. In 1948, this led to the recasting of the Office of Special Projects (OSP) and the creation of the Office of Policy Coordination (OPC).[15] Headed by former OSS agent Frank Wisner, the role of the OPC was to specialise in psychological (psyops) and paramilitary operations. Another war which was to have a significant influence on the development of US intelligence services was the Korean War (1950-1953). Seeing both the Soviet Union and China provide help to North Korean forces led, once more, to the need to provide reliable intelligence as well as the need to provide more weapons and weaponry. In respect of these needs, National Security Council directive 10/2 saw the creation of the Psychological Strategy Board (PSB) on 4 April 1951. Its task was to weigh up the "desirability and feasibility" of proposed covert programmes and major covert operations and to focus its efforts on psyops, or attacking communism through winning the 'hearts and minds' of populations in areas under threat.[16] In addition to its activities abroad, its role also included convincing the American public that its way of life was in danger and that a common approach to the threat was needed. The formulating of this consensus would be achieved through the publishing of anti-communist propaganda; through the use of buzzwords such as 'containment' to persuade populations of the evil nature of the enemy's intentions; and through radio stations such as Voice of America (VOA). Extensive broadcasts by VOA were to be heard in Eastern Europe and in Latin America with audiences being promised that they might hear 'bad news' but, at least, it was the 'truth'.[17]

However much the CIA attempted to disrupt communist-inspired political activity in France or in Italy, the modifications to the geopolitical landscape brought on by the defeat of once powerful empires and the withdrawal of others introduced the need to adopt more direct methods of determining the outcome of conflict between nationalist and communist forces. A case in point is China, where after the Second World War Mao Zedong of the Chinese Communist Party (CCP) and Chiang Kai-shek of Kuomintang (KMT) reignited an ideological feud which threatened to upset the political balance in the Far East. Confronted with the news that the CCP had made rapid territorial gains in Manchuria against the KMT, barely five weeks after Bockscar had dropped "Fat Man" over Nagasaki, the United States was already toying with the idea of deploying troops to key points in China to 'aid order restoration'.[18] It did so in September when the first of 50,000 marines entered Tientsin in northern China to protect key infrastructural installations.[19] After securing this city made famous by the Boxer Rebellion of 1899–1901, these marines fought against Zedong's Eighth Route Army using heavy machine guns and spotter aircraft.[20] Though the use of official regular forces was one means with which the US could counter communist aggression and limit its spread to neighbouring areas, the conflict in China also opened the CIA's eyes to the possibility of using unofficial irregular forces as a proxy army to represent United States' interests. In this respect, it is linked historically to the story that will unfold at a later stage in this book.

The United States had already gained some form of unofficial representation in China through the creation of a mercenary air unit known as the 'International Squadron' or the 'Flying Tigers' in 1937.[21] Formed after US Army Air Corps Captain Claire Lee Chennault had befriended Chiang Kai-shek and had become his chief air advisor, the International Squadron would then become the American Volunteer Group (AVG). This was a unit which fought under the colours of the Chinese Air Force (CAF) from 1941-1942 and which was a highly effective force. It gained 297 confirmed victories and lost only four pilots.[22]

Disbanding the AVG in 1943 and taking an early retirement Chennault was drawn back to China on seeing Chiang Kai-shek struggling to overcome Zedong's forces. Spotting an opportunity for another business venture in 1946, Chennault entered into a business partnership with former special assistant to the US Department of Justice Whiting Willauer. Together, they decided that the quickest and easiest way to make money was to start a new airline.[23] Following legal advice from former Roosevelt advisor Thomas Gardiner Corcoran and using his friendship with Chiang Kai-shek to obtain finance, Chennault and Willauer then set up Chinese Air Transport (CAT). Subsequently purchasing over twenty C-46 and C-47 cargo aircraft from the Philippines and from Honolulu,[24] it meant that CAT was able to provide essential supplies to nationalist forces in the fight against Mao Tse-Tung. This type of work proved to be perilous, however, and flights were often carried out in the face of attacks from communist forces. A number of pilots were taken prisoner.[25]

If CAT ran into financial difficulty towards the end of 1948, the CIA had realised by that time how effective a makeshift air force could be. Acquiring CAT and running it as a private business venture, the CIA could operate undetected under the noses of communist forces and, concurrently, it could provide the United States with the plausible deniability it needed when operating covertly in a conflict. Changing the name of the airline to Civil Air Transport in 1949, the CIA's first proprietary airline would form the basis of Air America. Its success then led the CIA to expanding its network of civilian covert contacts. From now on the CIA's tentacles included military operatives such as contract pilots, weapons technicians and arms dealers. Former US Army weapons specialist, Sam Cummings, became one of the CIA's main suppliers. Cummings had snaffled up guns left over from the Second World War and the Korean War and his supplies could be found in use in a number of conflicts. As a sideline, Cummings provided weapons for Hollywood productions,[26] but the CIA used them for more pragmatic purposes such as overthrowing foreign leaders. The first to be overthrown military was Jacobo Arbenz in Guatemala.

2
How to Overthrow a Foreign Leader: Guatemala, 1954

Since the earliest developments in US foreign policy Latin America had held a special place. Indeed, James Monroe's Doctrine of 1823 and Theodore Roosevelt's Corollary of 1904 both provided forewarnings to European powers on the dangers of straying into areas perceived as coming under US influence. Such was the importance of maintaining this influence, some years later Richard Nixon would declare that without it "the United States could not expect to achieve a successful order elsewhere in the world."[1]

From a more specific perspective, the popular revolution which took place in Guatemala in 1944 posed a serious threat to US financial and political interests in the country. Up to that point having backed Jorge Ubico Casteñada but seeing him deposed and replaced by Jacobo Arbenz Guzman, Guatemala's subsequent adoption of socialist policies generated fears in the State Department that it would soon turn towards experimentation with communism. As the Domino Theory dominated political beliefs on the best methods to contain communism, it was thought that Guatemala's example would be followed by its neighbours and that soon the whole of Central America would fall under Soviet influence. This had to be prevented by hook or by crook.

As irony would have it, the first foreign ventures in Guatemala were set up in 1844 by Belgian King Léopold I, the father of King Leopold II and the father of the man who would lead Belgium into the Congo through the acquisition of still unclaimed land. In similar circumstances, King Léopold I laid claim to carry out commercial activities and to exploit the natural resources that lie in the Izabal region of eastern Guatemala.[2] Some years later, it was Germany's turn to broaden the extent of its economic interests when it also set up coffee plantations in Guatemala's northern regions. As well as being a highly profitable affair for investors, Germany's forays into this part of Central America were highly influential in cultural terms and explain why many Guatemalan's can boast of being of German origin. One Guatemalan who was able to make this claim was future president Jacobo Arbenz.

The influence of the United States in Guatemala was to increase significantly after it had defeated Spanish forces in 1898. Becoming the dominant power in the region and warning other powers that they would be attacked without hesitation, it was commercial interests that played an important role in bringing American businessmen to a country sandwiched between Mexico to its north, and Belize, Honduras and El Salvador to its east and south respectively.

Though dotted with lakes and covered by tropical jungles, Guatemala possessed climatic conditions which were perfect for the growing of sugar, coffee and fruit. Taking advantage of America's increasing ties to the region and encouraged by the opportunities offered by Guatemala's fertile soil, the United Fruit Company (UFCO) was one of the first American companies to expand their business interests to Guatemala.[3] As American political influence expanded concurrently through the invasion of Nicaragua in 1909 and subsequent interventions in Cuba, Panama and the Honduras so did UFCO's activities. Throughout the first decades of the twentieth century UFCO extended its interests to Jamaica, Cuba, the Dominican Republic, Colombia and Ecuador. Eventually possessing up to 40% of Guatemalan farmland, and thus having enormous influence over political decision-making, UFCO also found itself in a position in which it could virtually make its own

Jacobo Arbenz (second from left) with his Salvadorian wife, Maria Vilanova (Latin American Studies)

The United Fruit Company owned up to 40% of Guatemalan territory (Author's collection)

laws. Indeed, the company was exempt from paying taxes and import duties.[4]

As UFCO held such a dominant position in the Guatemalan economy, it is hardly surprising that a popular socialist-inspired revolution was considered as an immediate threat to a purely capitalistic enterprise. These threats were confirmed after Juan José Arévelo Bermojoa came to power as classing himself as a 'spiritual socialist', Arévelo set about introducing social and economic reforms such as the establishment of a minimum wage and the development of Guatemala's agrarian-based economy.[5] His policies were a far call from those of Ubico who opposed industrialisation, and who forbade the use of terms such as 'communist', 'trade union', 'strike', and 'labour rights'.[6]

Very soon after the introduction of Arévelo's reforms, more concerns were raised by UFCO over the government's increasing empathy for the rights of workers and its lack of sympathy for the demands of business and the need to make profits. In effect, new labour laws enabled workers to set up representative bodies and, therefore, to demand higher wages while UFCO believed that it had become a victim. Matters were not helped when strikes over pay and conditions at UFCO plantations in Bananera and Tiquisate led to significant losses in production. These two plantations covered hundreds of square miles of Guatemalan land and employed up to 40,000 Guatemalans.[7]

In this context of social reform and increased rights for Guatemala's workers, a number of federations were created to represent not just farm labourers but also those working in the health and education sectors. As the 1940s came to a close, and as the 1950s saw the growth of federations such as the Confederación General de Trabajadores de Guatemala (CGTG), the Confederación Nacional Campesina de Guatemala (CNCG), the Sindicato de Trabajadores de Educacion de Guatemala (STEG), or the Instituto Guatemalteco de Seguridad Social (IGSS), US intelligence services began to take a far greater interest in their affairs believing that these federations had undergone a certain degree of communist infiltration. Intelligence reports issued in 1952 noted that these organisations had put themselves into a position whereby they could dominate the administrative machinery. In turn, this would enable federations to influence government decisions, and while they presented themselves as representatives of a "People's Democracy", their true objective was to reduce the influence of the western world to a minimum and leave the door open to communist penetration.[8] One Act of parliament in particular, the Agrarian Reform Law, or Decree 900 was perceived as an attack on US business interests. Introduced in June 1952 by the government of Jacobo Arbenz, this law redistributed unused lands to local peasant farmers. Though around 100,000 Guatemalan families benefitted from this reform,[9] the forced appropriation of land greatly angered UFCO. Not only did it stand to lose an ever-decreasing influence in Guatemalan political affairs, it also faced losing substantial financial involvement.

Of the political groups which had come to prominence during the debates on land reforms, the most prominent was the Partido

José Manuel Fortuny was the founder of the Guatemalan Workers' Party. (Latin American Studies)

Richard Helms was Deputy Director of Central Intelligence in 1952, becoming Director in 1966. (Author's Collection)

CIA Director of Intelligence Allen Dulles pictured with John F. Kennedy. Dulles oversaw operations to remove Jacobo Arbenz and replace him with Carlos Castillo Armas.

Guatemalteco del Trabajo (PGT) founded in 1949 by José Manuel Fortuny. Overtly declaring itself to be communist in its political orientation, the PGT had long been considered by the CIA as a vector through which the Soviet Union could establish a beachhead in Guatemalan affairs and, indeed, in South America as a whole.[10]

Although PGT activists were few in number and had previously failed to spread communist ideology,[11] by March 1952 an increase in its activities and influence led the CIA to produce National Intelligence Estimate 62 (NIE-62). The contents of the report described how communist sympathisers in Guatemala were exercising an influence far out of proportion to their numerical strength, how communist activity could adversely affect US interests, and how this influence constituted a threat to US security. If they had been so successful despite their limited numbers, the CIA concluded this was because there was a lack of opposition to communist ideology.[12] As fears grew in Washington in respect to possible outcomes in Guatemala, the CIA began to examine the ways in which it could create some form of opposition, and began to make contact with the Catholic Church, Guatemalan business leaders, university students, and workers' unions as it had done earlier in France. Above all though, the CIA saw the solution to its quandary in Guatemala as lying in the hands of fervent anti-communist Colonel Castillo Armas. Having taken part in a previously unsuccessful coup against Arévelo in 1950, instead of making further attempts at deposing him Armas had chosen to seek exile in Honduras.

On 17 March 1952, the Deputy Director of Central Intelligence Richard Helms received a report informing him that contact had been made with Armas to discuss the possibility of mounting a coup d'état. Though Castillo Armas initially doubted that he could due to a lack of resources, he was encouraged by the promise of support from ex-President Tiburcio Carias of Honduras, current Honduran president Manuel Galvez, President Anastasio Somoza of Nicaragua and President Rafael Trujillo of the Dominican Republic.[13] Now that Castillo Armas had been identified as a valid candidate to fight

Carlos Castillo Armas became Guatemalan president following the CIA's Operation PBSUCCESS. (Latin American Studies)

against communism, the next step for the CIA was to find 650 men suitable for the job and to equip them with enough weapons. As for these arms, the CIA was able to purchase 500 hand grenades, 180 machine guns, 500 automatic rifles and around 600,000 rounds of ammunition from a person of "utmost confidence".[14]

Despite everything having gone to plan and approval for Operation PBFORTUNE having been given by President Truman in September 1952, by October CIA Director Walter Bedell Smith was informed that the project had been uncovered and that all operational planning had been terminated.[15] Nonetheless, by early summer 1953 and with further reports that Arbenz was becoming increasingly pro-communist, the question of his removal became, once more, the subject of discussions in official circles. The resolve of the CIA to overthrow him hardened over the coming months, and by 18 September 1953 it had come up with a new plan. Described as an "extremely difficult and sensitive operation" that would take eight months to develop, the plan had a preliminary budget amounting to some $3 million.[16] Codenamed PBSUCCESS, its cryptonym gave an indication of the level of confidence involved. Using firstly the creation of an internal insurrection to destabilise the government, the second phase of the operation would involve a paramilitary invasion with the complicity of US allies. In short, these were the classic characteristics of a CIA covert operation.[17]

The first phase of the operation was one that the CIA had very recently perfected in August 1953 when with the cooperation of Great Britain, it had organised the overthrow of Prime Minister Mohammad Mosaddegh of Iran. What it planned to do in Guatemala was to use similar psychological warfare techniques such as drawing up of a list of the 25 most dangerous Guatemalans, and once this was done the CIA would then subject them to character assassination abroad. Another interesting technique, one also

Rafael Trujillo served as president of the Dominican Republic from 1930-1938 and again from 1942-1952. Trujillo strongly supported the overthrow of Jacobo Arbenz. (ThoughtCo)

used during operations against Cuba some years later,[18] was the broadcasting of anti-government propaganda through radio stations such as *Radio Internacional* or *La Voz de la Liberación*. The latter, calling for resistance to communism and support for Castillo Armas gave broadcasts from Miami in an operation known as SHERWOOD.[19] As such, its activities echoed those of Robin Hood and his fight against a tyrannical leader. With 'black' propaganda operations such as these continuing well into 1954, by May of that year Operation PBSUCCESS was ready to move from the propaganda phase to the paramilitary phase.[20]

It was at this point that the CIA's network of covert operators had really come to the fore, and at the end of March in the scope of Operation PBCABOOSE Air America pilots were offered $2,000 per month to take part in missions transferred from operations in the Far East to Miami.[21] Recruited by Whiting Willauer of Civil Air Transport fame, these pilots were to fly around a dozen aircraft some of which had been purchased by Nicaraguan president Anastasio Somoza. They included three C-47 Cargo aircraft, six F-47 Thunderbolt fighter bombers, one P-38 Lightning fighter aircraft, one Cessna 180 and one Cessna 140. As a sign of his friendship and his willingness to cooperate with the United States, these aircraft were based at Puerto Cabezas, Nicaragua.[22] This is the same base used by Cuban exile forces during the Bay of Pigs invasion.

In addition to the Air America pilots, it is interesting to note that many of those involved in PBSUCCESS would also be involved in later operations in Cuba and in the Congo. William 'Rip' Robertson is one man in question. From an early stage Robertson had taken part in the CIA's Executive Action programme, a programme dealing with the removal of foreign leaders, and as far as Guatemala was concerned, Robertson had unsuccessfully attempted to attack a train carrying weapons to support Arbenz's regime.[23] Seven years later Robertson commanded Cuban exile ground forces during the Bay of Pigs operation, and ten years later he led a commando unit made up of other Cuban exiles sent to rescue American hostages held in Stanleyville in the Congo.[24]

Operations to dispose Arbenz included bombing the Guatemalan capital and ports. (Latin American Studies)

As of the summer of 1954 with plans for paramilitary invasion still in the preparatory stage, it seemed that Arbenz was doing everything in his power to convince the Americans that he was aware of their invasion plans and that he was seeking assistance from the Soviet bloc in order to resist it. In June of that year the CIA's Deputy Director of Plans Frank Wisner reported that a shipment of Czechoslovakian arms had been transported by a Swedish-registered vessel named the *Alfhem* to Puerto Barrios. Then, the shipment of mortars, howitzers, grenades, machine guns and other items were taken to inland points. According to Wisner's report, the purchase of these arms valued at $100,000 had taken place in January and February of 1954 when Alfonso Martinez, a personal aid to Arbenz, visited Prague. This visit coincided with Jose Manuel Fortuny's trip to Moscow in order to establish diplomatic relations with Czechoslovakia. Until recently, Fortuny had been the Secretary General of the Guatemalan Communist Party (PGT), and as such he had pressured the Guatemalan government into adopting the agrarian reform laws perceived as so negative by the USA.[25] In addition to the June shipment, the CIA expected Guatemala to continue to bring in arms and noted that various cargo vessels carrying weapons were known to be loading or were at sea.[26]

To all intents and purposes Arbenz's fate had been sealed through his dealings with Soviet powers, and despite his efforts to broker a peace deal with the Americans, by mid-June 1954 the residents of Guatemala City began to expect an invasion by US forces any day. Among them was Ernesto Guevara who had arrived in December 1953 to lend his support to Arbenz. In the meantime, by 17 June in Honduras and in Nicaragua the CAT pilots contracted to the CIA awaited the order to board their P-47 Thunderbolts or P-51 Mustangs. Joined by 480 of Armas's best troops who had gathered in the Honduran towns of Florida, Nueva Octepeque and Macuelizo, the plan was to make small-scale incursions across a broad front to give the impression that a much larger force was at work. Around 200 troops would then attack Puerto Barrios in the northwest of the country while another large group would march on Zacapa. This town near the border with Honduras housed the Guatemalan Army's largest frontier garrison. Other invaders would cross the Guatemalan border from El Salvador to the south.[27]

Insofar as the actual invasion, on 18 June at 2020 hours Armas crossed the border into Guatemala and by 0150 hours his troops had already blown up a bridge at Gualán. Others captured the town of Esquipulas close to the Honduran border the following day and it appeared as if Arbenz was powerless to stop the invasion. Though Armas did suffer a humiliating defeat when attempting to take Puerto Barrios, CIA aircraft strafed trains transporting

Anastasio Somoza Garcia led a dynasty that would rule Nicaragua for over 40 years. Similarly to Trujillo, Somoza provided the CIA with assistance in overthrowing Jacobo Arbenz. (Author's collection)

William 'Rip' Robertson was part of the CIA's Executive Action, a programme that sought to remove leaders seen as unfriendly to US interests abroad. Robertson also played a role in the Bay of Pigs invasion and led a group of Cuban exile commandos in the Congo. (TangoDown63)

Guatemalan troops to conflict zones. After Matamoros Fortress in the Guatemalan capital was bombed on 25 June, Arbenz knew that the time had come to hand in his resignation. Two days later, he walked into the Mexican Embassy to seek political asylum, and two months later the plane taking him to safety landed in Mexico City.[28]

As Operation PBSUCCESS had been so effective and success had been acquired relatively quickly and cheaply, it more or less convinced the Eisenhower administration that covert operations were an inexpensive substitute for the use of armed force in "resisting communist inroads in the Third World."[29] This being said, the CIA's failure to recognise the specificity of the Guatemalan situation lulled Agency and administration officials into a complacency that would prove fatal just a few years later at the Bay of Pigs.[30]

3
From Guatemala to Cuba, 1961

An island of sugar cane plantations, rum and cigars, in the 1950s Cuba gained a reputation as a playground for the rich and famous that frequented hotel casinos such as the Riviera, the Capri, or the Havana Hilton. Underneath the glitz of the lifestyle enjoyed by visitors to the island such as Frank Sinatra and Ava Gardner there lay, however, a culture of corruption, involvement with American Mafioso and drug trafficking. Mobsters such as Al Capone made regular visits to the island during the Prohibition-era to take advantage of the 95-mile distance which separated Cuba from his home on Palm Island, Miami. Charles 'Lucky' Luciano was another. In December 1946, he believed that Cuba was such a safe haven for illegal activities that he even used the capital Havana as a base for a conference with the Sicilian Mafia. Sinatra provided the evening entertainment.

At the root to develop Cuba as a tourist destination and a playground for the rich and famous was President Gerardo Machado. Recognising in the 1920s that prohibition offered his country the opportunity to take the gambling business away from its traditional strongholds, Machado loosened laws and began to construct a mirror-image of a country and lifestyle he greatly admired. Following his election in 1925, Machado even had the Cuban capitol building rebuilt as an exact likeness to the one in Washington, D.C.[1]

Cuba's diplomatic relations with the United States had eased greatly since the Spanish had left the island in 1898, and Machado's position as leader seemed to be secured through Franklin D. Roosevelt's Good Neighbour Policy of 1933 in which the 32nd President of Cuba's northerly neighbour declared that the US was now opposed to intervention in Central and South America. Roosevelt's sentiments were repeated later that year in Montevideo by Secretary of State Cordell Hull. Extending the remits of the Good Neighbor policy, Hull openly declared that the intention of

Carlos Prio Socarras served as Cuban president from 1948 to 1952 until he was deposed by a military coup d'Etat led by Fulgencio Batista. (Author's collection)

Fulgencio Batista served as president of Cuba from 1952 to 1959 before being overthrown during the Cuban Revolution. (Author's collection)

the United States was henceforth to isolate itself from international conflict. This was a stance which held firm until the December 1941 and the Japanese attack on Pearl Harbour.

For much of the Cuban population, the timing and intentions of the Good Neighbor policy could not have come at a worse time. Since 1928 and the beginning of Machado's second term in 1928, it appeared as though the Cuban president was intent on holding on to power by eliminating any source of potential opposition. He embarked on a programme of political repression which saw university organisations shut down and in 1932 created a secret police force called the Porra. This group used violence to repress the activities of the ABC organisation which had vowed to depose and even assassinate Machado.

Political pressure of this type and the intervention of Roosevelt's envoy Summer Welles eventually forced Machado to resign in May 1933. Succeeded in August by Carlos Manuel de Céspedes y Quesada leading a provisional government, a constitutional crisis broke out shortly after De Céspedes assumed power.[2] In spite of efforts to calm the crisis by promising elections to be held in February 1934, on 3 September 1933 Sergeant Fulgencio Batista was at the root of a military known as the Sergeants' Revolt. Starting at Camp Colombia, disorder quickly spread to other military bases. Before long, the revolt had gained the support of some of Cuba's student organisations. Between 10 September 1933 and 10 October 1940 Cuba had a succession of leaders each attempting to manage the economic hardships caused by the fall in world prices for sugar, the island's main export. Some like Jose Barnet or Miguel Gomez lasted for up to seven months while others like Manuel Marquez Sterling only remained president for a matter of hours. In October 1940, Batista, himself, became president remaining in power until October 1944.

Given Batista's second term as president from 1952 to 1959, his first was surprisingly socialist in nature: he carried out numerous social reforms, supported labour unions, and even tolerated communist domination of the largest union, the Cuban Confederation of Workers (CCT).[3] After mounting a second military coup in March 1952 and deposing President Carlos Prio Socarras, it soon became clear, however, that Batista's only loyalties lay not with the Cuban people but with foreign business interests including the Mafia. Consolidating his position by encouraging relations with the US, he severed relations with the USSR and also encouraged division between his political opponents.[4]

Despite growing animosity towards communism forcing many of its advocates to go underground, during his seven years in power, Batista implemented a socially-minded programme including the improvement of the economy, sanitation, roads, and social housing. This was achieved through the Sugar Stabilisation Fund, the Economic and Social Development Plan and the Federal Housing Administration (FHA) which provided low cost housing for Cuba's poor.[5] On the other hand, Batista revoked political liberties such as the right to strike, and similarly to events in Guatemala pre-1944, he favoured wealthy plantation owners over their labourers. The gap between rich and poor widened enormously during Batista's tenure. [6] Similarly to Machado, in order to stifle any political opposition Batista also set up a secret police force called the Bureau for the Repression of Communist Activities (BRAC). Led by Mariano Faget who served in Batista's first government and who was responsible for tracking Nazi's, Batista used the BRAC to carry out widespread acts of violence, torture and executions. Some estimates put the total number of people killed by the BRAC at as many as 20,000.[7]

In regards to any political opposition to Batista, it was mainly centred on political parties which had been denied any representation in the government after the 1952 coup d'Etat. Of these parties, the Partido Revolucionaro Cubano (PRC) or Autenticos led by Prio Socarras, and the Partido del Pueblo Cubano (PPC) or Ortodoxo led by Eduardo Chibas, were the most valid contenders to Batista's regime. Though these parties were hopeful that they would gain political representation through further elections, one member of the PPC, a lawyer named Fidel Castro, believed that Batista should be removed forcibly using military means.

In attacking the Moncada Barracks in Santiago de Cuba on 26 July 1953, Castro sent a clear message to Batista that if his political hegemony could not be challenged he would be brought down using military means. Armed with a variety of pistols and rifles, some which had been hoarded in secret locations since 1898, the attack by around 150 rebels on Moncada left 18 soldiers and policemen dead. If in some ways this was a positive start for Castro, over the next few days Batista's army bore its teeth and cracked down heavily on any subversive activity in the area: over 50 members of Castro's forces were captured and subsequently executed by Batista's forces.[8] Castro, himself, was far luckier. Escaping uninjured but caught shortly after and sent for trial in Havana, he was sentenced to serve up to 15 years in the circular-shaped Presidio Modelo prison on Isla de Pinos. Released in 1955 following an amnesty granted by Batista, Castro then headed to Mexico to plan the next phase of his revolution.

Now joined by Ernesto Guevara, Castro set up a rebel base in the Sierra Maestra mountains in south-eastern Cuba from where he intended to ambush army patrols and capture weapons. Though Batista limited Castro's activities by reinforcing his positions in the area, two developments of a political and military nature eventually contributed to ending Batista's term as president. In Havana, demonstrations against Batista's regime were led by a student organisation called the Directorio Revolucionario Estudiantil (DRE) and in the Escambray mountains in Cuba's south, Spanish citizen Eloy Gutiérrez Menoyo set up the Second Front of the Escambray. Amongst Menoyo's troops were a number of foreign recruits including former US Army soldier William Alexander Morgan. Possibly acting for the CIA in Cuba, in 1961 Morgan turned against Castro and with Menoyo created a CIA-sponsored counterrevolutionary group called Alpha 66.

After the Catholic Church decided to lend its support to the revolution in 1958 Batista found it necessary to employ increasingly repressive measures to maintain power.[9] For example, constitutional guarantees that protected the rights of Cuba's citizens were suspended in March of that year. Despite having shown himself to be sympathetic to the United States and being part of the bulwark against the spread of communism in the Caribbean, the ways in which Batista chose to deal with political challenges to his regime greatly angered US government officials such Ambassador Earl Smith. Declaring that "it was no longer possible to gender any support in the State Department for the Batista government",[10] on 14 March the US imposed an arms embargo. Contributing significantly to the weakening of their military firepower, Batista's forces were also coming under considerable strain as the strength of rebel forces grew throughout the summer of 1958. They encountered heavy resistance at the battles of La Plata and Las Mercedes fought in July and August and, in late December suffered defeat during the battles of Yaguajay and Santa Clara. By the time, Castro's forces had captured the town of Cienfuegos on 2 January 1959, most of Batista's army had capitulated and their president had already fled. Taking up exile in Portugal and Spain, Batista died of a heart attack on 6 August 1973.

The composition of the first government in post-Batista Cuba was largely uncontroversial. Headed by liberal Cuban lawyer Manuel Urrutia, the cabinet was made up of men such as university professor José Miró Cardona as Prime Minister, philosopher Roberto Agramonte as Minister of State, Raúl Chibás as Minister of the Treasury, and Manuel Ray Rivero as Minister of Public Works. All of these four men were fervent opponents of Batista, and all four of them would become fervent opponents of Fidel Castro in the months following the Cuban revolution.

Also a member of Urrutia's cabinet and holding the grand title of Delegate General of the President to the Armed Forces and the Maximum Leader of the 26th July Movement was Fidel Castro himself. Another uncontroversial figure nicknamed *El Caballo* (The Horse) by his followers, Castro was for many the "romantic, quixotic, legendary liberator from the hills".[11] Within a short space of time, nonetheless, Castro would demonstrate that he possessed a highly ruthless streak, was bent on obtaining as much political power as he possibly could, and that he was prepared to substantially radicalise Cuban politics by bringing them ever more closer to communist ideology.

Though Castro projected the figure of a kindly uncle and of a friendly neighbour to the United States during his goodwill tour of North America in April 1959, back home in Cuba Castro had embarked on a programme of brutal repression aimed at purging any perceived threat to his increasing authority. Becoming Prime Minister in mid-February after the resignation of Cardona, Castro gave himself the authority to do so by replacing the Constitution of 1940 with the Fundamental Law. The resulting legislative change gave the 26th July Movement the power to imprison anyone seen as having remotely assisted Batista without charge. By mid-February operating under what was termed as the "Revolutionary Code of Justice", over 1,000 people found themselves in over-crowded conditions. Military prisoners including former members of Batista's Buró de Represión de Actividades Comunistas were held at La Cabana prison. Formerly the Fort of Saint Charles, prisoners who had sometimes be found innocent of any crime were tortured and executed by firing squads. These executions were overseen by Ernesto Guevara and it is estimated that over 200 people were killed in the same way between January and June 1959. They joined those Guevara had personally murdered in the Sierra Maestra in 1957-1958.[12] Otherwise, Castro suppressed any efforts to criticise either himself or his movement. The US Embassy in Havana reported that any expression of independent opinion or an opinion which diverged from Castro's own view disappeared. This was the case for several publications in towns such as Cienfuegos, Camagüey and Santiago. Their printing presses were taken over by representatives of the movement who promptly began to disseminate Castro's propaganda.[13]

Arguably the most controversial measures taken by Castro in the early months of 1959 was the promulgation of the Agrarian Reform Law. Crafted by Guevara who became head of the National Institute for Agrarian Reform (INRA), this law limited the size of farms to 3,333 acres and real estate to 1,000 acres. Holdings over these limits were expropriated by the government then redistributed to peasant farmers or used by the Cuban state as communal lands.[14] To supervise the realisation of this programme, the INRA employed a 100,000 strong militia.

Whereas land reforms greatly benefitted subsistence farmers and the policy gained the support of the popular masses, the propertied classes who had been deprived of sometimes thousands of acres of farmland and real estate were less than impressed. Seeing the confiscation of land as a sign that communism was mushrooming in Castro's Cuba, according to official US sources these classes were concerned that Soviet ideology was infiltrating the educational system, the armed forces and the public information media.[15] A reputed Communist had reportedly been recruited to revise text books used in schools, and "pro-Communists" featured in military training given at G-6, the Army indoctrination section at Camp Libertad and at Cabana Fortress.[16]

With observers on the alert for more signs of Communist influence over Cuban affairs, towards the end of April there were also signs of embryonic opposition to Castro's programme. This opposition came from several quarters including the nationalist *Auténticos*, ex-army personnel, and business leaders, the latter which was already weighing up the means to overthrow Castro.[17] While these elements are important when the question of counterrevolution is taken into consideration, the most significant source of disaffection from Castro's ideology, nevertheless, was that shown by the Catholic Church. Although the church was institutionally weak and closely identified with Spanish colonialism,[18] it did, however, have substantial support among those who associated socialism with communism and saw the latter as the repudiation of God, the persecution of the faithful, and the rejection of the values of Christian civilisation.[19] Moreover, given that the Cuban Catholic hierarchy was dominated by Spanish priests of strong Falangist inclination,[20] it was inevitable that once Castro's regime chose to pursue a pro-Soviet line the church would attempt to use its position in Cuban society to mobilise popular support against the revolutionary government.[21]

One of the strings to the church's bow that would provide it with the kind of support it needed to oppose Castro was the presence of a significant number of Catholic lay organisations which were particularly popular amongst Cuba's middle classes. Of these lay organisations that became increasingly active in the coming months was the Agrupación Católica Universitaria (ACU), or the Group of Catholic Universities. Indeed, it was the only one that continued to function on American soil after the Cuban exodus of the 1960s.[22]

The ACU was a sodality founded in 1931 by Spanish Jesuit Priest Felipe Rey de Castro. "Tightly structured and governed association of carefully selected university students and professional men", the nearly 600 *agrupados* (members) of this organisation included university professors, lawyers, medical doctors, engineers and newspaper editors who were expected to live up to the standards of the organisation's motto *Confortare et esto vir* (Be courageous as a true man).[23] The ACU was particularly productive in the 1950s publishing more than 50 papers on a variety of topics and selling over half a million copies. These were activities which transformed the ACU into a relatively influential entity. Though the ACU initially welcomed the arrival of the new regime, it quickly turned against Castro as the repressive measures contained in the Fundamental Law began to take effect. This included its own publication being banned.[24]

As the revolutionary government also started to gain control of most mass organisations in Cuba including the Federacion Estudiantil Universitaria (FEU), the ACU began to spawn its own student-based organisations as a counterbalance. While organisations such as the Movimento Demócrata Cristiano (MDC) led by José Ignacio Rasco, and the Directorio Revolucionario Estudiantil (DRE) became prominent opponents of Castro's policies, arguably the most important organisation to emerge from the ACU in mid-1959 was the Movimento de Recuperación Revolucionaria (MRR) or the Revolutionary Recovery Movement led by Dr. Manuel Francisco Artime Buesa. Bearing the Catholic trident as its emblem,[25] and its name professing a return to the fundamental tenets of the Cuban revolution, the MRR finds particular importance in this monograph through its association not only with the Bay of Pigs invasion but with events that would take place some six years later during the Congo Crisis.[26]

A nephew of Cuban poet José Angel Bueza, and raised as a devout Catholic by Jesuit priests, Manuel Artime was born to a family of wealthy sugarcane planters on 29 January 1932 in Camagüey. Aged 24, and studying to be a psychiatrist at the University of Havana, it was in 1957 that Artime had his first encounter with the ACU which, at that time, was heavily critical of Batista and which had supported Castro's earlier agrarian reforms in the Sierra Maestra. This was when Castro's burgeoning regime had taken control of the area in 1958. This contact with the ACU consisted in joining one of its sub-branches situated on the Catholic right called the Partido de Liberación Radical or the Radical Liberation Party (PLR). Then, becoming more inclined towards a military solution to deposing Batista, in December 1958 just before the end of the revolution, Artime joined the Rebel Army. Though it is not clear if Artime took part in any offensives against Batista's forces, on the creation of the INRA in May 1959 Artime was rewarded for his opposition to the former President by being appointed second in command of an agricultural zone in the Sierra Maestra. Under the sponsorship of Minister of Agriculture Humberto Sori Marin, Artime's role was to coordinate the work of a group known as the *Comandos Rurales*. Sponsored in turn by the ACU, the role of this group was to provide peasant farmers with the knowledge to develop their lands.[27]

As Castro's power grew through the resignation and dismissal of some of the more conservative figures in his cabinet – including Urrutia himself in July – the first clear signs that Castro was assuming the role of a dictator rather than a Prime Minister came on 19 October 1959 with the resignation of Major Huber Matos, one of the highest-ranking officers in Castro's rebel army and a man who had fought alongside Castro and Guevara since the early days of the revolution. Resigning as a protest to Castro's ever-increasing acquaintance with the Soviet Union, and denouncing his former comrade-in-arms as a communist, the next day Matos was arrested, charged with treason and sentenced to 20 years in prison. A few days later during a meeting of the INRA in Havana, the fears of both Matos and Artime were confirmed when Castro outlined a plan to communise Cuba within three years. It was at this moment that Artime realised that he was "a democratic infiltrator in a Communist government" and began to prepare a group of peasants and university students to fight against Castro's regime.[28]

At a time when Cuban intelligence services, the G-2, were repressing any political or social activity suspected of being subversive it was almost inevitable that they would get wind of Artime's plan to use the Sierra Maestra as a base for his counterrevolution. The G-2 uncovered Artime's plot as early as June 1959 when it received intelligence sent by a delegate of the Manzanillo Agrarian Bureau named Rodrigo Rivas Vega. The report which was sent to the Cuban Bureau of Investigation at Moncada Barracks tells of how "established interests", i.e. the clergy, and Artime as their agent were attempting to create a division within the masses in order to break up Castro's popular support which was perceived as a revolutionary tactic.[29]

Though it does not appear that any immediate action was taken on the basis of this intelligence, after Artime resigned from the Rebel Army and the INRA on 7 November, a warrant for his arrest was ordered alleging that he had embezzled some 100,000 pesos from La Sierra cattle cooperative.[30] Artime's letter of resignation addressed personally to Castro and published on the front page of the Havana newspaper *Avance* explained why he was leaving what he labelled as a "Red Army" and the "Red masquerade" led by Castro himself.[31] Realising that he would soon be taken into custody and tried on charges of treason, Artime disguised himself as a priest and made his way to the American Embassy in Havana. It was in the Cuban capital that Artime would meet CIA officials for the first time and from where he was smuggled out of Cuba.[32]

The Cuban Project

As observers of the Cuban revolution have pointed out, the American position in regards to Fidel Castro was highly ambivalent. Though US State officials believed that Castro was "motivated by certain ideals", had a "predilection for violence", and had had contact with Communist-front groups during his days at university, there was no firm indication that Castro was a Communist sympathiser himself nor that Communists held a dominant position in the 26th July Movement.[33] On the other hand, by early February 1959, the views of the State Department on possible Communist infiltration in Cuban affairs had changed, and this was mostly due to reports that Guevara wished to take the Cuban revolution to neighbouring Nicaragua, Haiti, the Dominican Republic and Paraguay.[34] This ambivalence continued well into the early months of 1959 even after Castro's appointment as Prime Minister and even after Castro's tone towards the United States had become far more belligerent: despite Castro's threat that there would be "200,000 dead gringos" in the streets if ever the US attempted to intervene in Cuba, this

Ernesto 'Che' Guevara and Fidel Castro were both prominent figures in the Cuban Revolution of 1959.

Felix Rodriguez (left) took part in early paramilitary operations to overthrow Castro. Later becoming a Paramilitary Operations Officer with the CIA's Special Activities Division (SAD), he oversaw operations that led to the capture and death of Guevara in Bolivia in 1967. (Donated by Felix Rodriguez)

was excused by his impetuousness and his emotional state. Castro's worst enemy, it was believed, was "his tongue".[35]

Castro's visit to the United States in April 1959 served a massive publicity coup for the Cuban leader as he charmed the press with a broad smile and gained its sympathy by explaining how his revolutionary movement had overthrown the tyrannical Batista and how the new regime had initiated reforms to provide farmland to poor peasants, was alleviating problems linked to unemployment and was bringing improvements to health care and education. Nevertheless, while Castro emphasised that he wished for a "real friendship" with the United States, and while he repeated that he wanted to establish a "real democracy" in Cuba, as was pointed out by analysts there were concerns over Castro's plans to expropriate lands and his brother Raul's contacts with Soviet Premier Nikita Khrushchev.[36]

Whereas the association of Castro, Guevara and Raul Castro with the Soviet Union would occupy the thoughts of US Cold War analysts for years to come, in May 1959 it was more pragmatic commercial considerations that were to come to the table during a secret meeting between Vice-President Richard Nixon, US Ambassador William Pawley, senior executives of Pepsi Cola, Esso, Standard Oil, UFCO, and the Mafia. Dismayed at the direction being taken by Castro and losing vast tracts of lands through the agrarian reforms, a pact was made whereby Nixon would be supported in his bid to become US President in the forthcoming elections if he promised to overthrow Castro.[37] This was no empty threat: as well as being an advisor to Eisenhower and to CIA Director Allen Dulles, Pawley was a close friend of Claire Lee Chennault of Flying Tigers fame. He had also played a significant role in Operation PBSUCCESS some five years previously.[38]

The discussions of May 1959 marked the beginning of US attempts to bring down Castro by hook or by crook and to ensure that the spread of Communism could be contained to Cuba alone. Over the next five years or so, there would be at least eight plots involving the CIA to overthrow Castro, and although they involved methods as diverse as using high-powered rifles, poison pens, poison pills and bacterial powders to kill Castro, the most serious and most organised attempt to depose the Cuban leader came through the CIA's association with the Cuban exile organisations which had transplanted their counterrevolutionary activities from Cuba to large American cities such as New York and Miami, the home at the end of the 1960s to some 200,000 Cubans who had fled their homeland.[39]

As Cuba was perceived by US authorities to be "proceeding methodically to solidify its control over all the major institutions of the society and to employ them on the Communist pattern as instruments of repression", in early 1960 the CIA was requested to "set in motion the organisation of a broadly based opposition to the Castro regime and the development of propaganda channels, clandestine agent nets within Cuba, and trained paramilitary ground and air forces wherewith the opposition could overthrow the Cuban regime".[40] Despite the programme of action being sponsored by the US, it was made clear, however, that the United States should not be seen as having any involvement in order to provide it with plausible deniability, one of the bedrocks of US shadow foreign policy. Known collectively as the Cuban Project, the programme to remove Castro would eventually become known as Operation Mongoose in November 1961.

The concept of this programme with an initial budget of $4.4 million came straight from the CIA's handbook on covert intervention and, indeed, on 17 March 1960, President Eisenhower authorised operations on the basis of a CIA report entitled "A Program of Covert Action Against the Castro Regime".[41] The first stage of the project involved putting CIA personnel documented as a group of businessmen in contact with Cuban exiles. The exiles would then be used as cover for action which became known publicly, and this enabled the hand of the US government to remain hidden.

According to official sources, as early as August 1959 the Chief of the Agency's Paramilitary Group attended a meeting to discuss the creation of a paramilitary capability that could be used in "Latin American crisis situations."[42] Next, in September 1959, the Chief of the Western Hemisphere Division – Colonel Joseph Caldwell King – prepared a series of studies on limited covert warfare. As well as calling for the setting up of a division paramilitary staff, King also set up a small proprietary airline to be used in operations. By December 1959, these studies had produced a plan whereby a number of Cuban exiles would be used as paramilitary instructors who, in turn, would train exiles in a Latin American country so that they could be infiltrated into Cuba to lead counterrevolutionary activities.[43]

Following National Security Council approval of King's report, in January 1960 the Agency established a working group whose role it was to oversee operations and to recommend possible courses of action. Known as Operation 40, this group took its name from a subcommittee of the NSC called the Special Group, or the 5412/2 Special Group.[44] It was reportedly presided by Richard Nixon, and its members included Chief of Naval Operations Admiral Arleigh Burke, Livingstone Merchant of the State Department, NSA advisor Gordon Gray, and CIA Director Allen Dulles.[45]

The Democratic Revolutionary Front or Frente Revolucionario Democratico (FRD) was formed by Manuel Artime, Jose Perez San Roman Antonio Maceo Antonio de Varona. The military wing of the FRD was called Brigade 2506. (Latin American Studies)

In the latter respect, a first phase would consist of training carefully screened recruits to become instructors and, in a second phase, these instructors would train forces in locations outside the US capable of launching an armed offensive against Castro. To infiltrate operatives into Cuba, the CIA planned to use one of its many secret airlines and, in order to establish the programme, a period of six to eight months was required.[52]

As plans were made to set up training centres, and CIA officers searched around Miami for suitable recruiting offices, communications centres and warehouses to store material, Manuel Artime was in the midst of a speaking tour which would see him travel to Costa Rica, Panama, Venezuela, Chile and Brazil. Towards the end of March 1960 when in Rio de Janeiro, Artime received a call from a certain Jaime Castillo asking him to fly to New York and to go to the Statler Hilton on Seventh Avenue presenting himself as George L. Ringo. Once he had reached his destination, Artime met Oscar Echevarría and another friend from Cuba named Angel Fernandez Varela. They explained to Artime that some prominent anti-Castro Cubans were interested in meeting him to enquire about Artime's joining them in a move to depose Castro.[53] One of these Cubans was Justo Carillo, the leader of the Agrupación Montecristi

As had been the case for Operation PBSUCCESS in Guatemala, former Office of Strategic Services (OSS) operative and the CIA's Assistant Deputy Director of Plans Charles Tracy Barnes was appointed to manage the Cuban Task Force and to head Operation 40. Calling a meeting which was held in his office in Quarters Eyes near the Washington Memorial on 18 January 1960, Barnes addressed a gathering which included future Watergate burglar Howard Hunt, Gerry Droller (aka Frank Bender), David Atlee Phillips (another veteran of PBSUCCESS), and Jacob Esterline, the deputy chief of operations to remove Jacobo Arbenz.[46] Inevitably, David Sanchez Morales,[47] Frank Sturgis[48] and Pedro Diaz Lanz were also present. Morales was allegedly involved in Executive Action, the programme to assassinate foreign leaders and was involved in Operation PBSUCCESS; and Sturgis and Lanz had both been involved in anti-Castro operations in December 1959.[49] Lanz was the former head of the Cuban Air Force.

Through Operation 40's subsequent meetings, by 16 March 1960 the 5412 Committee was ready to submit its report entitled "A Program of Covert Action Against the Castro Regime" for approval by President Eisenhower. The report proposed that a series of actions targeting the replacement should be implemented and that a regime "more devoted to the true interests of the Cuban people and more acceptable to the US."[50] Containing four major courses of action, the programme required the creation of:

1) a "responsible, appealing and unified Cuban opposition located outside of Cuba
2) psychological warfare of the type used in Guatemala whereby a propaganda offensive could be initiated [51]
3) the creation of a covert intelligence and action organisation within Cuba
4) the development of a paramilitary force outside of Cuba

John McCone served as Director of the CIA from 1961 to 1965 and oversaw operations to overthrow Fidel Castro. (Autor's collection)

The CIA's Theodore 'Ted' Shackley was involved in the plot to overthrow Arbenz and Castro. In early 1962, Shackley was appointed as deputy chief of JM/WAVE, the CIA's station in Miami. (Latin American Studies)

The CIA's David Atlee Phillips was another involved in operations in Guatemala and Cuba as well as the Bay of Pigs. (TangoDown63)

David Morales was also involved in the plot to overthrow Arbenz and Castro and worked directly under Ted Shackley in Miami. (TangoDown63)

Thomas 'Pete' Ray was a pilot in the Alabama National Guard that carried out attacks against Cuban installations in April 1961. (Janet Joy Ray)

(AM),[54] and others were Manuel Antonio de Varona, a former Prime Minister of Cuba and the leader of Rescate,[55] José Ignacio Rasco of the Christian Democratic Party (CDP), and Aureliano Sanchez Arango of the Triple A group.[56] In May 1960, these men had formed a group called the Frente Revolucionario Democratico, or the Democratic Revolutionary Front (FRD). Its military wing was called Brigade 2506, the force which fought in the Bay of Pigs Invasion in April 1961.

Of all the anti-Castro organisations which sprung up either on mainland Cuba or in the United States, Artime's MRR was the one which was seen as the most promising by the CIA operating in the agency's station codenamed JM/WAVE in Miami, or from offices located in the business district of Coral Gables.[57] Not only had Artime shown that he was willing to use armed force to overthrow Castro, he was also fast becoming a respected figure that made him the perfect vector for the recruitment of men prepared to join the fight. With a base of 28 men which included Rafael Quintero, the MRR had rapidly established itself as one of the most hard-line groups based in Miami. Subscribing to an "*ideario*" of which the main intention was to overthrow Fidel Castro, Artime described the MRR as a group whose objective was to "permanently fight for an ideology of Christ; and for a reality of liberating our nation treacherously sold to the Communist International".[58]

If the initial stages of covert operations in June 1960 involved the training of only a few dozen men at bases in Panama, by November the CIA was in a position to report from its Miami base that liaison with the FRD had already resulted in 475 air and ground trainees being dispatched to training camps Guatemala.[59] Indeed, after an agreement had been reached with President Ydígoras of Guatemala, the men of Brigade 2506 underwent training in the mountainous region of Retalhuleu. The number of exiles rallying to the cause through appeals made to different associations, through friendships and by word of mouth meant that by the end of January 1961 the exile strike force had grown to 644. By early February, it numbered 685, by early March it numbered 826, and by the 22nd of that month the figure had risen to 973. As the fateful day approached, the number finally grew to 1,390.[60] Many of the men were married,

A B-26 of Brigade 2506 as seen during attack on an oil refinery on Cuba. (Stephen Rookes Collection)

many had children, many had no previous military experience, but all were willing to overthrow Castro.

With newly installed President John Kennedy approving the invasion (also known as Operation Zapata) on 4 April, by then the Landing Craft Infantry (LCI) *Blagar* and *Barbara J.* had already left Stock Island, Key West, Florida on 28 March and were making their way to the Brigade's embarkation points situated at Puerto Cabezas in Nicaragua.[61] Brigade 2506 itself had two commanders on whom the CIA could count implicitly: Grayston Lynch was a member of the CIA's Special Activities Division (SAD), as was the second commander William 'Rip' Robertson. An experienced counter-intelligence officer, we shall see more of Robertson when we deal with the question of the Stanleyville rescue operations in the Congo.

The two landing craft reached Puerto Cabezas in Nicaragua on 2 April 1961 just over two weeks before the planned invasion. Told to wait for their final instructions, Lynch and Robertson were then informed that the assault on Cuba consisted of a multi-pronged attack on three landing areas: Playa Giron (code-named Blue Beach), Playa Larga (Red Beach), and Caleta Buena Inlet (Green Beach). After landing two battalions of Brigade 2506, tanks, trucks and other military vehicles would then provide support. A second phase involved landing two further battalions of troops. These reinforcements would be transported on a cargo ship named the *Houston* and would land at the Bay of Pigs. Anchored some miles out to sea, the aircraft carrier USS *Essex* carrying platoons of US Marines waited to provide more support should Cuban military resistance be difficult to overcome by Brigade 2506. Airborne troops were also to be dropped inland using USAF C-46 transport aircraft.[62]

Further preparations continued in the days preceding the attack during Operation Puma. This consisted of Exile pilots making bombing raids on key Cuban installations. Flying B-26B Invaders carrying the markings the Cuban Revolutionary Armed Forces (FAR), attacks were made on airfields at San Antonio de Los Baños, at Cuidad Libertad, and at Antonio Maceo International Airport. The intention of the attacks was to destroy Castro's air force and to eliminate any airborne threat to Brigade 2506.[63] A day before the

Captured members of Brigade 2506 are led through the streets in April 1961. (Latin American Studies)

invasion itself, the ships *Caribe*, *Atlantico*, *Barbara J.*, *Houston* and the *Rio Escondido* joined the *Blagar* before heading off towards the respective landing points. However, hampered by problems such as damaged propellers and coral reefs, progress was slow. Overcoming these setbacks, on the morning of 17 April, the different battalions of men moved ashore. Within 30 minutes, it became evident that the objectives of Operation Puma had not been reached. Within the space of 20 minutes, and with Castro's forces waiting for the landing forces, Brigade 2506 was attacked by a Cuban Air Force B-26, Hawker Sea Fury fighter aircraft and T-33 jets.[64] To add to the Brigade's woes, both the *Houston* and the *Rio Escondido* were hit and were reported to be sinking. This came as a severe blow as these ships carried the vital military hardware needed to back up the ground forces.

Those captured by Castro's forces underwent frequent beatings. (Latin American Studies)

The last of those captured at the Bay of Pigs remained in prison until the mid-1970s. (Author's collection)

The situation for the invading forces did not improve during the day. Air cover that had been promised failed to materialise, and troops were forced to take on a defensive rather than an attacking role under protection of the trees and swamps lining the beaches. The next day, Castro's MiG fighter jets were joined by over 20,000 members of his armies. Within the next 48 hours, any resistance to these attacks had faded. Despite some incursions made inland by paracommandos and despite an attempt by pilots of the Alabama National Guard to launch a counterattack, by 21 April 1961 38 of the invading forces lay dead and a further 1,209 had been captured. Those killed included Thomas "Pete" Ray and his flight engineer Leo Baker.[65] These Americans were shot to death after their plane was forced to make a landing. For those captured, over the following months in Cuban prisons they were to suffer torture and beatings at the hands of prison guards who considered them as traitors. After going to trial, some were sentenced to death and were executed by firing squad while those lucky enough not to suffer the same fate were sentenced to up to 30 years in prison.

In order to understand what had led to the invading forces being so overwhelmed, and something which underscores Kennedy's disappointment (or perhaps, guilt) in the failure, the morning after the surrender of Brigade 2506, Kennedy asked General Maxwell Taylor to establish a committee whose role was to examine the whys and wherefores of the debacle. Preliminary findings were presented to Kennedy on 16 May 1961, and for the purposes of this study, we draw on a review of the Taylor Committee's findings which was declassified at the end of December 1984.[66]

Drawing on testimonies of a number of organisers and escapees of the invasion, blame for the failure was laid rather harshly on a portion of Brigade 2506 described as "more lovers than fighters". Indeed, during the 72-hour battle, fewer than 150 of Castro's forces were

President Kennedy met Manuel Artime and released prisoners at the Orange Bowl, Miami on 29 December 1962. (Author's collection)

Despite Kennedy receiving the Brigade 2506 flag, his failure to send support at the Bay of Pigs made him an unpopular figure among the Cuban exile community (History.net)

killed in action. Even more unkindly, given the conditions which awaited Brigade 2506, was the suggestion that some of its members had reverted to cowardice once it was realised that Castro maintained control of Cuban air space.[67] That they had done so, and refuting the suggestion that there was insufficient ammunition provided for the invasion, was also the conclusion of a Cuban publication from August 1961 entitled *Playa Giron: Derrota del Imperialismo*. Here it was indicated that substantial quantities of munitions were abandoned in the face of Castro's advancing forces and that had the "mercenaries" of Brigade 2506 show more "spirited resistance", and had they fought "more courageously", then they could have held their territory for a greater length of time.[68] A more realistic, and possibly the most accurate evaluation of Brigade 2506's performance came from Fidel Castro himself in an article which appeared in the *New York Times* of 17 June 1961. Here, the Cuban leader was reported as saying that the invading forces fought "very well as long as they thought they had air cover. After it failed, it was an easy matter to get them to surrender".[69]

With Grayston Lynch drawing a similar conclusion in his own monograph published in 1998,[70] Kennedy's failure to authorise sufficient air cover was seen as being the principle cause of the failure. Moreover, with Kennedy also failing to authorise the intervention of the US Marines aboard the USS *Essex*, the perception was that that in the interest of avoiding a full scale war with Cuba, it appeared to many that the 35th president had abandoned the exiles to their own fate. In doing so, Kennedy rapidly became a hate figure in the Cuban Exile community as John Avlon notes in an article for the *Daily Telegraph* published 50 years after Kennedy's assassination.[71] If conspiracy theories are to be believed, there are many examples which go as far as implicating Cuban Exiles in the shooting which occurred in Dallas on 22 November 1963.

If Kennedy's lack of commitment when it was needed may have been due to diplomatic pressure exercised by the Soviet Union,[72] his subsequent efforts to dislodge the Cuban leader

Jacqueline Kennedy was also present at the Orange Bowl.

demonstrates that he remained sympathetic to the exile cause. Kennedy demonstrated this support by negotiating the release of the remaining 1,113 exile prisoners captured at the Bay of Pigs, and by personally welcoming them at Miami's Orange Bowl stadium on 29 December 1962.[73] Flanked on a rostrum by Manuel Artimé, José Miró Cardona and his wife Jacqueline, Kennedy was presented with the flag of Brigade 2506 and unfurled it to loud cheering from the exiles and their families gathered in the stadium. Speaking of how he wished to express his "great appreciation to the brigade for making the United States a custodian of this flag", Kennedy gave assurances to the crowd that the flag would be returned to the brigade in a free Havana.[74]

Despite Kennedy's rousing words Cold War imperatives meant that he would make no further organised attempt to remove Fidel Castro, and even made a compromise with the Soviet Union over the question of Cuba by agreeing to withdraw US missiles from Turkey. Going against the advice of his Joint Chiefs of Staff who advocated a full-scale attack on Cuba, Kennedy averted the possibility of nuclear war as the USSR agreed in turn to remove R-12 theatre ballistic missiles (TBM) from sites in Cuba. After the Cuban Missile Crisis of October 1962 Kennedy publicly distanced himself from attempts to remove Castro, preferring instead to leave the CIA to its own devices and preferring covert attacks on Cuba involving exile groups that continued well into 1964. Some of those who took part in these attacks launched from Nicaragua would subsequently be employed in the Congo, another area which the CIA feared was open to Communist penetration.

4
From the Caribbean to the Congo

The United States and Decolonisation

As regards US attitudes towards decolonisation there was often a clash between an ideological dogma which upheld the tenets of self-determination for non self-governing territories and more pragmatic considerations such as maintaining access to areas of strategic and/or economic interest in the context of the Cold War. Two cases which highlight political reality overriding political ideology were Indochina where the US gave assistance to French colonial forces, and South Africa whereby the US set aside condemnation of apartheid in order to secure supplies of high-grade uranium for the development of nuclear armaments. In the same year that D.F. Malan's government introduced racial segregation laws (1948), the US even went as far as financing the building of mining plants in order to extract uranium from South Africa's gold deposits.[1] In addition to what South Africa could offer in the way of rare earths and minerals, there was the question of its being seen as the "only independent state of European traditions and of substantial power and stability south of the Equator."[2] As well as making South Africa a "major stronghold of western ideology in the southern hemisphere" according to US analysts, it was also considered as bulwark against the spread of communism.[3] On a more practical level in US Cold War strategy, South Africa offered naval bases and deep-water ports at Saldanha Bay on the Atlantic Ocean and Simon's Town, Durban on the Indian Ocean.

As far as US strategic interests in East Africa in the 1950s were concerned, the United States played out a similar scenario to that in Indochina. Kenya aspired to independence from the British and was using the Communist-backed Mau Mau to press its case. It was, nonetheless, important for the United States that the Mau Mau did not succeed as the Kenyan capital Mombasa was the largest commercial port in East Africa. American imports of strategic materials from Uganda, the Belgian Congo, and northern Tanganyika flowed through it, and two American shipping lines maintain regular schedules between Mombasa and east coast ports in the United States and another operating from Gulf Coast ports. From a military point of view, Mombasa was Britain's principal naval base during the Second World War and it provided a geographical situation from which the Indian Ocean could be patrolled by ships. Logistically, the recently reactivated East African Command was headquartered in Nairobi and as such this allowed it to secure a 2,000 mile stretch of coastline from South Africa to Ethiopia. The base was being expanded in view of the expected loss of the Suez base area (at a time when Nasser of Egypt was negotiating the withdrawal of British troops) and the East African Railways and Harbors system was, in part, being funded by the US.[4] Again, the United States put aside ideological considerations on self-determination and declared, in the interests of containing communism, that the Mau Mau was

Larry Devlin became the CIA's Chief of Station in the Congo in August 1960. (Jeune Afrique)

a terrorist organisation and that full diplomatic support should be given to the British to uphold its colonial rule.[5]

When considering the question of containment as a threat to national security, what we should bear in mind is that the successful containment of communism did not boil down to a simple matter of developing a strategic framework. Indeed, any theoretical strategy needs to be complemented by the means with which it is to be implemented. In simpler terms, this signifies putting in place a military deterrent, and in the 1950s this deterrent consisted of tactical nuclear weapons, jet aircraft, and ballistic missiles. By the time innovations in jet and weapons technology were being made in the 1950s, the United States had long since put in place governmental structures that would assist it in acquiring minerals such as those mentioned above. These were the considerations which had brought the United States into indirect contact with the Belgian Congo and were considerations which would make it crucial after the country's independence that access to minerals was maintained and that access to the same minerals by the USSR was denied.

The demands of the First World War and the changing face of warfare forced the United States to re-evaluate its military capacity and to address the question of certain elements which were of great importance, particularly in war time.[6] In view of the shortages of these strategic minerals noted in 1917, in 1922 the US government established the Army and Navy Munitions Board of the US War Department whose role was to draw up a list of 15 strategic minerals considered essential to national defence which were to be found partly or entirely outside the United States. Fifteen critical minerals[7] were also added to this list.[8] With the increasing threat that imports of strategic and critical materials would be lost as a consequence of Japanese expansion in the Pacific,[9] and the threat of war in Europe, the 1939 Strategic Minerals Act authorised a $100 million budget for the Secretaries of War and the Navy, and the Army and Navy Munitions Board to purchase strategic and critical minerals needed for wartime production. This included the procurement of ferroalloys, chromite, manganese, natural rubber, and tin.[10] The Second World War did much to change US dependence on the import of materials necessary to its war effort.[11] The sinking of Allied ships led to stockpile shortages of materials such as copper, chromite, lead, manganese ore, tungsten and zinc concentrates, and the loss of skilled labour, meaning that mining equipment could not be sufficiently maintained, meant that the stockpile of these minerals was severely affected.[12]

In post-war America, the 1939 Strategic Minerals Act was supplemented by the 1946 Strategic and Critical Minerals Act, and the National Security Act of 1947 which created the National Security Resources Board. In addition to its advisory role to the President, this act also provided for the creation of "policies for establishing adequate reserves of strategic and critical material".[13] Importantly, on the question of US intervention in the Congo, and when we take into consideration the creation of the CIA through the same act, the National Security Act also stresses that policies will be created for the "conservation of these resources" and that the National Security Resources Board "shall utilize to the maximum extent the facilities and resources of the departments and agencies of the Government".[14] In respect to this last remark, the activities of an agency named the Advisory Committee on Uranium (ACU) illustrates perfectly how the government was able to procure materials which were essential to the development of weapons in the Second World War.

At the time when the Manhattan Project was being developed, and when scientists at the Pupin Physics Laboratories at Columbia University were attempting to create a nuclear chain reaction, the intervention of Leslie R. Groves of the ACU had an essential role to play in the creation of the nuclear bomb. In 1942, Groves was to learn of the presence of a quantity of high-grade uranium that had been shipped to the United States and was now to be found in a warehouse on Staten Island. This uranium had been shipped across the Atlantic Ocean by Edgar Sengier, an employee of the Union Minière Haut-Katanga (UMHK) who was fearful that Nazi Germany would attempt to procure the stock. Manhattan Project administrator Colonel Kenneth D. Nichols was to approach Sengier and was to purchase all 1,250 tons of the uranium ore.[15] Two-thirds of the uranium used in the Hiroshima and Nagasaki bombs came from the Congo.[16]

The case of uranium is just one example of how, over the coming years, the United States would sign international agreements in an attempt to maintain its supplies of strategic materials and, as we have seen with its relations with South Africa, the quest to maintain access to metals such as gold would often present the United States with a moral dilemma. A similar situation would later arise on the question of chromite ore imported from Rhodesia. UN sanctions imposed on this southern African country banned the import of a metal which was a key component to the production of stainless steel. However, the United States, which respected this embargo, relied on Rhodesia to supply around 40% of its requirements. With the US government also importing chromium from the USSR, Senator Harry Byrd successfully argued that the US government should be prohibited from banning the imports of strategic minerals from a non-communist country if an import from communist countries was not also prohibited. In 1971, Byrd's proposal led to an amendment to the Strategic and Critical Materials Stock Piling Act known as the Byrd Amendment.

The United States and the Congo's Minerals

Insofar as the Belgian Congo was concerned, the requirements for strategic minerals such as uranium and cobalt again led the United States to put aside its moral stance and to focus on Cold War necessities. In effect, just three years after the United States signed the Atlantic Charter and promised to allow peoples to choose their own form of government, it signed the Tripartite Uranium Accord with Belgium and Great Britain. Signed in 1944, this agreement stipulated that Belgium could only sell its uranium to the United States or to Great Britain. While it brought assurances that the US could continue to receive supplies for its nuclear programme, at the same time it gave reassurance to Belgium that its colonial presence in the Congo could be maintained.[17]

Whereas a certain strain of uranium is needed to provoke a nuclear reaction and the stockpiling of this mineral became essential, in the 1950s an access to the supply of cobalt became equally essential. In particular, cobalt was needed in the development of aviation and weapons technology.

The first generation of jet propulsion systems was made of steel. However, the main problem with this metal is that it cannot resist the extremely high temperatures at which jet engines operate for long periods of time. This placed severe restrictions on how jet fighters could be used in long-distance combat operations. It was discovered that this problem of over-heating could be solved by using superalloys, a group of nickel, iron-nickel, and cobalt alloys which were capable of withstanding temperatures of up to 950–1,300°C for long periods of time.[18] This discovery allowed for the development of the type of engines that would be used in the Boeing B-52 Stratofortress, a long-range strategic bomber which first flew

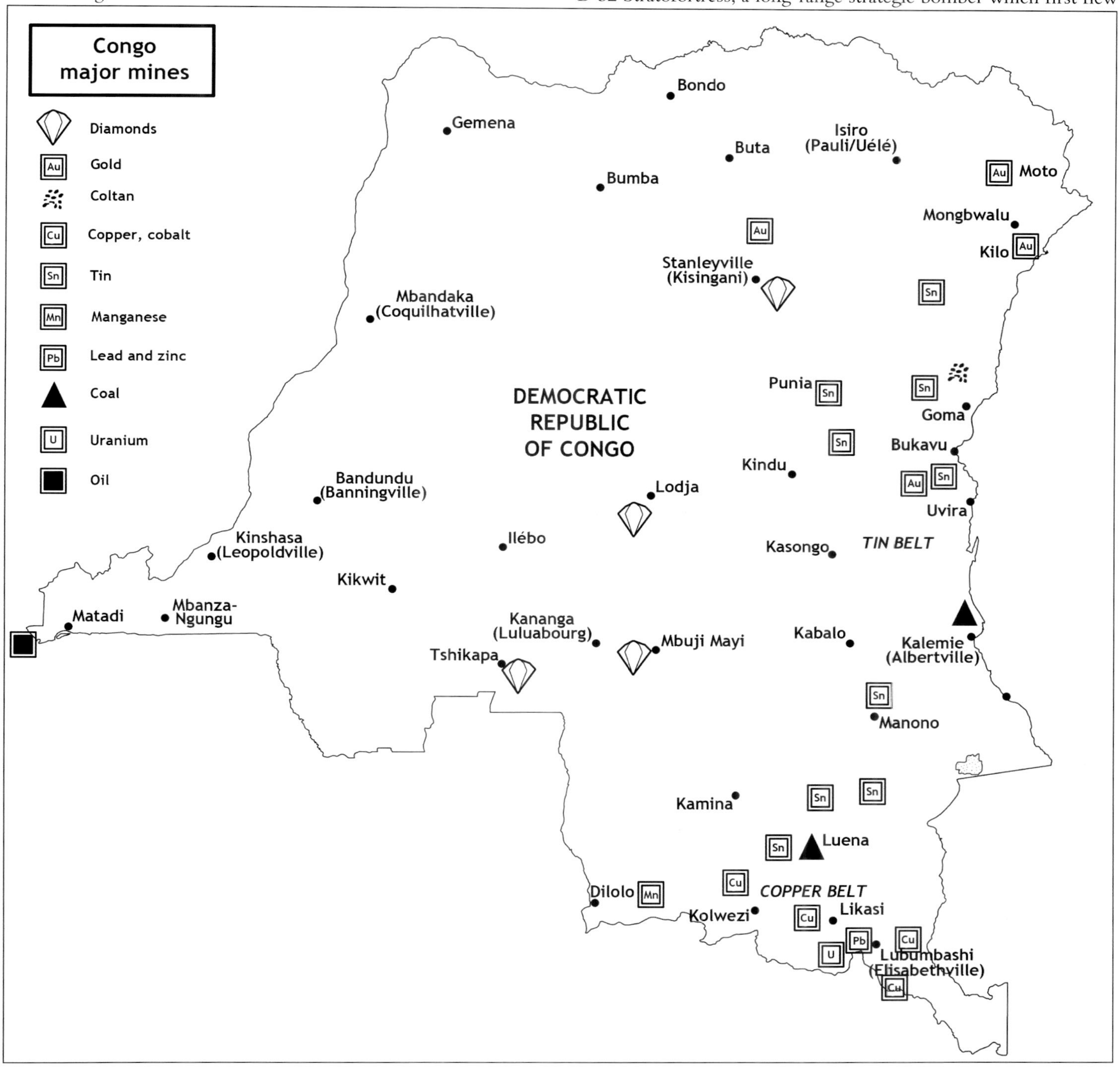

Mineral sources in the Congo.[31]

in 1952; the Lockheed C-130 Hercules, a transport aircraft first used in 1954; the Boeing KC-135 Stratotanker, a refueling aircraft first used in 1956; and the Lockheed U-2, a high-altitude spy plane first used in 1955.

The development of such aircraft was vital to the planning of strategic defensive measures. As a report from the National Security Council to Eisenhower demonstrates, concerns had been raised that the USAF had a "limited capability to defend the Western Hemisphere against air attack, owing chiefly to a shortage of all-weather jet interceptors." In Korea, following the onset of war, it was considered that the Air Force would have difficulty in carrying out measures "for the defense and maintenance of essential lines of communication" and, in the Far East it also had limited capability for carrying out a strategic offensive.[19] Along with the development of anti-aircraft systems capable of firing missiles to altitudes up to 60,000 feet, plans were made for the development of jet fighters capable of intercepting Russian bombers.[20] By 1957, in addition to those aircraft mentioned above, according to Butler (1966)[21] the USAF had produced just under 10,000 jet engines used in around 2,100 F-86 Sabres[22]; 760 F-84 Thunderjets;[23] 315 FH Banshees;[24] 600 B-47s;[25] 792 F-100 Super Sabres;[26] and 516 F-102 Delta Daggers.[27] This aircraft manufactured by Convair was designed to intercept Soviet aircraft such as the Tupolev (Tu-95) strategic bomber which had entered into service in 1952. To give some idea of US requirements in cobalt in the 1950s, according to Burrows (1971), the manufacture of jet engines required around 100lbs of cobalt. This meant that the military aircraft industry alone needed around just under a ton of this mineral.[28] As for the US industry as a whole, from 1961-1965 this figure would reach nearly six tons.[29]

If we return to the question of the United States maintaining access to supplies of strategic minerals in the 1950s, although in 1952 wartime requirements for many of the minerals could be met by domestic production, the Interdepartmental Stockpiling Committee had placed six minerals (beryl, cobalt, columbite, nickel, tantalite and tungsten) in the Band 1, thus making them as the most urgently needed. By 1958, in an African context in which total American investment in the sub-Sahara amounted to $500 million (and the majority of which was in the Union of South Africa), access to cobalt, asbestos, columbite, corundum, industrial diamonds and tantalum still remained an issue.[30] As the map on page 23 demonstrates, the Congo is particularly rich in cobalt, coltan (a mix of columbite and tantalite), diamonds, and manganese that were so needed by the United States. As we can also see, these reserves were to be found mainly in the east of the Congo and, in particular, in the provinces of Katanga, the Kasai, and the Kivu.

The Domino Theory comes to Africa

If the Congo was high on the list of countries in which access to minerals was essential, it should not be concluded that United States intervention in Congolese affairs was made purely on this basis. Rather, as demonstrated through the section on US strategic interests in southern and central Africa, any gambit relating to how the United States conducted its foreign affairs was taken in the interest of respecting long-established doctrines such as the Domino Theory. In other words, the United States was not predatory and was not looking to seize just any opportunity to lay its hands on minerals for the sake of a weapons programme and ensuring economic growth. It genuinely believed in a world free from subjugation and reiterated that it was prepared to provide support for nations still seeking to gain independence. US Presidents such as John F. Kennedy did not, however, wish to see one form of colonial control be replaced by a "far more iron tyranny", a desire he expressed in his inaugural address of 20 January 1961.[32] The reference to the Soviet Union given here does, however, underline Kennedy's determination to keep newly independent nations away from Communist influence.

The then Republic of the Congo was one of the sixteen sub-Saharan nations which gained its independence in 1960,[33] and one of the nations that Kennedy welcomed to the "ranks of the free".[34] Colonised by Belgium in 1908, the Congo had eventually shaken off its colonial yoke after negotiations at the Brussels Round Table talks held in December 1959. After holding elections to determine which of the country's many political parties would assume power on 30 June 1960, those eligible to vote decided that the country would be led by President Joseph Kasa-Vubu, and that Patrice Lumumba would become the Congo's first Prime Minister. Though Lumumba was not overtly communist, his association with Pan-Africanism and its loose association with Marxist ideology meant that his nomination as Prime Minister was viewed with some suspicion by the US State Department. Indeed, it had done as much as possible to avoid Lumumba gaining any access to a position of political power and in May 1960 had created a programme of political action designed to support pro-Western candidates and to "marginalise Marxist groups" in the Congo.[35]

As the Congo descended into chaos through the mutiny of its armed forces on 5 July and the secessions of the provinces of Katanga and South Kasai, US national security policy-makers became increasingly convinced that Lumumba was being manipulated by the Soviet Union and that the Congo was "experiencing a classic communist effort takeover".[36] Fears were consolidated in August 1960 when Soviet aircraft were used to transport the Congolese National Army (ANC) into South Kasai in an attempt to end its secession. Lumumba was then seen as a "stalking horse for what appeared to be a Soviet effort to take over the Congo,[37] and was described by some observers as Africa's Castro.[38] Shortly after Lumumba's arrival, therefore, the CIA's Chief of Station in Leopoldville Larry Devlin suggested that Lumumba be removed lest the Congo become another Cuba.[39]

Whether or not US perceptions of Lumumba's character were correct,[40] from mid-August 1960 the CIA started to draw up operational plans to replace Lumumba with a pro-Western group of leading Congolese political figures known as the Binza Group. With plans in place in September 1960, the CIA then assisted Army Chief of Staff Joseph Desiré Mobutu to engineer Lumumba's overthrow. The assassination of Lumumba was another option. In August 1960, Allen Dulles authorised the expenditure of up to $100,000 to achieve this objective. [41] Though attempts on Lumumba's life were made by CIA contract-killer Sidney Gottleib in September 1960[42] – the same man used in attempts to kill Fidel Castro – Lumumba's destiny lay in the hands of political opponents in Katanga who beat, tortured and shot him to death on 17 January 1961, just three days before Kennedy's inaugural address.

The news of Lumumba's death that filtered out of the Congo sometime in February occurred at a particularly sensitive and active time for the US State Department: plans were being made to invade Cuba and plans were being made to send military advisors to Vietnam in order to support the forces of Ngo Dinh Diem. With two military fronts on the verge of opening up in Latin America and in southeast Asia, Kennedy was now faced with a third in Central Africa.

Given that the Soviet Union had provided military, financial and political support to Lumumba it was bound to greet his assassination with consternation and accusations that the US and the United Nations had interfered in Congolese political affairs for their own purposes. In effect, Soviet premier Nikita Khrushchev had made his feelings very clear on the role of the United Nations Operations Congo (UNOC) and accused UN General Secretary Dag Hammarskjöld of doing the colonists' "dirty work" by paralysing the work of a lawful government. In doing so, the UN had facilitated the acts of "puppets in Katanga".[43] Unsurprisingly, given Khrushchev's sentiments, the Soviet Union then provided support to Lumumba supporter and former Deputy Prime Minister Antoine Gizenga. In December 1960, Gizenga had set up a revolutionary government in Stanleyville in the Oriente Province vowing to restore Lumumba to power. The Soviet Union reportedly helped Gizenga by providing his regime with weapons flown into Stanleyville on an Ilyushin-14 cargo plane.[44] There were also reports that the Soviet Union gave Gizenga $500,000,[45] and that another $500,000 was intercepted by the CIA in Sudan. According to Larry Devlin, this money ended up in the general fund of the US Treasury.[46]

Where Kennedy was concerned, he promised to practice a far more hands-on approach to the problems of the developing world as a whole and believed that the Eisenhower Administration had shown little imagination and missed too many opportunities in its relations with this area.[47] Intending to bring about change in US foreign policy and to establish new links with leaders of developing countries. These leaders included Gamal Nasser of Egypt, Kwame Nkrumah of Ghana and Sekou Touré of Mali.[48] To convince them of his goodwill and to allay suspicions that the United States had been involved in Lumumba's assassination, Kennedy continued to make attempts to demonstrate US neutralism in Africa. An example of this neutralism is the construction of Ghana's Volta Dam which was funded in part by the USA.[49] While this approach may seem magnanimous in nature, Kennedy's openness was not carried out purely in the interest of showing goodwill and reassuring Third World leaders that the US would not seek to interfere in their internal affairs. During his presidential campaign, Kennedy had underlined his commitment to protecting US interests abroad while, through showing more transparency in its affairs, it was hoped that non-aligned nations would take a favourable view of US foreign policy.[50] Insofar as the particular context of the Congo was concerned, although Kennedy believed that the country was for the time being "unable to advance toward normal political and economic life", US policy was based on the assumption that Congolese independence could best be advanced through a two-point approach: the provision through the United Nations of the economic, technical and military assistance so badly needed by the Congo, and that there would be no outside interference in the internal affairs of the Congo. Although this notion of non-interference was extended to include the United Nations, it was believed that the UN could be used to avoid direct confrontation between East and West.[51]

Although Kennedy's administration maintained this position in official circles, unofficially, the State Department and the CIA had every intention of ensuring that the political and economic direction of the Congo went in their favour.[52] Indeed, in June 1961, the Special Group met to discuss a programme of covert action of which the objective was to strengthen the position of Kasa-Vubu's central government by assisting members of the current parliament to gain a working majority. This, in turn, would offset the political actions of the Gizenga regime whose goal was to dominate parliament when it reconvened. If this goal was not met, there was a "real danger" that the country would come under the control of the Stanleyville government.[53] Consequently, with Gizenga receiving Soviet diplomatic support and military assistance, the Congo was wide open to the spread of communism.

The man identified as being most likely to bring a semblance of stability to the perilous situation in the Congo in mid-1961 was the political moderate Cyrille Adoula. A member of the Binza Group, it was recommended that the CIA be authorised to provide support to "key friendly elements" inside the Congolese government favourable to US interests.[54] However, while Adoula was able for the time being to resolve the Stanleyville issue by appointing Gizenga as one of his deputy prime ministers, other issues such as the secession of Katanga still represented the biggest obstacle to Congolese national integrity. Having declared the province's own independence on 10 July 1960, supported by powerful mining companies such as the Union Minière de Haut-Katanga (UMHK), since its secession the province had gradually built up armed forces comprising the Katangese Gendarmes, companies of mercenaries and an aerial unit known as the Force Aérienne Katangaise (FAK) or Avikat. Financial as well as military support for the secession made Tshombe resolute in his determination to maintain the *status quo* and to continue relations with Belgium. Terminating the Congo's reliance on Belgium had been one of Lumumba's Pan-Africanist-inspired objectives.

The Question of Katanga

If the question of the second secessionist state, South Kasai, was being resolved using sometimes brutal methods of repression used by the ANC, the question surrounding how to address the secession of Katanga and the failure to make any real headway against Katangan forces contributed to the feeling that control of the Congo was slipping from the UN's grasp. Compounding the idea that the UNOC did not have any clear objective in the Congo,[55] after noting the deaths of Lumumba, Maurice Mpolo and Joseph Okito in February 1961, the UN took a more aggressive stance and adopted Resolution 161 on the 21st of that month. This authorised UN peacekeepers to take all appropriate measures to prevent civil war in the Congo including the "evacuation" of foreign military, paramilitary, political advisors and mercenary personnel not under UN Command.[56] In spite of its being a move in the right direction and its leading to the arrest and repatriation of hundreds of mercenaries, it did little to blunt the overall effectiveness of Katangan military operations and the defence of the province given Katanga's air superiority at the time. The province's forces had not only repelled UN attacks, thus far, they had also fought off threats from Antoine Gizenga's Stanleyville-based rebel army and attacks emanating from tribal-based political organisations such as the Balubakat.

The FAK's greatest asset in its war against these opponents was the presence in its fleet of three French-made Fouga CM.170 Magisters. A jet trainer aircraft, armed typically with 7.62mm machine guns, bombs, rockets and Nord Aviation SS.11 anti-tank missiles, the Fouga Magister was an effective weapon that could be used to provide close air support for ground forces. An illustration of the aircraft's efficiency was seen at Jadotville from 13-17 September 1961. During the UN's Operation Morthor, an operation targeting mercenary units, the Fouga piloted by Belgian mercenary Joseph Deulin flying out of Kolwezi airfield was used to force Irish peacekeepers to surrender after a three-day battle. Somewhat ironically, the jets had been transported to Katanga aboard a Boeing 377 Stratocruiser operated by the Seven Seas Charter company. This company was later identified as a contractor for the CIA.[57]

Though two out of the three Katangan Magisters had been put out of action by September 1961 – one having crashed and the other captured – the last remaining aircraft's use at Jadotville and its attacks on UN supply lines meant that the battle for Katanga came to a deadlock. On 17 September, an already complicated situation was further convoluted when UN Secretary Dag Hammarskjöld was killed when his Douglas DC-6 crashed during its approach to Ndola airfield in Northern Rhodesia (Zambia). Hammarskjöld had been on his way to negotiate a ceasefire with Tshombe. The Burmese U Thant as successor to Hammarskjöld took a far more aggressive stance to the question of Katanga, and on 24 November 1961 authorised UN Resolution 169. Again containing the goal of maintaining the territorial integrity of the Congo and reaffirming many of the measures already stated in Resolution 161, it authorised U Thant to take "vigorous action, including the use of a "requisite measure of force" to put an end to hostilities.[58]

Sometime just before his death, Hammarskjöld had obtained the promise from UN member states that they would supply aircraft for UNOC operations. The United States had been approached and on 19 September 1961 Secretary of State McGeorge Bundy authorised the dispatch of US fighter aircraft and necessary logistical support to the Congo on a contingency basis. However, these aircraft would be used only if aircraft from other nations were not available, and only in the case of attack by Magisters on UN transport aircraft: they would not be used in offensives against Katangan forces.[59] As it turned out these US aircraft were never sent: Sweden provided five SAAB J-29 Tunnan fighter jets (nicknamed the Flying Barrel), Ethiopia sent four F-86 Sabre jets and India sent four B-58 Canberra light bombers. These UN aircraft were used to attack airfields at Kolwezi and Jadotville. Great Britain also supplied armaments: in December 1961, it provided twenty-four 1,000-pound bombs used to arm the Indian Canberras. On the other hand, it refused to transport them to the Congo given Katanga's opposition to Communism.[60] In the end, the bombs were delivered by US aircraft flying from bases in India.[61]

Whereas a period of relative calm followed the destruction of around half of the FAK's aircraft in early 1962,[62] the military position of the Congolese government was still unstable firstly because of the weakness of its national forces and, secondly because of the withdrawal by Ethiopia and India of their respective aircraft. This left the UN with only four J-29 fighter jets and had forced the United States to re-evaluate its position regarding its support for Cyrille Adoula. From July 1962, the US took a far more active role in Congolese internal affairs and moved away from its stance of maintaining neutrality in the face of increasing Cold War tensions with the Soviet Union. Firstly, the Department of Defense's Office of International Security Affairs sent a Special Military Advisory Team led by US Colonel M.J.L. Greene to the Congo and, secondly, it proposed a programme of assistance to the Congolese government in view of Adoula's Plan for National Reconciliation. While Greene gave subsequent advice on how the ANC could be modernised, trained, and turned into an effective fighting unit,[63] Adoula's plan was designed to bring Tshombe back into the fold of Congolese national politics thus ending the secession of Katanga.

Despite what appeared to be an opportunity for a peaceful outcome to this aspect of the Congo Crisis Tshombe knew that Katanga's economic might placed him in a strong position when it came to negotiating any agreement. Remaining steadfast in his determination to resist being forced into military submission, and frustrating attempts at reintegration, Tshombe even sought to strengthen his armed forces by buying more aircraft. Effectively, UN intelligence reports indicated that six T-6 Harvard aircraft, and a number of Dorniers, DHC-3 Otters and DH 104 Doves had been spotted at Kolwezi and at several new air strips.[64] Whereas these aircraft were remnants left by the Belgian Air Force (BAF) there was also evidence that Tshombe had bought six more Fouga jets. It was thought that they would be used for an attack on the UN airbase at Kamina.[65]

5
The Tools of Counterinsurgency

The Cuban Exile Solution to question of rebellion

As fighting continued between Katangese Gendarmes and the ANC in Northern Katanga in early October 1962, Chief of Staff Mobutu and other – unidentified – Congolese officials wondered why as a friend of the Congolese government the United States had not done more to assist it in the fight against an unfriendly regime. Comparing the Congo to Cuba, these officials warned that unless action was taken as soon as possible, the current national government would be replaced by a far-left regime that would almost certainly be unfriendly to the United States. This action consisted of sending "at least five jet fighters (together with mercenary pilots), several transport aircraft, trucks, and other equipment".[1] The mention of "mercenary pilots" being essential as the Congolese government had no other pilots at its disposal.

In a telegram dated 27 October 1962, the CIA station in Leopoldville proposed that the US government covertly supply five pilots to fly the Congolese government's existing force of five Harvard trainers and four transport aircraft. Preferably, these pilots should be made available before 5 November as this would provide the government with a "psychological and political lift out of all the proportion to the military value of the aircraft."[2] The proposal was studied at a meeting of CIA and State Department officials on 29 October during which the CIA stated that the that the "most readily available pilots were refugee [*less than one line not declassified*]". Two days later, a CIA memorandum added that only Adoula and Joseph Mobutu would know of the presence of the pilots, and on 2 November it notified the Stated Department that it was implementing the programme on an urgent basis.[3] Another telegram dated the 15 November 1962 and sent from the US Embassy in Leopoldville to the Secretary of State is important in that it is the first time that mention is given to the identity of the "refugee" pilots. Discussing "Adoula's 6 Cuban pilots from Caribbean Aero-Marine Corps",[4] it can be deduced that the airmen arrived in the Congo sometime in between the sending of the two telegrams.

Why use Cuban exiles?

In parallel to a plan to integrate Cuban exiles into US regular forces (see Chapter 7), by mid-1962 the CIA was looking at the ways it could best use Cuban exiles with the experience and knowledge to carry out covert operations on foreign soil. One idea was to create

The Terms and Conditions of a Pilot's Agreement with Caribbean Aeromarine

1. Agreement between Caribbean Aeromarine Co., a Florida corporation and signee pilot.
2. Duration of agreement – One year. During the first six months of the agreement, the signee's employment may be terminated by the employer at any time having given thirty days written notice. During the last six months, the agreement may be terminated by either the employer or the employee, a period of thirty days having been given as notice by either party.
3. Pilots will be paid at a basic, all-inclusive salary of $800 per month during the first six months of the agreement. During the last six months, the employee will be paid a basic, all-inclusive salary of $900. This salary is based on forty flying hours per month, and the employee shall be paid an additional $10 per flying hour for all flying hours in excess of forty flying hours per month.
4. The employer shall pay round-trip tourist class air transportation costs from Miami, Florida to destination and return, plus all other expenses directly relating to travel.
5. The employee shall have a two-month minimum salary guarantee under this agreement. However, in the event the said employer is unable to place the said employee within the two-month period, and the employee is released from the terms of this agreement to accept employment comparable to his last position of employment, then this guaranteed salary will cease, effective as of the date said employee accepts such re-employment.
6. The employer agrees to provide for the said employee during the term of this contract,
    a. A monetary benefit of $10,000 in the event of his death from any cause whatever during the term of this contract;
    b. An additional monetary benefit of $10,000 in the event of his death by accidental means while aboard a tested aircraft while operating in a non-war risk area and engaged in the performance of service under this contract, <u>provided</u> death occurs within 90 days of the accident;
    c. An additional monetary benefit of $30,000 in the event of his death by accidental means while engaged in the performance of services under this contract while aboard an aircraft being tested as to its airworthiness or when the aircraft is operating in a war risk area, provided death occurs within 90 days of the accident;
    d. That in the event the employee receives an injury or disability while directly engaged in the performance of services under this contract, he will be entitled to medical, surgical, hospital, transportation and disability benefits in such amount as in the sole discretion of the employer is proper, <u>provided</u> said benefits shall not exceed a total of $20,000 for the same injury or disability.
7. In the event, at the termination of this agreement, the employee accepts employment with an employer other than Caribbean Aeromarine Co., then the travel expenses and return transportation costs as hereinabove set forth shall not be paid to said employee.
8. In the event, during the term of this agreement, the employee should enter into a contract of employment with the Congolese National Government, then this contract shall terminate and shall be of no further force or effect.

The Congolese Air Force of 1964 comprised two squadrons: this T-6 was assigned to 21 Squadron and was photographed while taking off from N'Dolo Airport, outside Léopoldville. (Photo by Bob Houke)

A T-6 making a strafing run at Bumba.

a so-called Emergency Response Team (ERT) that could be used anywhere in the world and that could be deployed rapidly if needed. Using Roberto Medell as an intermediary for recruitment, those selected for the ERT underwent training at the Embry-Riddle School of Aviation in Miami.[5] A well respected member of the exile community, the CIA then called on his services in late 1962. Working out of offices situated on Miami's NW 36th Street close to the city's main airport, Medell informed anyone recruited that they would be working for Caribbean Aeromarine Corporation (Caramar),[6] one of any number of CIA front companies.[7] Those recruited had been pilots with a number of different services ranging from the Cuban Air Force and the Cuban Naval Aviation, to commercial pilots with Cubana Airlines or Aeropostal.[8] One Cuban exile recruited to start his second tour on 18 October 1963 was Captain Antonio Soto Vazquez.[9] A former Cuban military pilot, Soto had previously been the commander of a group of B-26s codenamed 'Paloma Two' at the Bay of Pigs.

The Birth of the Makasi

By the time the Congolese Air Force had become operational, the UN's Operation Grandslam was bringing the secession of Katanga to an end. Kamina Air Base was overrun by Swedish troops on 31 December, Jadotville came under UN control in early January 1963, and Kolwezi fell shortly after on 21 January. The battle for Katanga now over, any operation in which the CAF was due to take part was cancelled. In any case, their T-6s were still unarmed at that point.[10] Consequently, the role of the CAF at that point was to fly over Leopoldville and the surrounding areas making as much noise as possible as a show of government strength.[11] Mercenary commander Mike Hoare explains that the African mind associates great noise with great power.[12]

As was the case for all CIA covert operations at the time, the projects and the agents involved in them were each given a cryptonym. In the case of this particular Air Support Programme, it was decided that it would be denoted using the digraph WI (pronounced Y) due to the CIA's country code for the Congo, and to complete it with THRUSH in order to underline the avian nature of the project. As for the pilots themselves, though the official name of the group in which they served was 22 Wing, or Squadron, of the Congolese Air Force, the pilots never described themselves as belonging to this unit. Instead, they preferred to call themselves the Grupo Voluntario Cubano (GVC), or the Cuban Volunteer Group. At a later date, they would use the Lingala term *Makasi*. Describing something which possesses power, vigour, or vitality, the term would be used as a collective name for a pilot of any nationality attached to 22 Wing. Two French pilots, Jacques Roques and Robert Houke joined the squadron in early 1965, and former Royal Air Force (RAF) pilot, Terry Peet, joined the force sometime later the same year. The Cuban exile commando team arriving in the Congo in August 1964, and the naval force which operated on Lake Tanganyika from September 1965 were subsequently described as being "Makasi". On the other hand, these forces did not use the emblem adopted by the pilots. This was a black and yellow Cape buffalo that the pilots adorned the sides of all aircraft flown by 22 Wing as well as helicopter saddle

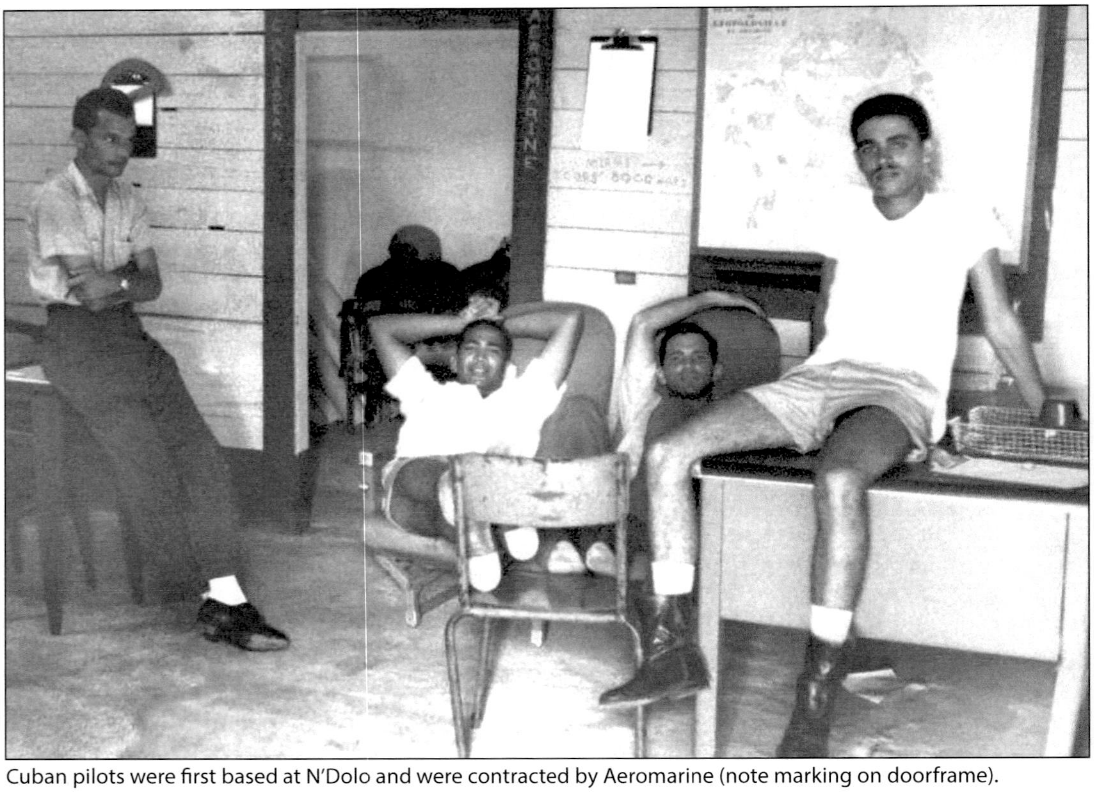

Cuban pilots were first based at N'Dolo and were contracted by Aeromarine (note marking on doorframe).

Not all Makasi pilots were Cubans. Standing to the left and right of one Cuban are Frenchmen Bob Houke and Jacques Roques. (Bob Houke Collection)

Jack Varela stands in front of a B-26, an aircraft he had flown at the Bay of Pigs in April 1961.

Cuban and British technicians loading ammunition into the battery of eight 12.7mm Browning machine guns of this B-26K: maximum load was 2,800 rounds. (T Spencer via Albert Grandolini)

tanks, flying jackets, coffee mugs, glasses and Zippo lighters.[13] The pilots, no doubt, adopted this logo during the time they "weren't doing any flying but just sat around drinking beer all day long", according to CIA pilot trainer Ed Dearborn.[14] Somewhat ironically, Patrice Lumumba had once been the Commercial Director for the Bracongo brewery.[15]

The first six Cuban exile pilots recruited by Medell's Aeromarine were based at N'Dolo Airfield located in the Lukunga district of the Congolese capital. Comprising Eduardo Herrera, Luis Cosme Toribio,[16] Antonio Soto Vazquez, Alfredo de la Maza,[17] Mario Ginebra Groero,[18] Rafael García Pujol,[19] these pilots were joined in the first few months of 1963 by fellow Bay of Pigs veterans Nildo Batista Hernandez[20], Raúl Solís Sariol,[21] Ernesto Peynó Inclán, and César Luaices Sotelo.[22] The commanding pilot was Joaquin Varela

The Makasi used a number of different airfields. Here, a T-28 takes off from Isiro. (Bob Houke Collection)

Two T-28s get underway from Albertville. (Bob Houke Collection)

Operations at Albertville provided spectacular views of Lake Tanganyika. This photograph shows T-28Cs FG-576 (right) and FG-292 (left).

who had flown a B-26 codenamed "Lobo One" on 17 April 1961.[23] His mission on that day was to bomb "Blue Beach" (Playa Girón), but he also bombed "Red Beach" (Playa Larga).[24] Also arriving in early 1963 were aviation gunner Francisco "Chiqui" Ginebra Groero,[25] radio operator Rafael "Toto" Quintero, and other support crew.

Rearming the Makasi

The sentiment held by many Congolese in 1963 was that the country's independence some three years previously had benefitted only a small proportion of the country's population. In particular, the inhabitants of rural areas such as the Kwilu Province, felt that their needs were being ignored by an elite made up of educated Congolese called the *évolués*, and that Patrice Lumumba's ideology of creating an egalitarian society had been scorned. This feeling of rejection and abandonment was the main cause of social unrest and was one which was to be exploited by Pierre Mulele from July 1963.

As former Minister for Education in Lumumba's first cabinet, and Foreign Minister in the Stanleyville rebel government set up by Antoine Gizenga in December 1961, Mulele was a revolutionary to the core. A Marxist-Leninist who had honed his ideology throughout the 1950s, in 1962 after Gizenga accepted a ministerial position in Adoula's government, Mulele sought exile from the Congo and spent the next year or so learning Maoist guerrilla tactics in the Peoples' Republic of China (PRC). By July 1963, Mulele felt ready to adapt these tactics to the Congolese context, and having trained hundreds of disaffected Congolese in order to form a militia, Mulele's goal was to bring down Adoula's government. A separate rebellion, but one which was linked ideologically, was also being prepared in the eastern Congolese province of the Kivu. Known more frequently as the Simba Rebellion, it was led by Gaston Soumialot, Laurent Désiré Kabila, and Christophe Gbenye. Overtly anti-American and spurred by political and ethnic grievances, this rebellion had the support of Baluba tribesmen, Tutsi warriors from Rwanda, and military and logistical assistance from the PRC and radical African nations such as Algeria. In April 1965, it was to be bolstered by the arrival of Che Guevara.

Despite (and because of) repressive measures intended to root out Mulele and his followers from September 1963, the Kwilu Rebellion started in earnest on 1 January 1964. Schools, religious missions, and industrial installations that the rebels saw as symbols of colonial rule were attacked and destroyed while, at the same time, teachers, nuns, priests and local government officials were beaten,

Table 1: T-28s flown by the Makasi, 1964-1967[31]

Serial	BuAerNo	Type	Date delivered	Notes
FA/FG-067	140067	T-28C	?? Sep 1964	crashed at Zongo Falls, pilot Giuseppe Gereghi killed, 13 December 1968
FA-111	138111	T-28B	27 May 1964	abandoned near Paulis after running out of fuel, 29 May 1965
FA-153	138153	T-28B	28 April 1965	crashed into Lake Tanganyika, pilot Jacques Roques killed, 20 November 1965
FG-244	50-244	T-28D-5	7 Mar 1966	ex-T-28A, to WIGMO, April 1966
FG-245	50-245	T-28D-5	7 Mar 1966	hit by ground fire, crash-landed Kamembe (Rwanda), pilot Simon M'Baki and passenger killed, 20 September 1967
FA/FG-252	146252	T-28C	15 Oct 1964	crashed during air display, N'Dolo, pilot Joseph N'Tambwe killed, 17 December 1968
FG-255	146255	T-28C	15 Oct 1964	written off after crash landing at Bunia, January 1965
FA/FG-260	138260	T-28B	28 Apr 1965	captured and blown up by anti-Mobutu mercenaries, Bunia, 2 August 1967
FA/FG-282	146282	T-28C	27 May 1964	crashed near Kalemie, pilot Vincent Ipoma killed, 20 August 1967
FA/FG-289	146289	T-28C	15 Oct 1964	withdrawn from service in 1975
FA-290	146290	T-28C	27 May 1964	hit by ground fire, crash-landed at Kabongo, pilot John Merriman died of injuries, 27 July 1964
FA-291	146291	T-28C	15 Oct 1964	crash-landed near Sudanese border, pilot Juan Peron safe, passenger Richard Holm badly wounded, 17 February 1965
FA-476	140476	T-28C	10 Mar 1965	abandoned near Paulis after running out of fuel, pilot Luis de la Guardia parachuted safely, 29 May 1965
FA/FG-477	140477	T-28C	27 May 1964	crashed on take-off from Albertville, pilot Mario Ginebra killed, 9 July 1965; rebuilt with parts from aircraft written off in 1968
FA/FG-485	140485	T-28C	15 Oct 1964	captured and blown up by anti-Mobutu mercenaries, Bunia, 2 August 1967
FA-490	140490	T-28C	27 May 1964	hit trees during strafing ground attack near Mahagi, pilot Fausto Gomez killed, 17 December 1964
FA-496	140496	T-28C	27 May 1964	crash-landed near Sudanese border after running out of fuel, pilot Juan Tunon killed by rebels, 17 February 1965
FA/FG-516	140516	T-28C	27 May 1964	withdrawn from service in 1975
FG-524	49-1524	T-28D-5	25 Feb 1969	crashed during air display, N'Djili, pilot Michel N'Gabu and passenger Jacques Mpasi killed, 7 February 1970
FG-528	49-1528	T-28D-5	2 Dec 1967	hit Congo River near Kwamouth, pilot Crispin Mwambi killed, 4 August 1968
FG-533	49-1533	T-28D-5	2 Dec 1967	hit by ground fire, ditched in Lake Tanganyika, pilot Flemming Friberg injured, 27 October 1970
FG-542	49-1542	T-28D-5	2 Dec 1967	crashed near Kinshasa, pilot Roger Makulu killed, 17 Jun 1968
FG-543	51-3543	T-28D-5	21 Sep 1965	crashed near Kinshasa, pilot Peter Wicksteed and passenger Desmond Parker killed, 10 May 1967
FG-559	51-3559	T-28D-5	21 Sep 1965	crashed near Kikwit (ferry flight), pilot Arturo Piqué killed, 12 October 1965
FG-563	51-3563	T-28D-5	25 Sep 1965	abandoned following engine failure, pilot Alberto Perez parachuted safely, 13 March 1967
FA/FG-576	140576	T-28C	15 Oct 1964	withdrawn from service in 1975
FG-634	49-1634	T-28D-5	25 Feb 1965	withdrawn from service in 1965

tortured and killed. In the face of a severe lack of resistance from the ANC, by mid-March 1964, the context had deteriorated so much through rebel activity that US military analysts in Leopoldville began to wonder if the ANC was capable of ensuring any internal security at all. At that point, Commander in Chief, Strike Command (CINSTRIKE) dispatched counter-guerrilla warfare specialist Colonel William Dodds to the Congo to evaluate the situation. Dodds concluded that if the rebellion was not "rolled back" before the end of June 1964, there was a serious danger that it would act as a catalyst for other insurgencies in the Congo.[26] As the last of the UN peacekeeping forces were due to leave in June, it was recommended that the ANC be provided with additional military equipment and transport capacity.[27] Furthermore, it was recommended that the programme of providing psychological non-combat air support be changed into "active combat participation".[28]

In view of Dodd's report, on 24 April 1964 President Johnson authorised the creation of a much more substantial air support force to assist the ANC in its operations against Mulele. The existing T-6s were armed with .30 calibre (7.62mm) machine guns and rockets and, then, were replaced by North American T-28 Trojan aircraft. Ten Piasecki H-21 Workhorse/Shawnee helicopters commonly known as the "flying banana" were recommended but it is unclear

The refuelling of the aircraft often gave the local children the opportunity to earn money. (Houke)

A T-28C FA-576, armed with a 250-round gun-pod and a rocket pod rolling down the tarmac behind two B-26s. This aircraft was delivered to the Congo in October 1964.

T-28C FA-252 arrived in the Congo in October 1964. Note the early-style, smaller Makasi insignia and the seven-tube rocket pod. (Albert Grandolini Collection)

if they were delivered. None of the Cuban pilots were qualified to fly helicopters at the time but it is possible that the craft were later used by the Force Aérienne Tactique au Congo (FATAC), a Belgian-staffed air unit used for logistical purposes. The multi-mission H-21 was to be used for rescue and as air support for the T-28s.[29] The rearmed T-6s were subsequently transferred for use by the FAC's 21 Squadron which was composed of British, South African, Canadian or Belgian pilots.

The six T-28s delivered through the US Military Assistance Programme on 25 May 1964 were far different from the 800-horsepower, two-bladed model used by the USAF at the time. Powered by the beefier air-cooled Wright R-1820-86A or 9HD Cyclone radial nine piston engine and a three-bladed Hamilton Standard propeller, it was capable of producing 1,425 horsepower and reaching a top speed of 300 knots (346 miles per hour). It was armed with two .50 calibre machine guns and two rocket pods each capable of holding seven folding-fin rockets. Eventually, the United States would supply three T-28Bs, fourteen T-28Cs and nine T-28Ds to the Congolese government. Twenty-five of these aircraft were delivered between 27 May 1964 and 7 November 1967, the end of the Congo Crisis. To fly the T-28Bs delivered at the end of May 1964, the CIA recruited two more Cuban exiles, namely Gustavo Ponzoa and René Garcia. Ponzoa had

Table 2: B-26s flown by the Makasi, 1964-1967[35]

Serial	BuAerNo	Type	Date delivered	Notes
RF/FR-644	64-17644	B-26K	18 Aug 1964	nick-named Shit-House Mouse/Cachita
RF/FR-645	64-17645	B-26K	18 Aug 1964	nick-named Rum Dum
RF/FR-646	64-17646	B-26K	18 Aug 1964	nick-named Boogie Bogey
FR-649	64-17649	B-26K	?? Jan 1964	
FR-662	64-17662	B-26K	?? Jan 1964	later FM-662

FA-496 was delivered to the Congo aboard a USAF C-133 in May 1964. (Albert Grandolini Collection)

The Makasi played a vital role in operations such as White Giant in early 1965. These operations involved mercenary forces as well as the ANC. (Photo by Bob Houke)

piloted "Gorilla One" at the Bay of Pigs while Garcia had flown "Linda Two".[30]

Because of the rapid advance of the Simba throughout June and July, and their capture of Stanleyville at the beginning of August, the CIA relayed an urgent message through the US Embassy in Leopoldville to the White House to provide a different type of aircraft to complement the six T-28Cs. This request was noted and followed by a search for aircraft capable of delivering extra fire power. It was decided that the craft the best suited to the job was the Douglas B-26 Invader: guns could be fitted to present a formidable ground-attack aircraft, and the Cubans knew the plane well having used it during the Bay of Pigs Invasion.

The only drawback with the B-26B model was that it was ageing having first entered service in 1942. It had been withdrawn from service from the USAF in February 1964 after two accidents related to fatigue. While the model had been brought up to date by its manufacturer, the On Mark company, and became the B-26K, four of the non-modified B-26Bs were sent to the Congo to join WITHRUSH. They had been decommissioned from service in Vietnam and were located at the USAF base at Clark Field in the Philippines. One of the four never made it further than Okinawa in Japan while another crashed in Aden on its way to Leopoldville.[32] For the two B-26Bs that did arrive, the Cubans refused to fly them for combat missions due to their structural fatigue. Instead, they flew the B-26K model which had undergone extensive improvements: the fuselage and wings had been reinforced and a new 2,500 horsepower engine installed. This gave the B-26K a maximum speed of some 300 mph. Extra fuel tanks were fitted to the wings to increase the extent of the aircraft's operational area, and its climb rate and operational ceiling had been improved. Modifications had also been brought to the cockpit, and pilot and navigator could now sit side-by-side. As for the B-26Ks' weaponry, those used in the Congo were fitted with eight .50 calibre machine guns mounted in the nose.[33] The delivery of the B-26Ks naturally led to the further recruitment of pilots. Those who arrived in the Congo in August 1964 included Fausto Gómez, Tristán Garcia, Tony Blázquez, Castor Cereceda[34], Reginaldo Blanco and Ignacio Rojas.

The Makasi Commando Unit

As we saw in Chapter 8 of *Ripe for Rebellion*,[36] the Makasi's B-26Ks were used to great effect during operations which took place in and around Stanleyville in late November 1964. An essential element in Colonel Vandewalle's plans to reconquer the Congo and to rescue over 1,300 hostages held in Stanleyville by the Simba and as part of the 5th Mechanised Brigade, the Makasi aircraft flown by Castor Cereceda, Tomás Afont, Francisco Alvarez and Reginaldo Blanco attacked Simba positions at Simi Simi Airport in Stanleyville. Disabling enemy artillery placements, these attacks cleared the way for the arrival of USAF C-130s used to transport Belgian paratroopers. During the landing of men and equipment, the absence of anti-aircraft weapons meant that transporters drew only rifle fire and suffered minimal damage.

Whereas the efforts of Belgian troops and 5 Commando have formed the basis for a number of studies on the Dragon operations, the participation of a group of Cuban exile commandos is often unknown or has been overlooked. Otherwise known as 58 Commando and, therefore, part of the 5th Mechanised Brigade, this unit had first arrived in the Congo in August as part of a plan to rescue the American consular officials held captive by Nicolas Olenga in Stanleyville. Known as Operation Low Beam and codenamed WIPEGASUS, this plan was eventually abandoned due

This B-26K (FA-644) was converted from an A-26C Invader in 1964. Note the rocket pod on the outboard underwing pylon. (Albert Grandolini Collection)

FA-649 arrived in the Congo in January 1965 and left in October 1966. (Albert Grandolini Collection)

Members of the Makasi Air Force in front of a B-26K, at Albertville, in 1964. (Reginaldo Blanco)

Max Rojas at the controls of a B-26K. Rojas was a veteran of the Bay of Pigs invasion.

FA-662 served in the Congo from January 1965 to February 1967. It then served in Vietnam.

Makasi Bell-47 taking off from Albertville. Notable are the big air blades, useful for landing in marshy areas or on the water. (Bob Houke Collection)

A Makasi Bell-47 at Baraka, during a CASEVAC operation. (Houke)

The Makasi fleet also included three C-46s like this one photographed at Baudouinville. (see colour section for details).

The wounded were evacuated by helicopter to hospitals like this one in Albertville. (Houke)

A wounded member of 5 Commando waiting to be evacuated.

The Congolese Air Force HQ in Stanleyville. (Bob Houke Collection)

Makasi commandos are alerted to events taking place at Kilometre 8. (Courtesy Miami Herald)

to the difficulty of the logistics involved in approaching the city and the fear that the detection of the commandos would lead to the hostages being killed.[37]

Though not much is known about the recruitment of men for WIPEGASUS, we do know that the operation was led by the CIA's William 'Rip' Robertson and seconded by another Company operative known only as "Mitch". Otherwise, as the table below shows, four of the 19 men in the group were members of Brigade 2506, and at least two had been involved in CIA operations since April 1960. One thing all 19 men had in common is that they were members of the MRR or associate groups.

By the time the Cuban commandos arrived in Stanleyville most of the Simbas had either fled, been captured, or had been killed by Belgian paratroopers as they made their way from Simi Simi Airport to the centre of Stanleyville. As for the different mercenary forces, they entered either from the south or, in the case of the Cubans, from the north where they were obliged to cross the Congo River.

The Makasi Commando Unit arrived in the Congo in 1964 and was later named 58 Commando. (Courtesy Miami Herald)

Makasi commandos Menedes, Silva, Castro, Blasque, Benitez, Valliciergo. (Angel Benitez Collection) (Courtesy Miami Herald)

The scene that greeted Makasi commandos at Kilometre 8, 24 November 1964.

Table 3: Makasi Commando Unit[38]			
Name	**Place and date of birth**	**Entry into US**	**Notes**
Arguelles Izquierdo, Santiago, J.	Havana, 30 September 1933	March 1960	Bay of Pigs veteran
Benitez, Angel Manuel	Consolacion del Sur, 22 November 1938	Early 1962	
Calas, Alicio Raque	Havana, 1 October 1936	15 February 1962	
Fernandez Martinez, Alfredo	Santa Clara, 17 January 1925	1 January 1959	Fled Cuba as soon Batista's regime ended. Nicknamed "Calviño"
Fernandez Morales, Conrado	San Juan de las Yeras, 18 January 1932	25 March 1962	
Fuentes Games, Felix	Marianao, 19 July 1933	22 December 1961	Nicknamed "Felo"
Garcia Duarte, Orlando	Mariel, 24 February 1935	12 July 1960	Sent to the Belle Chasse Louisiana Ammunition Dump (JMMOVE) for training in February 1961. This was a CIA controlled training camp used from February-April 1961 and used to provide training in the use of special explosives and underwater operations for Cuban exiles involved in the Bay of Pigs.
Gonzalez Castro, José Angel	Trinidad, Las Villas, 23 May 1940	15 August 1960	Bay of Pigs veteran and later USAF. Nicknamed "El Chino"
Hernandez Martinez, José Severino	San Jose de las Lajas, 1 October 1936	15 February 1962	Nicknamed "Juan Roque"
Lazo Gonzalez, Guillermo	Pinar del Rio, 10 February 1933	18 July 1962	
Lopez Cristo, Pedro	Vueltas, 26 May 1934	2 September 1962	
Martinez Gonzalez, Raimundo	Vueltas, 23 January 1934	3 September 1962	
Morales Navarrette, Ricardo Anibal	Havana, 14 June 1939	29 November 1960	Took refuge in the Brazilian Embassy in October 1960 and entered the United States at Miami as a Cuban refugee on 29 November 1960. A former agent of Cuba's G-2 intelligence services and nicknamed 'The Monkey', Navarrette Morales was a member of Operation 40. According to one source, Morales would later become one of Miami's biggest drug dealers. Bay of Pigs veteran nicknamed "El Mono".
Perez Martinez, Alberto	Havana, 15 November 1938	20 August 1960	Nicknamed "Dr. Kildare"
Rivero Coloma, Manuel A.	Havana, 11 September 1940	22 August 1960	Nicknamed "El Gallego"
Rodriguez Triana, Jorge Delio	Cardenas, 22 February 1941	Late 1961	
Romero Arias, Mario Andres	Guira de Melena, 20 January 1935	29 September 1961	
Silva del Monte, Jorge Luis	Havana, 26 June 1929	August 1960	Nicknamed "Fotingo"
Tamayo Cordovi, Juan Cornelio	Guaimaro, Camaguay, 24 June 1938	1 July 1960	Bay of Pigs veteran nicknamed "El Negro"

Pilot Profile – Reginaldo Blanco

Born in La Palma in Cuba's Pinar del Rio Province on 15 November 1942, Reginaldo de Jesús Blanco Gómez, known more commonly as Reginaldo Blanco arrived in Miami on 19 April 1961. Though missing out on joining the Bay of Pigs invasion force by a matter of days, Blanco was given the opportunity to renew his fight against Communism when, in 1962, he became one of the first Cuban exiles to join the Cuban Volunteer Programme. Sent to Lackland Air Force Base in San Antonio, Texas as a supply specialist, Blanco was then accepted for pilot-training and trained on T-6s. Learning of the Congo mission and recruited through his contacts with the MRR in mid-1964, in August with just nine hours of training on B-26s, Blanco took a Pan-Am flight from Miami to New York. Here he was told in no uncertain terms that he should never reveal the identity of his employer, and that if ever he was captured he was "on his fucking own". The next step in his journey was Leopoldville. Gaining the nickname "*Le Petit Mercenaire*" Blanco arrived on 12 August. During his time in the Congo, Blanco flew over 150 combat missions, and would see hand-to-hand combat in Kabalo and Katanga. These missions included the Stanleyville rescue operations on 24 November 1964.

Makasi pilot Reginaldo Blanco (second left) at the Lackland Air Base in 1963. Blanco arrived in the Congo in August 1964. (Blanco)

Panchito Alvarez and Reginaldo Blanco at the controls of their B-26K.

Table 4: C-46s and C-47s flown by the Makasi, 1964-1967

Serial	Registration	Type	Date delivered	Notes
42-3577	9T-PLJ	C-46A-30-CU	?? ?? 1966	purchased from Transair Sweden as a wreck, repaired; crashed in the Congo River due to fuel starvation, killing 45, 16 April 1969
42-3580	9Q-CRP	C-46A-35-CU	?? Dec 1967	purchased from Fairline Sweden, withdrawn from service in 1970
43-48241	9T-PKF	C-47A-30DK	3 Jun 1964	destroyed in Stanleyville to avoid capture by the Simbas

De Havilland Doves were also used for CASEVAC duties. This one was was photographed at Bouta.

Pilot Profile – Ignacio Rojas

Ignacio 'Max' Rojas was born in Santa Clara, Cuba in 1935. Qualifying as a pilot and joining the Cuban Naval Air Force, in 1958 was sent to Pensacola, Florida where as part of an agreement between the US and Cuban governments, he received training on T-34s and T-28s. Returning to Cuba after the overthrow of Batista, Rojas then flew for the navy in Castro's newly-formed armed forces. As one of thirteen pilots who received special privileges in Castro's Revolutionary Navy, Rojas was responsible for flying officials such as Castro and Guevara to meetings around Cuba. It was during this time that Rojas realised that Castro was 'truly Communist' and he was approached by another pilot to discuss the possibility of overthrowing the new regime. After applying for a visa to visit the US, Rojas was finally dismissed from the navy in the summer of 1960 after planning to steal an aircraft to escape Cuba and go to the US. He arrived in the US on 3 October 1960 for his honeymoon after being married the previous day. During his honeymoon around the Miami Beach area, Rojas was joined by five other pilots from the Cuban Revolutionary Navy (Paul Lazo, Demetrio Perez, Raul Vasquez, Tomas Afont and Octavio Soto). On October 12, 1960 they were flown by the CIA in a DC-4 to training camps in Retalhuleu, Guatemala where they would train for the Bay of Pigs invasion programmed for April 1961. Rojas was then sent to Nicaragua where plans to destroy Castro's air force were made. As the pilot of a group of three B-26s codenamed 'Gorilla Two', the mission was to bomb airports over a two-day period and to provide air cover at 'Blue Beach'. Gorilla Two shot down one of Castro's B-26s. Rojas's navigator was Esteban Bovo-Carás, another recruited for the Congo mission.

Aircraft Maintenance

As the number of aircraft, missions and operational bases increased – Kamina Air Base in Katanga being the largest and most important – so did the need for personnel for weapons and maintenance purposes. Inspired by the activities of a Panamanian-registered company named Aerovias Panama that had been operating in the Congo for some time, the CIA's Lichtenstein-registered Western International Ground Maintenance Organisation (WIGMO) was officially created on 21 September 1964 to manage a staff of some one hundred Cuban, British, Swedish, German, Polish, Spanish and Danish nationals.

The CIA used its own maintenance team composed mainly of Europeans. Notable is the application of the Makasi insignia on the fuel tank, and the serial number of this Bell 47: FH-944. (Photo by Bob Houke)

Insignia of the ill-fated Brigade 2506. (via author)

Flag of Brigade 2506. (via author)

The MRR's flag and arm patch, featuring a trident that symbolised its links to the Holy Trinity and the sea. (via author)

Wing badge of the flying crews assigned to Brigade 2506. (via author)

On arrival in the Congo, CIA T-28Cs were formally assigned to the 211th Squadron of the Congolese Air Force – even if the Congolese had no operational authority over them or their crews. All the aircraft were painted in the standard US Navy pattern consisting of light gull gray (FS 36440) on top surfaces and sides, and insignia white (FS 17875) on undersurfaces and the rudder. Both were applied in high gloss, but this rapidly dulled due to exposure to the elements and wear. They wore no other markings than the type designation ('T-28C' in this case) and the full BuAerNo in black, below the horizontal stabilator. Their armament consisted of two gun-pods with 125 rounds each, installed on inboard underwing pylons. A pair of underwing hardpoints on each wing was usually used for installation of one or two 68mm rocket launchers under every hardpoint. This aircraft (BuAerNo 140516) was unique in having its propeller head painted in orange: on all other T-28s, this was left in black. (Artwork by Tom Cooper)

Weeks after their arrival in the Congo, the CIA's T-28s began receiving a long black field along the centre fuselage behind their exhaust, to cover-up the heavy stain. Notably, all the aircraft still had their blind flying hoods mounted along the top of the cockpit. The first major modification arrived in the form of much bigger and heavier, 500-round gun pods. To further increase their firepower, CIA ground crews coupled three, and then four launch rails for 68mm unguided rockets under each of the two outboard underwing pylons. This aircraft (BuAerNo 146291) was lost when it ran out of fuel near the Sudanese border. Its pilot, Juan Peron, was recovered safely, but his passenger Richard Holm was badly burned. (Artwork by Tom Cooper)

The next major change in the looks of the CIA T-28s in the Congo was the application of national markings in July 1964. For a few weeks, just the roundel was applied on the rear fuselage: only two or three are known to have received it on the top of the right wing and under the left wing. This was followed by the emergence of serials: always in black, these were applied in fonts reminiscent of those used by the Royal Air Force, on either side of the roundel. Notably, most of the aircraft received the national insignia even before the long black field along the fuselage. The final addition consisted of the Congolese flag used as the fin flash. While the armament frequently remained the same, the inboard of two underwing pylons was meanwhile removed to decrease drag. This T-28C (BuAerNo 146290) was probably shot down by ground fire: pilot John Merriman managed a crash landing at Kabongo but died of injuries. (Artwork by Tom Cooper)

With the application of the long black field along the centre fuselage, the 'almost-definite' look of the CIA's T-28s in the Congo was complete. Some aircraft delivered to replace attrition – like this example, BuAerNo 140067, which arrived on 25 September 1964 – had their ruder painted in light gull gray. Moreover, the blind flight hood along the top of the cockpit was replaced by the green transparency, installed to decrease the effects of the sun. This T-28C survived its service with the CIA, but crashed at Zongo Falls on 13 December 1968, killing the pilot Giuseppe Gereghi. (Artwork by Tom Cooper)

Starting with replacement aircraft delivered from early 1965 onwards, the fonts of serials applied on the CIA T-28s in the Congo was changed to the 'Amarillo USAF' – the standard font for all aircraft operated by the US Air Force. This aircraft – BuAerNo 140476 – was the last T-28C delivered, and is shown in almost pristine condition because it was written off only two months after its arrival: it had to be abandoned in the air after running out of fuel. Pilot Luis de la Guardia parachuted safely but landed with some injuries. (Artwork by Tom Cooper)

The final look of the CIA's T-28s flown by the Cubans in the Congo emerged when ground crews began applying a 'unit insignia'. Inspired by the brand of beer produced in Paulis named Makasi ('very strong' or 'strong bull' in the Lingala language), this practice emerged in May-June 1965. Initially, the insignia consisted of a small, and crude artwork in mid-brown and black, together with the word MAKASI in black, worn on only a few aircraft. By June-July 1965, the second, much larger and better drawn version began emerging, which was applied on all of the T-28s in service at the time. This insignia is shown in detail in the insert. This aircraft, BuAerNo 140282 received a small individual nickname, 'Hot Dog', applied on the cockpit frame. It crashed near Kalemie after running out of fuel on 20 August 1967, killing its pilot, Lieutenant Vincent Ipoma. (Artwork by Tom Cooper)

The most powerful variant of this type to see service with the CIA in the Congo – and thus with the Cuban Volunteer Group, or the Makasi – was the T-28D. The first examples arrived in late 1965. Contrary to the earlier T-28Bs and T-28Cs, they were painted in the standard USAF gray colour (FS 36473), had their anti-glare panels in a slightly different shape, and all their maintenance stencils in USAF-style. Moreover, their USAF-serials – worn until delivery to the Congo – had to be overpainted, resulting in a slightly darker mark on the fin. T-28D-5s also received a much bigger roundel on the fuselage, resulting in their serials being spaced more widely. Finally, all of them received the definitive version of the Makasi insignia: introduced in late 1965 and early 1966, this was slightly larger than either of the earlier variants, and applied in black and yellow. (Artwork by Tom Cooper)

Following the deployment of T-28s to the Congo, the CIA realised that many of the 20-25 Cuban pilots were Bay of Pigs veterans that had previously flown B-26s. Correspondingly, it took care to deploy this type in the country. With the first three B-26B/Cs found to be in poor condition, the decision was taken to divert three B-26Ks – brand-new from being rebuilt by the On Mark company for the USAF. The aircraft were all painted in green (FS 14062) on top surfaces, and gray (FS 16422) on undersurfaces (the sole B-26B that was flown in the Congo is known to have been painted in gray FS 36373 overall). The sole national marking consisted of a roundel applied on the rear fuselage. The serial – applied in white on the fin – consisted of a prefix RF followed by the last three of their full B-26K serial. This is a reconstruction of the third of the first three B-26Ks – nicknamed Boogie Bogey. (Artwork by Tom Cooper)

During the second phase of their operations in the Congo, CIA B-26Ks retained their original livery, but received a fin flash in the form of the national flag, and had their serials moved from the fin to either side of the roundel on the rear fuselage. The Makasi insignia was initially applied starting in late 1965, on a white square below the front portion of the cockpit (on either side of the aircraft, and with the bull always pointing towards the nose). The CIA imposed strict restrictions upon the ordnance deployed by its B-26Ks in the Congo. Correspondingly, bombs were never used, and their internal bomb bay was occupied by extra fuel tanks. Instead, the primary armament was eight 12.7mm machine guns installed in the nose (with total capacity of 2,800 rounds), and pods for unguided rockets – of which the latter were rarely used. (Artwork by Tom Cooper)

The last of the five B-26Ks operated by the CIA in the Congo was the example with full serial number 64-17662. Originally wearing the Congolese serial FR-662, it was later re-registered as FM-662, and received the Makasi insignia in its final position, on the nose, right behind the gun barrels. As well as flying thousands of other combat sorties against the Simbas, Cuban-piloted B-26Ks led the C-130s involved in deploying the Belgian paratroops during Operations Dragon Rouge and Dragon Noir, and then supported foreign mercenaries – foremost 5, 6 and 10 Commandos – in mopping up. (Artwork by Tom Cooper)

For operations on the Lake Tanganyka, the CIA acquired two Seawart Seacraft Swift Mk I, 50-foot boats. They were delivered to the Congo on board USAF C-124 transports. Painted in medium sea gray, each had a crew of 20-25 and was armed with three .50 cal and one .30 cal machine guns, and a single 57mm recoilless rifle. Like the rest of the Cuban Volunteers Group in the Congo, they were supported by Curtiss C-46 transports: sadly, only the appearance of the front part of the fuselage of these is known, but it is certain that at least two had received the Makasi insignia in 1966-1967. (Artworks by Anderson Subtil & Tom Cooper)

The Simbas were famous for their flamboyant headgear and this man added an arrangement of flowers, Christmas ornaments and animal skins to his bush hat. This rebel wears old civilian boots and typically nondescript green field shirt of the Armée Nationale Congolaise, but his trousers are made from Belgian "brushstroke" camouflage material. In his belt, in addition to magazine pouches, he carries a large machete, and his main weapon iss a Belgian semi-automatic rifle SAFN M1949 in .30-06 Springfield. (Artwork by Anderson Subtil)

While considering themselves 'mercenaries', Cuban volunteers in the Congo were a part of an organised military force. Correspondingly, their pilots were originally issued with standard USAF flight overalls in green, and caps. Towards the end of their involvement, they were issued camouflaged flight overalls, as shown here: this pilot has added the Makasi bull emblem. Demonstrating their free (and 'Cuban') spirit, many pilots wore cowboy hats: this one was decorated by a piece of animal skin. Personal armament consisted of a .45 ACP Colt M1911 pistol in a shoulder holster. Around his waist he wears an M1936 pistol belt with a .45 magazine pouch and M3 trench knife. (Artwork by Anderson Subtil)

Like the pilots of the Cuban Volunteer Group, the Cuban sailors recruited by the CIA for operations in the Congo were members of an organised military force. Correspondingly, they were issued with standard US Navy uniforms - including shirts and trousers - in khaki. This artwork shows one of the MRR sailors involved in operations in the Caribbean, the attire of which was far more casual. In addition to blue shirt and jeans, he is shown wearing the 'Chukka Boots' - light shoes developed by the British for the war in North Africa during the 1940s, and much more appropriate than heavy military boots. His firearm consists of a 9mm Parabellum Vigneron submachine gun, a weapon virtually unknown outside Belgium and its zone of influence. (Artwork by Anderson Subtil)

Italian and Belgian personnel serving with the 21st Squadron of the Congolese Air Force, with one of their North American T-6s. The same aircraft were initially flown by Cuban pilots deployed in the country by the CIA. (Photo by Bob Houke)

A nice study of the T-28D-5 serial number FA-153, as seen while armed with the 500-round gun pod and a 7-round pod for unguided rockets. This photograph was taken before the Makasi insignia was applied. This aircraft crashed into Lake Tanganyika in November 1965, killing its pilot Jacques Roques. (Photo by Bob Houke)

The B-26K serial number RF-645 as seen relatively shortly after its arrival in the Congo, at Kitona AB, in Katanga, together with its Cuban crew (Max Rojas is furthest right). Notable is the nickname applied on the gun-bay cover: Rum Dum. (Photo by Bob Houke)

One of three C-46s operated by the Makasi, seen at Baudouinville in 1967. The inset shows the third and final version of the Makasi insignia, as applied on C-46s and T-28Ds. (Photo by Bob Houke)

One of the Bell 47s operated by the Makasi for CASEVAC purposes, photographed at Aketi, wore the serial FH-946. Notable is the application of the Makasi insignia on the fuel tank. (Photo by Bob Houke)

A mortar team of Makasi commandos providing protection for a CASEVAC operation at Aketi. (Photo by Bob Houke)

A map of the Congo in the 1960s, with principal air bases and airfields used by the Cuban Volunteer Group. (Map by Tom Cooper)

Regulations and Instructions for Pilots

When WIGMO became fully operational from September 1964, it was a well-oiled and highly-structured organisation that left little to chance. As Terry Peet described after being transferred from 21 to 22 Wing in January 1966, WIGMO's hangar and office complex situated about a mile east of the civilian terminal at N'Djili airport looked no different from the hangars used by Sabena or Air Congo. Inside the building, however, it was just like a USAF base. There were "proper tools, a huge store filled with every imaginable kind of spare part, and overflowing armoury, and fully equipped engine bays".

As one might imagine given this organizational efficiency and a hierarchal structure comprising a Senior Air Officer, a Chief Air Officer, Chief Pilots, Station Chief Pilots, and administrative services, a pilot arriving in the Congo was also expected to comply to certain regulations and obey instructions. If, in theory, he was a 'mercenary' and, as such, could be expected to fit a profile typically associated with a 'soldier of fortune', in practice the pilot was just like any other soldier acting within regular forces. What follows is adapted from a document obtained from a private source. Dated 20 April 1965, it contains the regulations for pilots and crewmen serving in the Congo.

A pilot typically arrived at N'Djili Airport in Leopoldville after having travelled from Miami via JFK Airport, New York. Other connecting flights could be joined at Dakar,

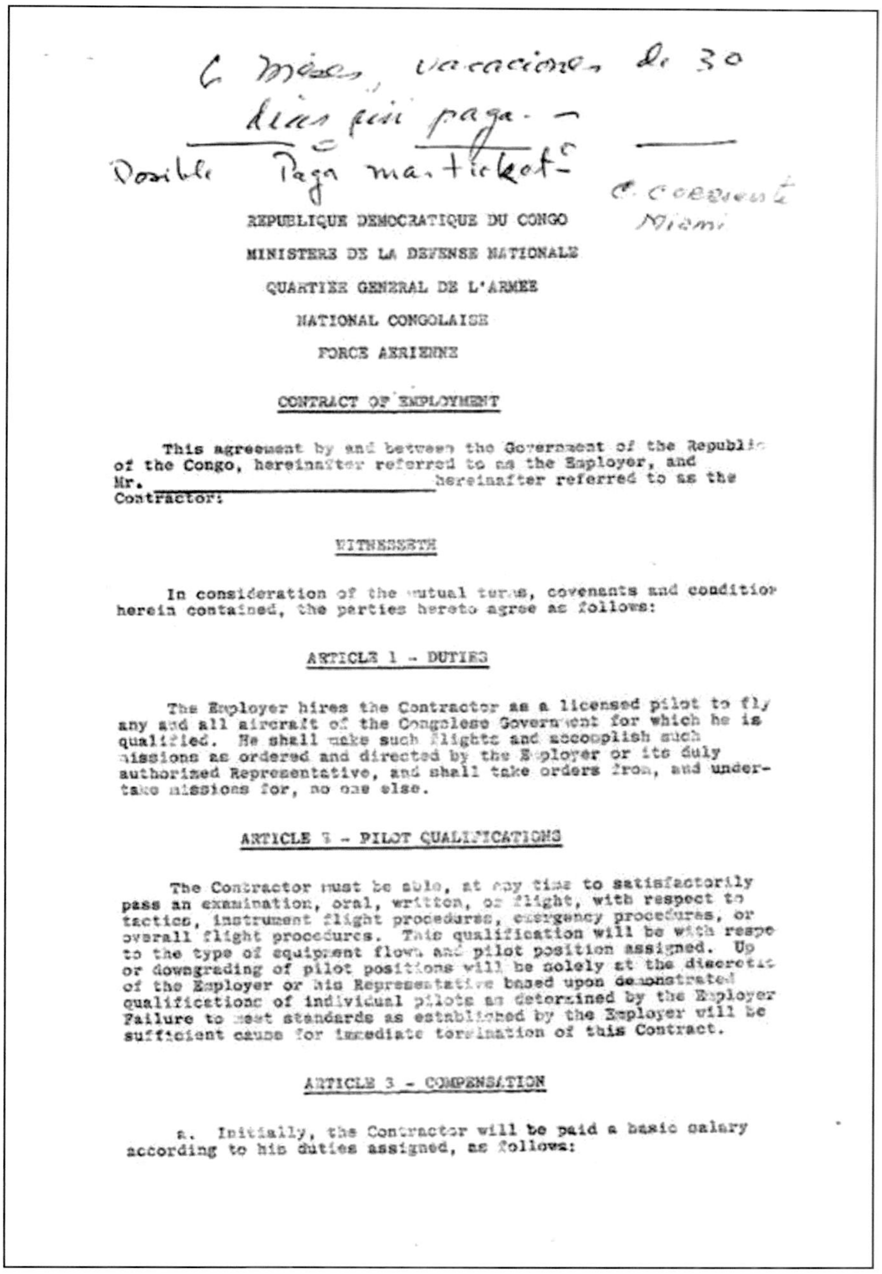

REPUBLIQUE DEMOCRATIQUE DU CONGO

MINISTERE DE LA DEFENSE NATIONALE

QUARTIER GENERAL DE L'ARMEE

NATIONAL CONGOLAISE

FORCE AERIENNE

CONTRACT OF EMPLOYMENT

This agreement by and between the Government of the Republic of the Congo, hereinafter referred to as the Employer, and Mr. ______________ hereinafter referred to as the Contractor:

WITNESSETH

In consideration of the mutual terms, covenants and conditions herein contained, the parties hereto agree as follows:

ARTICLE 1 - DUTIES

The Employer hires the Contractor as a licensed pilot to fly any and all aircraft of the Congolese Government for which he is qualified. He shall make such flights and accomplish such missions as ordered and directed by the Employer or its duly authorized Representative, and shall take orders from, and undertake missions for, no one else.

ARTICLE 2 - PILOT QUALIFICATIONS

The Contractor must be able, at any time to satisfactorily pass an examination, oral, written, or flight, with respect to tactics, instrument flight procedures, emergency procedures, or overall flight procedures. This qualification will be with respe[ct] to the type of equipment flown and pilot position assigned. Up or downgrading of pilot positions will be solely at the discreti[on] of the Employer or his Representative based upon demonstrated qualifications of individual pilots as determined by the Employer. Failure to meet standards as established by the Employer will be sufficient cause for immediate termination of this Contract.

ARTICLE 3 - COMPENSATION

a. Initially, the Contractor will be paid a basic salary according to his duties assigned, as follows:

Pages of the pilot contract signed by all that flew for the CIA in the Congo of the 1960s. (*Continued opposite.*)

Senegal or Lagos, Nigeria in order to maintain secrecy. On arrival in Leopoldville, a pilot was met by the Chief Pilot or his designated representative then expedited through customs and immigration. Temporary lodging – usually at the Hotel Memling – was provided until a permanent assignment had been found.

The following day, a pilot reported at 0800 to the Chief Pilot or the Administration Officer for processing. Assigned quarters during training carried out in Leopoldville, the next step was to fill out administrative papers and to sign a contract with the Congolese government. The pilot would be briefed by the Chief Pilot on operations and given general information about his role, then he would meet the Chief of Air Operations (CAO) and draw flight and personal equipment from the WIGMO supply department. This equipment was to be signed for, kept for the duration of the contract, and returned on completion of the aforesaid. Any equipment lost or not accounted for was charged to the pilot and deducted from his pay at twice the cost since it was not readily available in the Congo.

In normal circumstances a pilot's pay would be deposited into his bank account on the 30th day of each month. While in the field of operations, this pay would be distributed in cash by the Administration Officer on the 15th of each month. As for personal mail, it was to be sent through an administrative officer in Leopoldville where it would be checked before being dispatched to the receiver. As was the case with long-distance phone calls, pilots were

(1) $600 per month for co-pilots;

(2) $800 per month for single-engine aircraft pilots and captains of multi-engine aircraft;

(3) $1000 per month for rotary-wing pilots.

Basic salary shall continue at the initial rate for a period of six (6) months from the date of the Contractor's arrival in the Congo. Thereafter, the Contractor's basic monthly salary shall be increased by $100 per month for the duration of his employment hereunder. At the completion of one year's continuous satisfactory service, the Contractor may be recontracted for an additional year with an increase of $100 per month in basic salary.

In addition to basic salary, the Contractor will receive $10.00 as a pilot and $7.50 as a co-pilot per flying hour. Furthermore, the Contractor will receive an additional $5.00 per flying hour for all flights designated as hazardous by the Employer or his Representative. This additional compensation shall be computed and paid on a calendar month.

c. Payment of taxes on income earned hereunder is the personal responsibility of the Contractor.

ARTICLE 4 - METHOD OF PAYMENT

All monies due to the Contractor will be forwarded to any bank designated by the Contractor. Any monies due the Contractor and requested by the Contractor in cash in the Congo will be paid in Congolese Francs at the then current rate of exchange as established by the Brussels Currency Exchange.

ARTICLE 5 - TRAVEL

The Government will pay transportation costs and approved incidental travel expenses from ________________ to the Contractor's place of assignment in the Congo and return, via tourist-class air, except as otherwise provided in Article 3 below.

ARTICLE 6 - SUBSISTENCE

The Contractor will be provided lodging during his period of employment in the Congo when in Leopoldville, and meals and lodging will be provided when performing assigned duties in the Congo outside Leopoldville.

Pages of the pilot contract signed by all that flew for the CIA in the Congo of the 1960s. (*Continued overleaf.*)

forbidden from describing operational matters, missions, target locations, target areas, damage, casualties, etc. Pilots were advised not to make themselves "look like a hero by writing this garbage" as it could have an effect on their families or those of flying companions. Photos of a pilot, his friends, his aircraft and the countryside were acceptable, but those dealing with strikes, missions or targets were also forbidden. Any violation of this instruction would result in personal correspondence not being sent.

Transportation to and from the operational bases was normally provided by 2-3 VW buses from the motor pool. Running to a schedule devised by the Admin Officer, in case a pilot was on R and R, on medical leave or any other authorised reason, a bus could be requested on WIGMO-6062 to arrange transport. For medical visits, a doctor employed by WIGMO was available at the airport offices from 0900-1200 hours each day. If a doctor was needed outside the hours, he could be contacted (if in Leopoldville) at the WIGMO house codenamed "Fox Trot" or on WIGMO-9165.

For training purposes, a pilot was assigned by the Chief Air Pilot and then Chief Air Officer according to the pilot's flight background and to the needs of his anticipated field detachment. During training, the pilot was to follow Standard Operating Procedures (SOP) and given a handbook for the aircraft for which he was assigned. This was to be studied, and prior to flight training, the pilot was to take an examination covering the assigned aircraft. The schedules for flight training were posted on the WIGMO bulletin board outside the WIGMO supply room, in the Sabena Apartment building, or at the River House, the lodgings for some of the pilots.

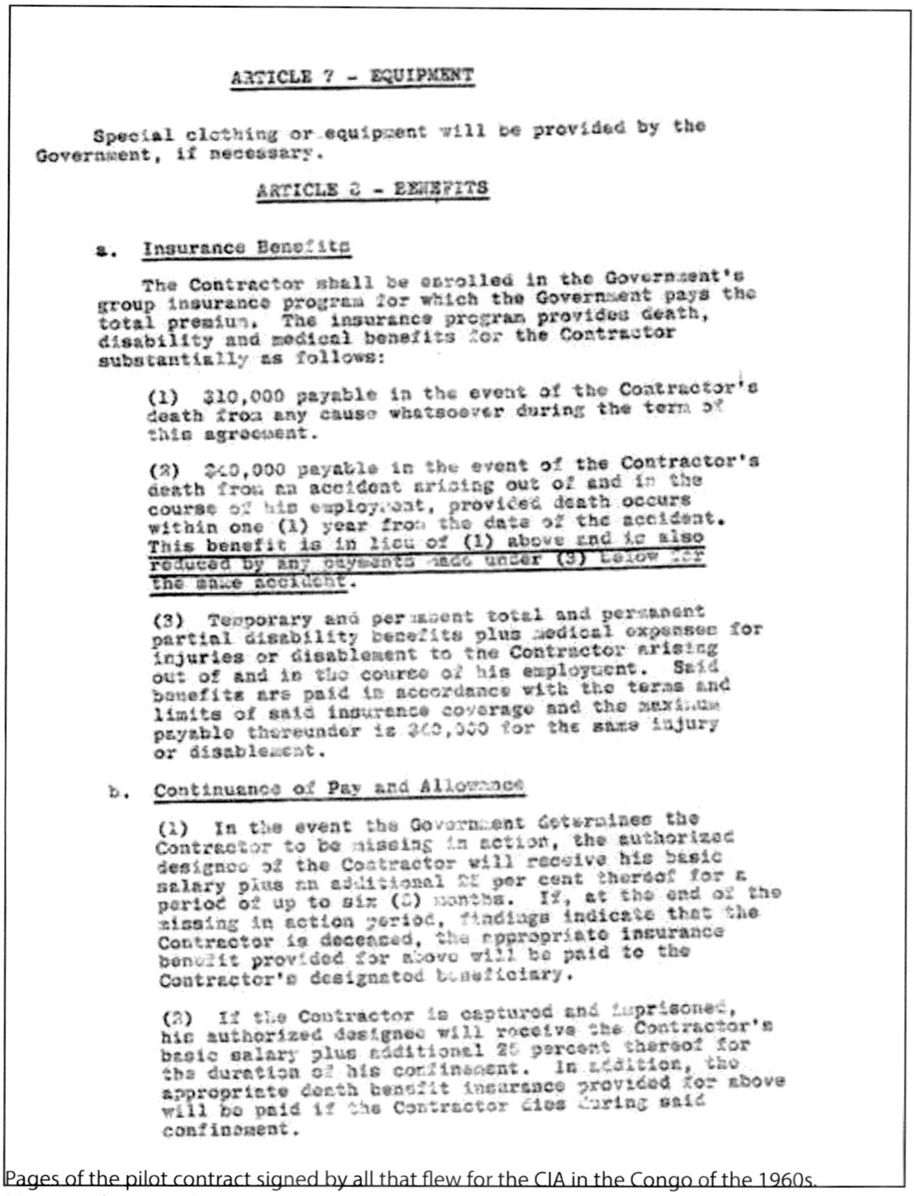

ARTICLE 7 - EQUIPMENT

Special clothing or equipment will be provided by the Government, if necessary.

ARTICLE 8 - BENEFITS

a. Insurance Benefits

The Contractor shall be enrolled in the Government's group insurance program for which the Government pays the total premium. The insurance program provides death, disability and medical benefits for the Contractor substantially as follows:

(1) $10,000 payable in the event of the Contractor's death from any cause whatsoever during the term of this agreement.

(2) $40,000 payable in the event of the Contractor's death from an accident arising out of and in the course of his employment, provided death occurs within one (1) year from the date of the accident. This benefit is in lieu of (1) above and is also reduced by any payments made under (3) below for the same accident.

(3) Temporary and permanent total and permanent partial disability benefits plus medical expenses for injuries or disablement to the Contractor arising out of and in the course of his employment. Said benefits are paid in accordance with the terms and limits of said insurance coverage and the maximum payable thereunder is $40,000 for the same injury or disablement.

b. Continuance of Pay and Allowance

(1) In the event the Government determines the Contractor to be missing in action, the authorized designee of the Contractor will receive his basic salary plus an additional 25 per cent thereof for a period of up to six (6) months. If, at the end of the missing in action period, findings indicate that the Contractor is deceased, the appropriate insurance benefit provided for above will be paid to the Contractor's designated beneficiary.

(2) If the Contractor is captured and imprisoned, his authorized designee will receive the Contractor's basic salary plus additional 25 percent thereof for the duration of his confinement. In addition, the appropriate death benefit insurance provided for above will be paid if the Contractor dies during said confinement.

Pages of the pilot contract signed by all that flew for the CIA in the Congo of the 1960s. (*Continued opposite.*)

After completing his training, a pilot was assigned to an operational base where the first step was to meet the Station Chief Pilot (SCP). Acting as a direct supervisor, it was his role to inform the pilot of local operations and conditions concerning weather, terrain, navigation and areas where ground fire was to be expected. Working in conjunction with the detachment Air Officer (OA), the SCP was then to make sure that each pilot knew what was required.

As operations were considered to be part of a "Bush War" and pilots flew for hours over stretches of jungle or savannah, according to instructions, there was a risk that flying could become a "bore" and that inattention could lead to taking a "few arrows in the can". Consequently, pilots were expected to maintain air discipline at all times. Before April 1965, it would appear that radio discipline had not been respected and pilots were reminded that there was "no excuse for continual chatter". It was important to maintain this type of discipline as it was probable that radio communications were being monitored.

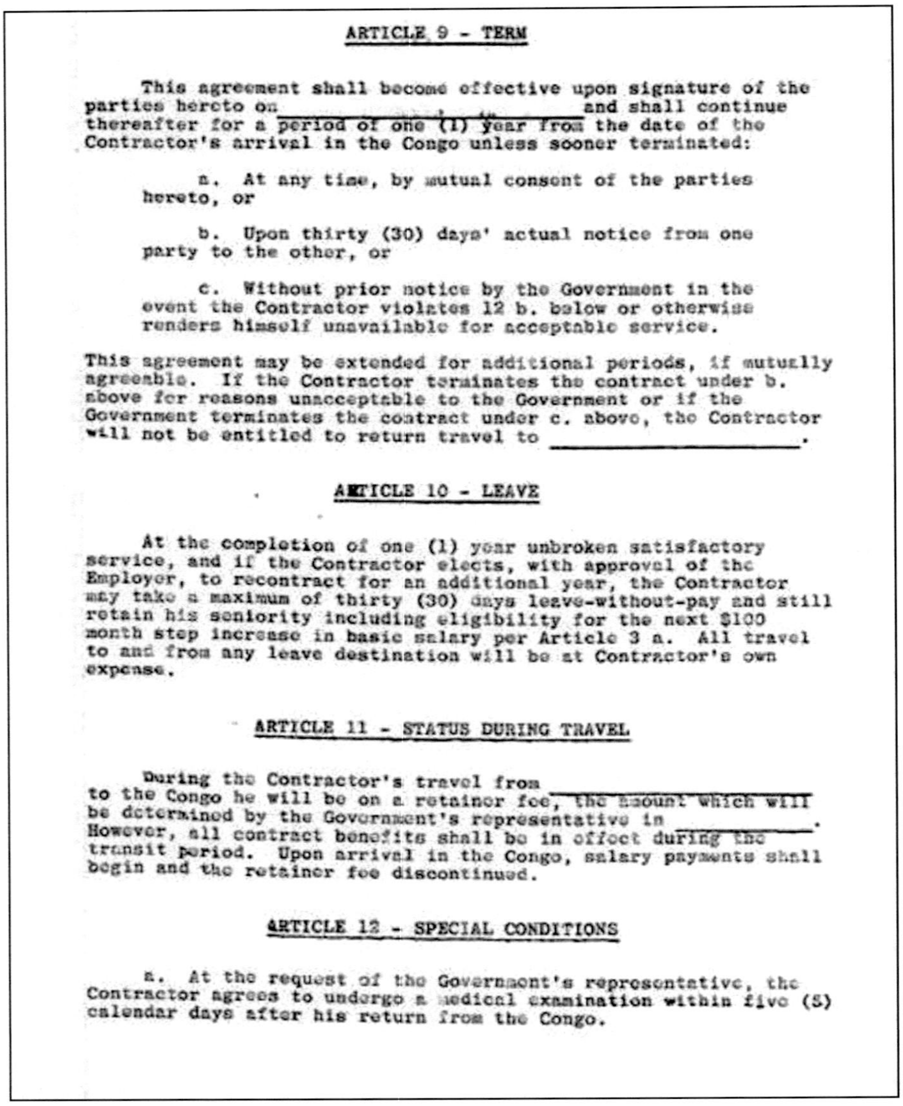

ARTICLE 9 - TERM

This agreement shall become effective upon signature of the parties hereto on ____________ and shall continue thereafter for a period of one (1) year from the date of the Contractor's arrival in the Congo unless sooner terminated:

a. At any time, by mutual consent of the parties hereto, or

b. Upon thirty (30) days' actual notice from one party to the other, or

c. Without prior notice by the Government in the event the Contractor violates 12 b. below or otherwise renders himself unavailable for acceptable service.

This agreement may be extended for additional periods, if mutually agreeable. If the Contractor terminates the contract under b. above for reasons unacceptable to the Government or if the Government terminates the contract under c. above, the Contractor will not be entitled to return travel to ____________.

ARTICLE 10 - LEAVE

At the completion of one (1) year unbroken satisfactory service, and if the Contractor elects, with approval of the Employer, to recontract for an additional year, the Contractor may take a maximum of thirty (30) days leave-without-pay and still retain his seniority including eligibility for the next $100 month step increase in basic salary per Article 3 a. All travel to and from any leave destination will be at Contractor's own expense.

ARTICLE 11 - STATUS DURING TRAVEL

During the Contractor's travel from ____________ to the Congo he will be on a retainer fee, the amount which will be determined by the Government's representative in ____________. However, all contract benefits shall be in effect during the transit period. Upon arrival in the Congo, salary payments shall begin and the retainer fee discontinued.

ARTICLE 12 - SPECIAL CONDITIONS

a. At the request of the Government's representative, the Contractor agrees to undergo a medical examination within five (5) calendar days after his return from the Congo.

Pages of the pilot contract signed by all that flew for the CIA in the Congo of the 1960s.

Travelling in three heavily armed jeeps, the Cuban force had encountered a number of ambushes along the way. Alberto Perez, Conrado Fernandez, and Rip Robertson had all been wounded in early confrontations with the Simba, and later that day Andres Romero and Ricardo Morales would also be hit. None of these injuries was life-threatening.

While Makasi pilots flying from Punia and Lisala were called in to attack pockets of Simba located in the outlying areas surrounding Stanleyville, and while 5 Commando heaped revenge on those they found in the city, the Cuban commando unit was approached by a man named Al Larson, an American missionary who had just been liberated. He told the Cubans that around 25 people were being held at a Christian mission known as Kilometre 8 situated some five miles away. Mistakenly believing their faith would provide them protection from the Simba, American, Canadian, and British missionaries and their families had been kept under guard for four months. This changed on 24 November as rebels heard the drone of aircraft over Stanleyville and realised they were under attack. After lining up the hostages and threatening to shoot them, the rebels ended up killing Canadian missionary Hector McMillan.

The Cuban commandos set off for the mission with little explanation from their commanding officer. This, as Angel Benitez later explained was because "That's always the way with the CIA, they don't tell you much".[39] Coming under constant fire, it took about an hour to cover the five-mile trip. Arriving at the compound and establishing a perimeter, the commandos laid down fire into the surrounding forest to which the Simba had fled. With the smell of cordite still in the air, the children at the mission were treated to Hershey bars that Tamayo carried in his ammunition pouch.[40]

6
Cubans versus Cubans in the Congo

International reaction to the Dragon Operations

Though the Dragon operations were hailed as a success in many quarters, extensive media coverage devoted to them only served to reaffirm suspicions that the US was supplying large amounts of military assistance to the government of Moïse Tshombe and that he had become nothing more than a puppet of the West. For example, when speaking at a meeting of the UN's Security Council in December 1964, the Soviet Union's Permanent Representative to the United Nations, Nikolai Fedorenko, accused western powers of using Tshombe to "transfer the Congo to the imperialists" and of intervening in the Congo purely for financial gain.[1] Diplomatic criticism of intervention in the Congo was not restricted to the Soviet Bloc. Kennedy's former Ambassador to Guinea and to Kenya, William Attwood, was also to denounce the fact that dozens of rebels had been killed by the rescue forces and that an "orgy of looting and killing" had been carried out by Tshombe's forces;[2] Jomo Kenyatta declared that he was "appalled" by the intervention of Western forces in Stanleyville; Julius Nyrere of Tanzania saw Stanleyville as another "Pearl Harbour"; and Kwame Nkrumah considered that the rescue missions to be a "flagrant act of aggression against Africa".[3] In addition to the war of words, protestors in Nairobi demanded that President Johnson be hanged, students in Cairo overran the US Embassy and set fire to a library, and other attacks were made on the American, Congolese, Belgian and British embassies in Moscow, Czechoslovakia, Bulgaria, China and Indonesia. More

Mercenary forces and the ANC were transported along the Congo's waterways using a variety of craft. This one makes its way along the Congo River to Basoko (now Yalemba). (Photo by Bob Houke)

Watercraft were used for the transport of men and machinery. (Photo by Bob Houke)

One of the watercraft operating on the River Congo was *Le Mons*. (Photo by Bob Houke)

worryingly from a military point of view, both Algeria's Ben Bella and Egypt's Nasser promised to supply weapons to rebel movements in the Congo in order to repel Tshombe's foreign forces.[4]

Cuba and the Congo

Given its history of providing support for different liberation movements in Africa it is unsurprising that the most virulent criticism of Western involvement in the DRC came from Cuba. After deposing Batista, Castro's revolutionary movement quickly turned its attention to Africa: Che Guevara and Raul Castro travelled to Cairo in June 1959 and in July 1960, while in September 1960 Fidel Castro castigated France over its war in Algeria, and promised Cuba's support for the Algerian people, the "remaining colonial peoples in Africa" and the "Negroes who are discriminated against in the Union of South Africa".[5] From December 1961, Cuba began supplying weapons to Algeria's National Liberation Front (FLN): in that month, the *Bahia de Nipe*, a Cuban vessel, left Havana and transported its cargo of 1,500 rifles, more than 30 machine guns, four US-made 81mm mortars, and a large quantity of US-made mortar rounds.[6] These weapons and ammunition had been captured from Brigade 2506 at the Bay of Pigs.[7] In addition to its support for Algeria, in 1961 Cuba allegedly supplied weapons to rebel movements in Zanzibar in 1961, and from early 1964 Cuban military personnel accompanied Algerian weapon shipments to Tanzania. Cuba also sent shiploads of weapons, including tanks, to Algeria during its brief conflict with Morocco in October 1963.[8]

While the Stanleyville rescue operations were taking place Guevara had left Cuba, and had headed to Moscow where he was to attend celebrations to mark the anniversary of the Bolshevik Revolution, and the opening of the new "Soviet-Cuban Friendship House", the inauguration of which he was to co-host with Soviet astronaut, Yuri Gagarin. As John Lee Anderson underlines in his study of the Argentine revolutionary,[9] the last months of 1964 were a good time to test Cuba-Soviet relations: China was encouraging support for its Maoist form of communism in South America, and in 1964 Peru's Communist Party had been weakened by the departure of a pro-Peking group; in Bolivia and Colombia there were similar factional splits; and, in Guatemala, a Trotskyite faction was emerging that would soon split the Cuban-backed Rebel Armed Forces (FAR). Through Guevara's discussions with various Politburo officials, it became apparent that the Soviet Union no longer supported

Le Mons had its own form of armament if needed. Here, it is pictured at Bumba in early 1965. (Houke)

This 13-year-old 'Major' was just one of the child soldiers captured at Stanleyville. (Photo by Bob Houke)

Cuban ideology on its armed struggle in Latin America. Guevara left the impression that he was determined to carry on the struggle; distrusted the Soviet policy of peaceful existence; and as far as Sino-Soviet relations were concerned "he was on the Chinese side".[10]

The first public indication of Guevara's dissatisfaction with the Soviet line was given during a speech in Santiago de Cuba on 30 November 1964, less than a week after the Stanleyville intervention. Preferring not to attend the Communist Party Congress being held concurrently in Havana, Guevara castigated "imperialist" wars in Algeria, Vietnam and Laos. After promising to provide continued support for struggles in Portuguese Guinea, Guevara's focus turned to the Congo and the recent rescue operations. For Guevara, the "storming" of Stanleyville by Belgian paratroopers and their slaughter of a large number of citizens under the statue of Professor Lumumba (sic) demonstrated two things: the "bestiality of imperialism", a bestiality that has no fixed borders, and that it is in the "very nature of imperialism to demean men to their wildest impulses, to turn them into blood-hungry beasts, willing to slaughter, to murder, to destroy until the last picture of a revolutionary, a supporter of a regime that fell under their boot, or who fights for his freedom".[11] Ignoring the fact that Lumumba had overseen the ANC massacre of thousands of Congolese citizens at Bakwanga in August 1960, Guevara promised to rebuild the statue of this "martyr of the revolution of the world".[12]

Guevara's denunciation of the United Nations in the same speech, and the insinuation that it was in some way complicit in Lumumba's assassination, did not stop him travelling to New York as Cuba's representative at the 19th General Assembly of the UN held on 11 December, 1964. Dressed in his customary olive-green uniform, Guevara wasted no time in welcoming the representatives of Zambia, Malawi, and Malta. Expressing the hope that these newly-independent countries would join the "struggle against imperialism, colonialism, and neocolonialism", Guevara also hailed the appointment of Ghana's Alex Quaison-Sackey as president of the assembly as the sign that an "historic stage of resounding triumphs for the peoples of Africa" had begun, and that colonialism was witnessing its final hour.[13]

In repeating much of the content of the speech given in Santiago de Cuba, the second half of Guevara's speech in New York was devoted to the question of the Congo. From the repetition of this content, and his evocation of support for "peoples in conflict" with "white colonial"[14] oppression in Southern Rhodesia, South-West Africa or in Swaziland, it would seem that Guevara's focus had turned away from struggles in Latin America and that his focus now lay on sub-Saharan Africa. That this is the case is confirmed by a number of things: Castro's plans for spreading the Cuban revolution to South America seemingly unfavourable in the eyes of the Organisation of American States (OAS);[15] the belief that the export of revolution as "essential to justify and protect the Cuban revolution itself";[16] the fact that Guevara did not return to Cuba preferring, instead, to embark on a three-month tour which would take him to Africa, China, France, Ireland and Prague. Acting as a goodwill ambassador for Fidel Castro, Guevara saw Africa as part of his dream to form a "Tricontinental" alliance against the West.[17]

Guevara arrived in the Congo in April 1965 disguised as a salesman. This explains why he appeared there without his emblematic facial hair. (Albert Grandolini Collection)

With the objective of making this strategy become reality through establishing and consolidating Cuban relations with radical African governments and liberation movements, Guevara left Cuba in December 1964. His first port of call was Algiers to discuss the Congo with Ben Bella, Cuba's closest friend on the African continent, and a nation with which Cuba had formed a 'brotherhood'.[18] On 14 January, Guevara arrived in Ghana where he was greeted enthusiastically by waiting crowds,[19] and after meeting Kwame Nkrumah, Guevara was led on a tour of the development projects being put in place in the Ghanaian capital, Accra.[20] The tour also included visits to Mali, to Guinea, to Dahomey (now Benin), and to Congo-Brazaville where Guevara would meet Alphonse Massamba-Débat (Congo-Brazaville),[21] and Angola's Agostinho Neto.[22] Following a meeting with leaders of the Congo's Conseil National de Libération (CNL) in Dar es Salaam on 11 February 1965, the contents of which we will discuss shortly, Guevara's continent-wide odyssey was to take him to Algiers where on 24 February, 1965 Guevara was to give speech at the Afro-Asian Conference.

Attended by no fewer than 63 representatives from Asian and African countries as well as representatives from 19 national liberation movements, as a member of the conference's presiding committee,[23] the meeting provided an ideal platform for Guevara to present his vision of the Tricontinental Alliance. Undoubtedly with events in the Congo in mind, Guevara called for the creation of an alliance between the "underdeveloped peoples and socialist countries" to be used in the fight against the United States, or any other "imperialist enemy".[24] Although Guevara offered praise for the Soviet Union and the Republic of China in that both had offered military aid to liberation movements, he was to castigate the USSR, albeit implicitly, through the mention of "mutually beneficial trade based on prices forced on the backward countries by the law of value and the international relations of unequal exchange that result from the law of value". "How", Guevara argued, could it be "mutually beneficial" to sell at world market prices the "raw materials that cost the underdeveloped world immeasurable sweat and suffering, and to buy at world prices the machinery produced in today's big automated factories?"[25] As Anderson notes, it was clear to all who were listening that Guevara was making a clear attack on the Soviet Union:[26] in Havana, Guevara had been very vocal in his denunciation of what he saw as Soviet "profiteering" in its trading relations with developing nations. Furthermore, Guevara chastised the USSR for not demonstrating "unconditional solidarity" with North Vietnam, a country which had been the target of recent bombardments by the United States.[27]

Some observers suggest that Guevara's speech in Algiers and his condemnation of the Eastern Bloc made Guevara's position in Havana untenable: Guevara's demonstration of sympathy for China in his speech was in direct contradiction to Fidel Castro's denunciation of China's recent split from the Soviet Union, and it was thought that Guevara should move on to pastures new.[28] Other observers, however, note that any dispute between Castro and Guevara has been exaggerated, and that nothing more than "strong words" would have been exchanged between the two.[29] This is due to Castro's earlier criticism of the Soviet socialist model, and the indirect indication that Cuba would not accept Soviet attempts to impose this model on the island. Guevara's speech in Algeria did, however, make Castro's task of defending him from accusations that he was a Maoist more complicated, [30] and it was suggested that Che be sent to lead a group of Cubans already in training for a mission in the Congo.

The Mercenary Naval Force

The defeat of the CNL at Stanleyville and the loss of several hundred of its Simba fighters put an end to any aspiration it might have held to capture Leopoldville from northern and central Congo. However, as Tshombe's forces began clearing up what remained of rebel resistance in the Oriente, Kwilu and Equateur provinces, the efforts to march on the capital simply shifted eastwards to where Laurent Désiré Kabila was in the midst of building up his forces. As well as being able to bolster his army by recruiting Baluba tribesmen living in the Kivu and Northern Katanga, Kabila gained the support of Tutsi soldiers from Rwanda.

In which ways this shift of focus would affect US plans in the Congo was summed up in a report submitted by Robert W. Komer of the National Security Council to McGeorge Bundy, President Johnson's Special Assistant for National Security Affairs. In this report dated 26 January 1965, Komer sought to "counter all the gloom" that had been "purveyed", and stated that he could see "blue sky in the Congo".[31] His optimism had been fermented by the wishes of the Organisation for African Unity (OAU) which had expressed its desire to seek an "African way to reach an African solution to an African problem". The most important consideration for Komer was to "get the fighting stopped" before a rebel counter-offensive put the US "back in the soup".[32]

Though the diplomatic intervention of the OAU brought the promise of peace for the Congo, by 25 February 1965 the military situation in the Congo had deteriorated so badly that Harold H. Sanders of the National Security Council Staff feared that a rebel counter-offensive may have already begun".[33] In addition to the Baluba and the Rwandans, Kabila was by now being backed by regular forces of the Ugandan Army in north-eastern Congo. Intelligence reports also indicated that the Ugandan president, Edward Mutesa, had issued a call for Chinese and Algerian aircraft to fight off attacks allegedly made by the Makasi on towns situated along the border with his country. The reports joined others which warned of arms shipments from Algeria and from the United Arab Republic (UAR). These weapons were swelling already substantial arms caches and the rebels were being trained in how to use them by "Arab mentors in East African safe havens".[34] This, Saunders believed, made Tshombe's forces ill-equipped to fight off a "well-run rebel push supported from outside."[35] Evidently, this kind of military escalation was not one which the United States wished to see in the area.

As further – yet unconfirmed – reports spoke of Chinese and Soviet weapons being supplied to CNL bases in Congo-Brazzaville, therefore bringing the threat of a second front opening in the west, as far as US policy in the region was concerned at the beginning of 1965 there were very few options: as there was nobody to present a viable alternative to Tshombe the US must help him win. On the other hand, the question of the ANC's efficiency still remained. Although he thought that Tshombe should refrain from employing South Africans in order to promote African unity, he also believed that the US should continue to support friendly foreign forces fighting in the Congo as the "ANC were practically worthless unless led by mercenaries".[36]

In the face of the increase in attacks carried out by rebel forces, by early March 1965 a coalition of mercenary forces directed by US intelligence services and Belgian officers again coordinated their efforts to counter support being provided to rebels in operations known collectively as White Giant. These operations would seek to seal off the Congo's north-eastern border with Sudan and Uganda using two infantry battalions under the command of Mike Hoare. Other objectives included taking back control of large towns in the Oriente Province such as Watsa, an important gold-mining centre. Advances made by mercenary forces aided by Makasi B-26s and T-28s resulted in Operation Violettes Imperiales being launched at the end of May 1965. Again, the objective was to cut off rebel supply routes, but this time operations involved attacking Buta and Bondo, two towns situated on the Congolese border with Sudan and the Central African Republic.

A concentration of rebel strongholds found along the Fizi-Baraka axis were providing stubborn resistance and destroying them had become an objective for the Fifth Mechanised Brigade as early as December 1964. To make matters worse, from April 1965, local intelligence indicated that the rebels were receiving supplies of Chinese-manufactured land mines, machine guns, 76mm cannons and a "good supply of "bamboo bazookas", and that these weapons were being shipped into the Tanzanian port of Dar es Salaam, carried along former Arab slave trading routes that criss-crossed the country to the Tanzanian port cities of Ujiji or Kigoma, and ferried across Lake Tanganyika.[37] In order to stop the flow of weapons from reaching the rebels led by Laurent Kabila and assisted by Guevara, Lieutenant-Colonel Roger Hardenne, a former Belgian paratrooper, was given command of Operation South in the summer of 1965. Headquartered in Albertville (Kalemie), the plan was to carry out a three-phase offensive against APL forces using 5 Commando and ANC infantry battalions. Air cover was to be provided by the Makasi whose fleet of aircraft was supplemented by the arrival of a T-28C and three T-28Bs in April and May 1965. For casualty evacuation and rescue operations, it had also brought in three Bell F-47 helicopters. Their pilots, Frenchman Robert Houke and South African Bob Brannon, were transferred from the FAC's 22 Wing to the Makasi in March 1965. Later in 1965, the helicopter pilot force was joined by former Royal Air Force pilot, Terry Peet. Another Frenchman named Jacques Roques was recruited to fly one of the newly arrived T-28s. He was killed when his plane crashed during an attack manoeuvre over Lake Tanganyika in November 1965.

In order to vary the methods and angles of attack, it was decided that waterborne operations would be launched against rebel positions situated along the western coast of Lake Tanganyika. Be this at it may, a substantial problem lay in the fact that a naval force capable of transporting men and equipment had to be created from scratch. This task was handed over to the CIA's Maritime Branch of the Special Operations Group (MBSOG) headed by Bill Hamilton and Thomas Clines. [38] In turn, they appointed a certain 'Jordy McKay' to find vessels and men for what was to become the Force Navale Congolaise (FNC).[39] In regards to how the FNC would be constituted, it was decided that existing members of 5 Commando would be commissioned to navigate two old, but seaworthy, boats capable of hauling a force of 300 mercenaries, their vehicles, weapons, and equipment around a vast stretch of one of the world's largest waterways. McKay managed to track down and acquire a 120-foot cargo ship called the *Ermans* which was subsequently converted into a gunboat. Captained by South African Ian Peddle, it carried a 75mm recoilless rifle on the stern, .50 calibre Browning machine guns, and would eventually be armed with 12.7mm Russian machine guns.[40] It was also equipped with radar so that it could navigate the dark waters of the lake at night. Next, McKay acquired the *Urundi* from a Belgian-owned maritime company. This vessel was equipped to carry troops and to tow several barges each with a specially designed ramp for offloading jeeps, five-ton trucks and Ferret armoured vehicles. To provide greater manoeuvrability, the FNC's fleet was completed by six Seacraft-21 patrol boats.[41]

As operations continued with attacks on rebel positions around Fizi, Baraka, Uvira and Mwenga, by his own admission Hoare found that the resistance put up by rebel fighters was much stronger than he had faced in previous encounters with the Simba. Indeed, instead of "melting away into the hills" as they had done in previous encounters, this time opposing forces had stood and faced their enemy.[42] He suspected that these enemy soldiers had undergone some sort of professional military training and his suspicions were confirmed after rebels had attacked military installations at Bendera in the South Kivu province on 29 June, 1965. Among the items found on one of the enemy killed in the attack were identity papers and a personal diary. They indicated that the dead soldier had travelled to the Congo from Havana *via* Prague and Peking.[43] As well as this discovery, radio messages in a type of Spanish used by Cubans were intercepted by one of Hoare's Spanish-speaking signallers.[44] That the dead were, indeed, Cubans was confirmed when radio messages were picked up by the American spy ship USNS *Private Jose F. Valdez*. Carrying crew fluent in either Russian, French, Spanish, or Portuguese, it sailed around the Indian Ocean in the hope of intercepting enemy radio communications. Though Guevara was aware that overly frequent use of the radio would expose the Cubans to detection and had given instructions that the frequency of these communications had to be reduced, his radio operators had been sloppy. US intelligence services already knew that Castro was communicating with Dar es Salaam, and that his messages to Cuban guerrillas were being relayed from the Tanzanian capital. Every day at 8.00 am, at 2.30 pm, and at 7.00 pm, Cuban radio operators based in Kigoma on one side of Lake Tanganyika would receive updates on the situation, and requests for supplies from Cuban troops on the other side.[45]

Che Guevara in the Congo

A revolutionary with Guevara's experience and knowledge should have known when and where to continue his brand of activism. Unfortunately for Guevara, it would appear that the Soviet Union's decision not to support armed struggle in Latin America had rather forced his hand, and he found himself obliged to seek out revolutions in other areas of the world. Given US involvement in Central Africa, and Guevara's deep-rooted hatred of what he called 'Yankee imperialism', the Congo presented a perfect opportunity.

During his tour of Africa, Guevara had met many of the leaders he hoped would support his efforts to continue the revolutionary struggle. As we have seen, he met with Ben Bella, with Nasser, with Nkrumah, and had promised his support for independence movements in Angola through his meetings with Angola's Agostinho Neto. But it was while in Tanzania that Guevara had also had the chance to meet Laurent Désiré Kabila and his deputy Gaston Soumaliot who were residing in Dar es Salaam. Kabila made an "excellent impression" on Guevara: he had made a "clear, specific, and resolute" presentation of the situation in the Congo and realised that "the main enemy was North American imperialism". What Guevara failed to recognise was that Kabila was more or less alone in thinking along these lines, and that other 'Freedom Fighters', as Guevara referred to them, did not hold the same point of view. These other leaders of the Congolese rebel movements merely saw rebellion as a means of getting rid of Tshombe: they did not share Guevara's view that the fight in the Congo was part of a larger struggle against an enemy common to both the Congolese and the Cubans.[46] Despite early warning signs that Africa had a long way to go before it reached "real revolutionary maturity",[47] and despite warnings from Nasser, [48] Guevara promised Kabila that he would provide a group of 30 instructors to help train Congolese rebel forces. On Kabila's insistence, these instructors would be black so as not to arouse suspicion of Cuban help.[49]

Towards the end of January 1965, Victor Dreke (Cruz)[50] received an order from the Cuban Army High Command to start the recruitment of men for an assignment which could last for a period of up to two years. Not yet being informed of where the mission would take place, Dreke selected men from the Cuban Revolutionary Army (FAR) and began training at the Piti 1 Camp in Pinar del Rio. At some point during the next two months, it was decided that a force totalling nearly 500 recruits would be divided into two units named Columna 1 and Columna 2. The 113 men of the first unit would be assigned to Kabila's forces and travel from Dar es Salaam to the Fizi-Baraka area of the Congo whereas the second unit Columna 2, or the Patrice Lumumba Battalion, would be sent to Congo-Brazzaville to carry out a number of missions. Although this unit's primary function was to act as a reserve for Columna 1, its other missions were to fight alongside MPLA guerrillas in the Angolan enclave of Cabinda, and to protect the Republic of the Congo's border to the DRC.[51]

The training of Cuban troops and the destinations of their respective missions were, naturally, a matter of extreme secrecy.[52] For this reason, since Guevara's return from Africa on 15 March, 1965 he had been somewhat elusive, making only one public appearance in the weeks that preceded his departure for the Congo. In the interest of this secrecy and to avoid the detection of Guevara's movements, at the end of the month Guevara was to undergo a physical transformation that would make him unrecognisable even to former comrades such as Victor Dreke. In a television documentary made for the French-German television channel *Arte,* in 2007,[53] Dreke explained how Castro had invited him to dinner. In the presence of Raul Castro and a few friends, Dreke was then asked to identify a clean-shaven man wearing glasses and a homburg hat. Unable to do so, Dreke was told amid roars of laughter that the person in the photo was Guevara. To complete the disguise, the French-speaking Guevara would travel under the assumed name of Ramón Benitez and would be introduced to the Congolese as a doctor and translator. [54]

Guevara's goodbye to Cuba would come in the shape of a farewell letter. Addressed to Fidel Castro and dated 1 April 1965, Castro was to read aloud in front of Cuban television cameras. Guevara averred that he felt he had fulfilled his duty that tied him to the Cuban revolution, and in wishing his comrades well for the future, he declared that "other lands of the world summoned" his "modest efforts of assistance" and that he would "carry the faith" taught by Castro into new battles. Guevara's letter expressed his revolutionary spirit and the sense that his most sacred of duties was to fight imperialism.[55]

Leaving Havana on the same day, Guevara arrived in Dar es Salaam on 19 April and had hopes of meeting Kabila. Unaware that Guevara would be joining the fighting in the Congo, Kabila was in Cairo with other members of the CNL where, paradoxically, as things would turn out, he was to discuss areas such as combat unity and the constitution of the revolutionary organisation.[56] After the arrival of the first batch of Cuban troops on the 20 April, Guevara travelled to Kigoma before crossing Lake Tanganyika and set up his headquarters at Kibamba some 30 kilometres inland. In the Congo Guevara would be known as 'Tatu' (Swahili for the number three), Dreke would become 'Moja' (one), while Jose Maria Martinez Tomayo (Dreke's second-in-command) would become 'Mbili' (two).[57]

The strategy that Guevara hoped to adapt to the type of asymmetric warfare[58] he would find in the Congo would later be known as *Foco*, or Focoism. Its tenets being developed by Guevara in the 24-page booklet *Guerrilla Warfare: a Method* published in 1961,[59] this theory of *Foco* advocated the principle that it was not necessary to wait for conditions to be right in order to start a revolution.[60] Instead, a small band of revolutionaries acting as a vanguard could launch small-scale guerrilla warfare to serve as the focus and inspiration for a more general uprising. With the Congo bordering nine other countries, it presented to ideal opportunity to put this theory to the test.

One of the foundations of Guevara's strategy relied on the "unity of people's forces in order to counter the unity of repressive forces".[61] However, he was soon to realise that his own willingness to share the hardships of the peasant farmers in the Congo were neither matched by rebel leaders who spent most of their time in Dar es Salaam nor by members of the rebel forces who would pilfer food from the peasants and steal what luxuries they possessed.[62] This lack of unity extended to the Rwandan forces sent to support the Congolese and Guevara notes that the "Rwandans[63] and the various Congolese tribes treat each other as enemies, and the frontiers between the ethnic groups are clearly defined".[64] It was to make Guevara's task of creating a regional union to fight a common enemy extremely complicated, and it was a phenomenon that was repeated all over the Congo. In his own account of the Congo mission, Victor Dreke was to conclude that it was not possible to bring together Africans from other countries to form a consolidated unit.[65]

If the creation of some sort of unity and common purpose was of primary concern for Guevara, when it came to the question of the individual elements which were to constitute a complete rebel force, the concern was no less important. From the outset, Guevara was dismayed at the behaviour of his troops who, many of them, had contracted venereal disease in the brothels of Kigoma. A second problem was that drunkenness was widespread: the consumption of *pombe*, a spirit distilled from the juice of corn and manioc, caused havoc when, imbibed with this potent liquid, Guevara's army spent its time brawling and causing general mayhem.[66] Whereas frequenting brothels and getting drunk are part and parcel of service in the armed forces, when coupled with a strong belief in tribal traditions such as taking a *dawa* to ward off enemy gunfire, it would prove to be a disastrous combination: if one soldier was seen to have been killed or injured by a bullet which was supposed to be deflected through protection from this potion, others involved in a battle would flee believing the *dawa* to be faulty. In an attack on the town of Katenga on 30 June 1965, for example, out of 160 men 60 were to desert the ranks.[67] Another problem linked to tribal beliefs was that the Congolese would not dig trenches (for the Congolese, trenches were holes, and holes were for dead bodies), and were incapable of closing one eye so as to aim a weapon.[68] At Katenga, most Congolese opened fire nearly always shooting into the air, and kept on firing until their ammunition ran out. While doing so, they were decimated by enemy fire.

The inability of Congolese rebels to mount any kind of coordinated attack was extremely disheartening for Guevara and his fellow Cubans. By the end of June 1965, Guevara had reached the conclusion that if the behaviour of the Simba off and on the battlefield did not change, Guevara's dream of creating an epicentre for widespread revolution was a very optimistic target. In Guevara's own words, "the possibility of this happening seemed more remote with every passing day".[69]

While morale amongst the Congolese was to improve on 7 July with the visit of Kabila, to add to the fragility of Guevara's military situation Guevara was to learn that political events inside and outside of the Congo were to play an important role in determining the outcome of operations: in Algeria, Houari Boumedienne had overthrown Ben Bella on June 19, 1965, causing friction between Cuba and its North African ally; and on the Congolese front, further friction between leaders of the CNL meant the promise of further disunity and, potentially, factitious conflict. One source of reassurance came through the continuing arrival of Chinese weapons, but even this positive aspect was countered by the fact that shipments brought in from Tanzania were missing firing pins or ammunition or, more significantly, as Guevara would point out in a letter in which he would summarise the situation: "If the Yankees have learnt the lessons of other revolutions, now is the moment they should strike hard and take pre-emptive measures such as the neutralisation of the lake [Tanganyika]: that is, to do everything necessary to close our main route for supplies of all kinds."[70]

Little did Guevara know, at that time, that the CIA was preparing to do just that. In cutting off the supply route which had thus far facilitated Guevara to sustain the rebellion, to all intents and purposes it could snub out any further threats. What the CIA needed now was a naval force to patrol the waters that divided the Congo and Tanzania, and a force that had experience of this type of maritime operations. In the end, the CIA was able not just to find men and craft that fitted the bill: they were also able to find men who wanted Guevara dead.

The Cuban Exile Naval Force: From the Caribbean Sea to Lake Tanganyika

Some 7,300 miles from Kigoma, and some two years before Guevara made an appearance in the Congo, the US government continued to wrestle with the question of how to deal with Fidel Castro. Although Operation Mongoose was still up and running, there seemed little prospect that the United States would be able to unseat the Cuban leader in the near future. Instead, by mid-October 1962 Castro was in the process of cementing his position as an ally of the Soviet Union by setting up installations for Soviet SS-4 ballistic missiles. Additionally, over 1,000 Cuban exiles remained imprisoned in Cuba's jails: they represented non-negligible bargaining chips that could be used as collateral should the need arise. Paradoxically, the so-called Cuban Missile Crisis and the East and West's mutual realisation that the outbreak of nuclear warfare was frighteningly close created the conditions necessary for the release of Brigade 2506.

Freedom for men who had spent the past 18 months at Castro's mercy came on 23 December when they arrived at Homestead Air Force Base some 37 miles south of Miami. Greeted by their families, US government officials and the Secret Service, the next and last time the members of the Brigade would find themselves together was at Miami's Orange Bowl Stadium on 29 December 1962. Their release had been secured upon payment of $53 million donated by a variety of US companies and was calculated on what value was accorded to each prisoner. The sums involved for each prisoner ranged from $25,000-100,000 while fines imposed on the US government for its involvement with leading exiles amounted to half a million dollars.[71] Others who were not so fortunate such as MRR co-founder Emilio Martinez would remain imprisoned until 1977. Sentenced to 30 years hard labour as well as losing Cuban citizenship, Andrés de Jesús Vega Pérez died in prison on 23 July 1982.

The 40,000 friends, relatives and families of the Brigade gathered in the stadium situated west of Miami's Little Havana cheered loudly when Brigade chief Pepe San Roman presented Kennedy with a flag bearing the words Brigado Assolto. Joining her husband on the rostrum placed on the playing field, Jacqueline Kennedy sang the praises of the men and charmed the crowd by addressing them in Spanish. Though it appeared that Kennedy's perceived betrayal at the Bay of Pigs had been forgiven, underlying the surface-level joviality and the smiles on the faces of the massed ranks of seated exiles ran a hatred for Kennedy that would never fade. According to Howard Hunt, one of the CIA's liaison officers with the Brigade and the future Watergate burglar, the flag-passing ceremony nearly did not take place. Indeed, in the Brigade's eyes Kennedy had committed a second act of betrayal by promising Castro that the US would discontinue its support for anti-Castro activities.[72]

As if almost to make amends for his past errors, in September 1962 Kennedy asked the US Department of Defense (DOD) to modify a programme that would enable Cubans resident in the United States to join its regular armed forces. Initiated in May 1961 shortly after the Bay of Pigs, the DOD embarked on a recruiting campaign and Selective Service boards for applicants wishing to join the Cuban Volunteer Program (CVP). Up to 4,000 exiles applied for the programme but, finally, only 142 were recruited. Many applicants were disqualified due to their age and number of dependents while others lost interest when told they would not be serving in Cuban units. Of the 1,000 who were registered after the first phase of selection, the majority was then rejected at the Armed Forces Examining Station for reasons of "moral and security". Disqualification occurred when the volunteers were given lie detector tests,[73] and admitted histories of sexual deviation. One hundred and thirty-five of the applicants failed on medical grounds.[74] The failure of the programme in its present state led to its closing in July 1962.

In September 1962, then, the Joint Chiefs of Staff acting on recommendations given by the Special Group (counterinsurgency) prepared a new plan which would take into consideration the specificities of the Cubans: from then on they would join specially created all-Cuban units to satisfy their own political goals and, on the question of the language barrier, all training was to be provided in Spanish. Induction would be for a period of two years, and after 20 weeks of basic training a volunteer could be discharged, transferred to reserve status or integrated into a regular military unit. If they met the standards required, some would even be considered for integration into the special forces.[75] As with the plan of May 1961, volunteers could be tracked in such a way as to "permit their consolidation into a Cuban unit should the need for such a unit ever develop".[76] In other words, the plan enabled the US government to create an army of third-nation nationals within its own army so that it could plausibly deny its implication in a given conflict. Despite their extreme dislike of Kennedy, nearly half of Brigade 2506 was to take up his offer of service in the rejigged version of the Cuban Volunteer Program. As well as making it easier for them to obtain a green card, it set them on the path to obtaining US citizenship. A number of those who joined the US Army and who trained at Fort Benning would later serve in the Vietnam War – one example being Colonel J.R. Lopez de la Cruz, the current president of the 2506 veterans association – while others who chose the USAF later flew with the Makasi.

Successful as it was, many Cuban exiles still felt that Castro had to go and that the United States' own wars had little to do with their own personal political objectives. One, in particular, was Felix

Table 5: MRR, Organisation Structure

Name	Position
Manuel Artime and Ricardo Lorie	Secretary General
Jose M. Mole	Secretary of Intelligence
Manolin Gutierrez	Secretary of Naval Affairs
Rafael Quintero	Secretary of Military Affairs
Ricardo Chavez	Secretary of Operations
Edgar Sopo	Secretary of Press Affairs
Felix Gonzalez	Secretary of Communications
Jaime Varela	Secretary of Propaganda
Sixto Mesa	Secretary of Finance
Manuel Guillot de la Serrana	Secretary of Miami Delegation
Eddy Suarez Rivas	Secretary of New York Delegation

MRR Leaders (from left to right) Ricardo Chavez, Rafael Quintero, Reynaldo Gonzales, Tony Inglesias, Eddie Suarez Rivas, Manolin Gutierrez.

MRR Leaders Ricardo Chavez (left), Manuel Artime and Rafael Quintero. Chavez later recruited the crews of the Makasi naval force. (latinamericanstudies.org)

MRR base at Monkey Point, Nicaragua. This base was used for training and for launching attacks on mainland Cuba. (Santiago Alvarez)

Rodriguez. Born in May 1941, Rodriguez was devoted to the anti-Castro cause and had previously participated in the plan to overthrow the Cuban leader in August 1959 organised by Rafael Trujillo's Anti-Communist League of the Caribbean. Following this failed attempt, he was recruited as a Paramilitary Operations Officer with the CIA's Special Activities Division (SAD), and prior to the Bay of Pigs Rodriguez had infiltrated Cuba in order to provide intelligence. In 1967, Rodriguez became the last Cuban exile to see Guevara alive. Having married in the summer of 1962, and promising his wife that he would settle down and leave behind all thoughts of taking part in operations against Castro, Rodriguez accepted a commission as a second lieutenant in the US Army and was sent to Fort Benning in Georgia. However, when he met Manuel Artime and Rafael "Chi Chi" Quintero in March 1963, they informed him that the MRR was organising a Cuban-run and Cuban-led operation against Castro, he immediately resigned from his position.[77] By that time, Artime had become a highly organised operation and had even established offices on 1035 NW, 10th Avenue, Miami. The offices produced its own stationery, provided the false identity papers used by Artime to pose as a travelling salesman, and the MRR had its own organisational structure.[78]

If Kennedy and his Attorney-General brother Robert had seemingly distanced themselves from the Cuban exile cause, in reality they had authorised the setting up of a new operation labelled with the cryptonym AMWORLD. This, as a number of CIA Chiefs of Stations and Bases learnt from Chief of the Western Hemisphere Division, Joseph Caldwell King in July 1963 was a CIA (cryptonym KUBARK) operation targeted against Cuba (PBRUMEN). Administered and directed by Artime (AMBIDDY/1), the activities involved in the programme were to be based outside the United States (PBPRIME). Any participation of the CIA was to be kept to a minimum, and its role was limited to supporting Artime financially and logistically. The United States government (ODYOKE) was aware that there were risks involved when using autonomous exile groups and individuals "not responsive to KUBARK guidance" and, ominously as things turned out, that it would have to face the consequences of using what it termed as "a lowering in professional standards adhered to by autonomous groups", as opposed to using "fully controlled and disciplined assets". However, this was a price the United States government was willing to pay in order for it to deny involvement in the operations. Coordination between the CIA and Artime was to be made using the agency's station in Miami (JMWAVE).[79]

Given that Artime's objectives in the Caribbean were based on using naval vessels to infiltrate guerrillas into mainland Cuba, the first step was to set up bases from which they could operate. Next

Members of the anti-Castro MRR at Monkey Point, Nicaragua. (Santiago Alvarez)

The MRR received regular supplies of material from the CIA: these troops were photographed while greeting a supply ship. (Santiago Alvarez)

came the task of acquiring the vessels, their crews and the weapons they would use. Most importantly, though the CIA was backing operations, no trace could be left that indicated the United States had any role to play in Artime's plans. Naturally, this meant that a network of clandestine contacts built up sometimes over many years would have to be deployed in order to satisfy demands.

As of late June 1963, and based in Tortuguero in Costa Rica, Artime already possessed a Seabird boat powered by two 140 HP outboard Mercruiser engines with a maximum speed of 38 knots.[80] To work alongside this craft named *Monty*, the CIA envisaged the purchase of a mother ship which could blend in with the type of maritime traffic found in the Caribbean. It could be registered to a foreign country, and as such could have every reason to dock in a port like Puerta Carezas in Nicaragua, the other country ostensibly behind Artime's operations. It was believed that the Colombian-registered *Olga Patricia* would be ideal for the purpose.[81] A 178-foot light cargo ship (LCS), it was believed the vessel could be purchased for between $125,000 and $150,000 using the AMRUN Corporation.[82] Otherwise, it could be leased for a monthly rate of $5,500.[83] In addition to the mother ship, it was suggested that a Forest Johnson Prowler could be used as a strike boat and a Bertram Moppie for infiltration missions. They would be supplemented by short range strike boats and rubber rafts. The purchase of RS-12 rubber boats was recommended due to silent outboard motors. Thirty-six men were needed for Artime's initial operations: they included cooks, carpenters and an electrician.[84]

As Manuel Gutierrez took care of the MRR's purchases, in September 1963 Artime was able to report that the MRR's military missions to Cuba had already begun. In order to accelerate and fulfill the number of future missions, an MRR recruitment centre was set up in Miami. In total, 300 men would sign up to Artime's naval forces. They included a number who left the CVP, others such as radio technician and Bay of Pigs veteran Roberto Pichardo Snr., and Santiago Alvarez. Alvarez had formerly been a member of Alpha 66 and a radical exile group known as Commando L. While these men were sent to training camps at Zenon Viera naval base compound at Monkey Point in Nicaragua, another transport boat, the *Joanne*, was purchased and sent from Baltimore to training camps in Costa Rica. Its job was not just to carry supplies, but also to carry "Black Infiltration" combat personnel from PBPRIME (United States).[85] What role nine members of the "Black Nine Resistance Team" mentioned in a CIA cable reporting the purchase of the *Joanne* is unknown.

While the naval force eventually comprised two large ships, eight smaller vessels, two speed boats, three aircraft, more than 200 tons of weapons and armaments and around $250,000 dollars worth of electrical equipment,[86] (mostly made by Decca and fitted by Roberto Pichardo Snr.), the MRR's forces spent most of the time between mid-1963 and early 1965 conjuring up plans to destroy Castro's economic installations. On the question of weapons, these would be acquired from Interarms, or Interarmco (International Armament Corporation), the company upon which the CIA had relied for its supply of covert weapons for a number of years.[87] In this case, the MRR's representative in Monaco, a certain Manuel Hernandez,

MRR aboard the *Gitana*. The captain, Santiago Alvarez (sunglasses), was a long-standing anti-Castro fighter and was also member of the radical Alpha 66. Like Generoso Bringas (beret) the *Gitana* was soon to travel from the Caribbean to Lake Tanganyika. (Santiago Alvarez)

would act as an intermediary for payment to Interarmco. In all, $326,262.82 was paid into Interamco's account held at the Banque Genevoise de Commerce et de Crédit (BGCC) situated at 2 rue Diday in Geneva, Switzerland.

The MRR carried out its first raid against Castro when it attacked the Cabo Cruz sugar mill, Puerto Pilon in the Oriente Province on the morning of 13 May 1964.[88] 70,000 sacks of sugar were destroyed during the attack codenamed Operation Zenon Viera II.[89] Next, on 1 September, the MRR announced that one of its raiding parties had destroyed a radio station at Cabo Cruz. A further attack came on 4 February 1965 when the MRR shelled an oil depot in Cas Ida, Las Villas Province but by March 1965, Artime had announced a complete change in strategy. From then on, it would cease its naval operations and focus on internal subversion.[90]

Now what caused this change of strategy is a matter which continues to resound in the Cuban exile community and is an event which would change the entire course of the exile's fight against Cuba as a whole. Occurring on 13 September 1964 about 130 kilometres off Guantanamo, it involved the *Gitana*, one of the two Swift boats used by the MRR and the sister-ship to *Monty*. Commanded by Santiago Alvarez, on the day in question it mistook a Spanish cargo ship called the *Sierra Aránzazu* for a vessel of the of the Cuban merchant navy. The attack led to death of three men aboard the ship, caused an international uproar and, from then on, led to the CIA being forced to distance itself from MRR activities in the waters of the Caribbean Sea.

While the MRR's operations were wrapped up and financial support withdrawn, both the *Monty* and the *Gitana* would soon have another role to play. Around one year after the attack on the *Sierra Aránzazu* the CIA came looking for boats and their crews to take part in another mission. Instead of making incursions into Cuban waters, the MRR's craft and men were now to be sent to patrol the waters of Lake Tanganyika. Being informed that their target was Che Guevara only made the mission more tempting.

The success of Operation White Giant generated a great deal of optimism in Washington. So much so, that on 25 August 1965 National Security Advisor McGeorge Bundy was able to confirm to Johnson that the "back of the rebellion [was] broken", and that the US government was working with the Belgian government on "longer range military and administrative programs to get the Congo back on its feet." Nevertheless, Bundy struck a note of caution by informing Johnson that one area was still under rebel control.[91] Just over a month later on 29 September, Peter Jessup of the National Security staff also warned that the "ability of the Tshombe regime to reestablish stability in areas many miles away from Leopoldville [was] negligible." Main population areas had been captured and garrisoned, but the outlying areas remained "chaotic and filled with marauding bands."[92] The situation in the Fizi-Baraka area was gravely concerning. Rebels continued to be supplied across Lake Tanganyika by "Russians and/or Chinese", and the rebel units are well armed and undergoing extensive training by Cuban guerrillas.[93] This said, according to Jessup, the CIA had begun to address the problem by harassing the supply route using several boats based in Albertville. However, the size of the lake (40 miles wide, 300 miles long) meant that a far more substantial "pocket Coast Guard" was necessary. To make matters worse, the "mercenary adventurers" and various Congolese used to crew the boats so far had proved to be "disastrous as to discipline and ability to carry out their missions, to say nothing of maintaining the equipment".[94] What was needed, in Jessup's view was a nucleus of reliable covert boat operators.[95]

The question of how to provide a more efficient pocket navy had already been raised during high-level talks between Department of State officials on 30 August. Attended, also, by Ambassador McMurtrie Godley and Larry Devlin, discussions turned towards a recommendation by the Country Team[96] that two 50-foot Swift boats be dispatched to Lake Tanganyika.[97] Though the problem of crewing the boats with personnel familiar with this type of craft the only real option was to man them with 20-25 [not declassified].[98]

The origin of the two Swifts and the identity of the personnel were to become clearer in July 1965 when Navy SEAL James Hawes was by Bill Williams and Colonel Bruce Cheever of the CIA's Special Operations Division (SOD) in relation to the Congo programme. "Meeting their standards", in his own words, Hawes left the military and the Vietnam War behind to join the CIA.[99] The next stage for Hawes was an "OpsFam" course at what was then known as the Marana Air Park in Tucson, Arizona,[100] a USAF base which became the headquarters for all CIA air operations during the Vietnam War. Marana was also the primary facility of Intermountain, the CIA front company which provided training to Makasi pilots in the Congo.

Arriving in Leopoldville aboard a commercial flight from Paris two weeks later, Hawes was met by 'Dick Johnson', his CIA contact.[101] Taken to the US Embassy, Hawes then met Larry Devlin and Ambassador Godley. As he was to repeat during the Country Team

Weapon training aboard the *Gitana*. (Photo by Alvarez)

MRR cremembers. (Photo by Santiago Alvarez)

meeting Godly held on 30 August, Godley expressed his concerns over the mercenary navy and any negative publicity that it might give to the US government.[102] Godley also expressed concern over the imminent arrival of "imported Cuban personnel." They were proven fighters, and had experience of covert missions, but Castro's fighters were already helping the Simba rebels. Supplying anti-Castro fighters to combat pro-Castro fighters was a notion to which Godley and the State Department objected.[103] As it would take several months to train European naval personnel, something suggested by the State department, there was, nonetheless, no other option than to use the Cuban exile crews. As Hawes made his way to Albertville aboard a WIGMO-owned C-46 where he saw the Makasi B-26Ks and T-28s, in the Caribbean Sea, Tom Clines of the Maritime Operations Branch was making contact with Artime's MRR and arranging for the *Monty* and the *Gitana* to be transported to the Congo for service on Lake Tanganyika. Based at JMWAVE, Clines had worked closely with the Cuban exiles and was a personal friend of Nicaraguan president Anastasio Somoza.[104]

Now, how two 50-foot Swift boats made their into the inner reaches of Central Africa is a story which is a reminder of a plan devised some 50 years earlier when Lieutenant-Commander Geoffrey Spicer-Simson of the Royal Navy was attempting to find ways of defeating the Kaiserliche Marine during the Battle for Lake Tanganyika (1915-1916). On this occasion, and in order to secure Lake Tanganyika from German forces, two motorboats named HMS *Mimi* and *Toutou* were transported from Cape Town to Lukuga. This journey involved taking the boats by train to Bulawayo in Southern Rhodesia, then to Elisabethville in the Congo. From here, Congolese carriers, oxen and mechanical tractors would drag the boats through nearly 150 miles of dense bush. The boats then sailed down the Lualaba River before crossing Lake Kisale and arriving at Kabalo on 22 October, 1915.[105]

The 1965 version of the trek across large parts of Africa began when it was decided that due to the size of the boats it would be impractical to transport them by sea: they were not built to travel the distance which separated the two continents, and the sight of the two craft could have raised suspicions. The idea was, then, for Ricardo Chavez and Santiago Alvarez to sail the MRR's Swifts from Monkey Point in Nicaragua and to take them up the Gulf of Mexico to Morgan City, Louisiana. Here, at the facilities of the Swift's manufacturer, Sewart Seacraft, the boats would be cut up into three pieces. Once this was done, the pieces would be loaded on to C-124 Globemasters and, once

The *Monty* and the *Gitana* arrive in parts in the Congo, September 1965. (Roberto Pichardo Snr.)

The *Monty* (background) was also transported to the Congo after having been cut into three pieces at Sewart Seacraft's premises in Louisiana. (Photo by Alvarez)

The crews of the Makasi naval force pictured at Albertville in 1965. The CIA's James Hawes (top left), Generoso Bringas (seated, first left), Ricardo Chavez (seated third from left), Eulogoi Reyes (crouching, left), Roberto Pichardo Snr. (crouching, centre). (Roberto Pichardo Snr.)

in the Congo, the boats would be reassembled by Sewart employees.[106] The boats were then fitted with three .50 calibre machine guns, one .30 calibre machine gun, and a 57mm recoilless cannon. Each Swift carried enough fuel to carry out a 720 kilometre patrol.[107] When it came to the question of personnel for the two Swifts, Clines had no hesitation in recommending their current crews. "Well trained, disciplined, and devoted to combating communism across the globe"[108], in Cline's opinion, the exiles were perfect for the role they were about to undertake.

The crew of the *Monty* in Albertville, 1965. (Roberto Pichardo Snr.)

Though Santiago Alvarez chose to continue his fight against Castro from Miami, something he would do for many years to come,[109] the CIA had no trouble in making up the numbers for the Congo mission. Long-term MRR associate Ricardo Chavez was used as a go-between, and he was joined by 15 others, many of whom had taken part in operations against Cuba either at the Bay of Pigs or during subsequent missions. Eulogio 'Papo' Reyes was one of the MRR's most fearless operatives,[110] Generoso Bringas and Serapio Cepedo were among the first to join MRR activities in 1963. Roberto Pichardo was recruited to act as the navy's radio and radar technician. Born in 1936, Pichardo was a member of Brigade 2506 and was captured in April 1961. Released in December 1962, Pichardo was working in a radio shop in Miami when he was contacted by Luis Cosme. Although married and the father of two boys, Pichardo was made aware that Guevara was in the Congo and saw the coming mission as a way in which he could avenge the defeat.[111] According to James Hawes, this was a sentiment shared by the Cubans. They held the "fundamental belief that they were different from mercenaries" and that they were a "professional military force operating within certain moral and ethical lines". They had been staunchly anti-Communist since Castro had taken control of Cuba, and they were paid modestly for their services. They did not go to the Congo to "get rich" and did not necessarily believe that their contribution would win their country back. What they wanted was to fight the spread of Communism.[112]

The role of the Makasi naval force was to stop weapons being transported from Tanzania into the Congo. Typically, weapons and supplies were ferried across the lake in small fishing boats like this one. (Albert Grandolini Collection)

On the understanding that they would be working for Oceanus Cargo Line, yet another CIA front company, and with their salaries paid into banks in Miami, the Swift's crews boarded commercial Pan Am flights and flew to Leopoldville *via* New York and Senegal. Once in Albertville, the crews were given their instructions and were informed that they would be working alongside 5 Commando in order to give training to its personnel, to transport 5 Commando up the lake into battle zones and to patrol the lake. Jock Cassidy remained in charge of 5 Commando's naval branch while the CIA's Marcell Rene "Gooch" Gough acted as the liaison officer between the agency and 5 Commando and who was in charge of coordinating joint operations involving the two forces. Gough, a veteran of WW2 and a retired navy frogman, was killed in a car crash in the Congo in November 1965.[113]

Though stopping weapons being transported from Tanzania was the main role of the Makasi navy, what they wanted more than most was the chance to confront and possibly capture Guevara. On one occasion they believed this time had come. It happened when *Lobo-1* (the codename for *Monty*) set out at night to patrol the lake around 15 to 20 miles from their base. Sighting a possible target but, at first, believing they had stumbled across another mass of floating vegetation common to the lake, the crew of *Lobo-1* moved closer in order to make an inspection. Quickly realising that the mass was, in fact, five boats, the order was given to open fire. Whereas four of the boats continued to return fire, one suddenly headed back to the safety of Tanzanian waters. Though never confirmed, the exiles firmly believed that Guevara had been aboard the fifth boat. Their suspicions gained credence when 5 Commando discovered the wreckage of one of the four boats destroyed in the attacks and found documents indicating a Cuban presence. [114] As for Guevara, this may have been one of his last incursions into the Congo. Faced with the problem of not being able to train soldiers, with troop indiscipline, and with a serious lack of weapons and food supplies, Guevara became increasingly desperate. In a telegram sent to Cuba on November 10 he explained that "Enemy pressure [was] increasing and [the] attempts to block lake [were] continuing",[115] and on 14 November Guevara wrote that it was "Indispensable that [the boats carrying supplies] come today: we are starving and encircled".[116] On 20 November, he was eventually forced to concede defeat, to leave the Congo, and to try his hand at stirring rebellion in Bolivia.

One of the objectives of the Makasi naval force was to either capture or kill 'Che' Guevara.

Makasi Navy Crew Member Profile

Born in Pedro Betancourt, Cuba in 1942 to a family of devout Catholics, Felix Toledo's first contact with the MRR came through an encounter with a priest who had once been a member of General Franco's nationalist forces in the Spanish Civil War. The priest in question, Father Francisco, opened Toledo's eyes to the dangers of the communist ideals which were beginning to take root in Cuba after the overthrow of Batista, and advised Toledo to escape to the United States. Imprisoned for association with the MRR in 1960, it was at this point that Toledo fled the island and travelled to Miami. Though he did not take part in the Bay of Pigs invasion, Toledo took advantage of the Cuban Volunteer Program and in 1962 was sent for military training at Fort Wayne, Indiana. After further training at Fort Knox, Kentucky and Fort Jackson, South Carolina, Toledo was dismayed at Kennedy's decision not to attack Castro and then decided to join Artime's movement in December 1963. Based in Costa Rica and trained in communications, in 1964 Toledo was transferred to Monkey Point from where he took part in raids on the Cuban mainland. Proud to this day of his anti-communist activities, in the early 1980s Toledo returned to Central Africa as part of a medical team based in Miami. He put his experience in the Congo to use by providing help to UNITA rebels in Angola. Later, as part of his continuing commitment to defeating communism, Toledo returned to Nicaragua to train the Contras. His biggest regret was that, "You can't shoot communists anymore".

7
Mobutu, the Mercenary Revolt and the Makasi

Mobutu Comes to Power

The maritime operations carried out by the Cuban exiles did much to convince Guevara that the Central African version of focalism was a lost cause and that the time had come to try his hand elsewhere. This said, while the Congo saw one potential threat distanced from its eastern shores, all too familiar forms of internal political unrest would come to the fore almost immediately after Guevara's departure. Over the past five years the Congo was never more than a breath away from a rebellion or a coup d'Etat and the period between November 1965 and November 1967 proved to be no different. While new threats to political stability came from familiar quarters, others were largely unexpected.

The political turmoil that took place in 1965 began as soon as a new constitution had been promulgated on 1 August 1964 and parliamentary elections had been programmed for March 1965. Fearing that the elections would provide Kasa-Vubu with the opportunity to restructure his government and to distance the popular Moïse Tshombe from the reins of power, the US Department of State believed that the Katangan leader would retire to his homeland from where he would make a renewed bid to obtain

The Makasi naval force worked alongside 5 Commando in a training role. (Photo by Bob Houke)

There was, however, the chance for some R&R. (Roberto Pichardo Snr.)

secession for the province.[1] Given what had taken place the last time Katanga had unilaterally declared its independence, there were good grounds to keep a watchful eye on developments that could unhinge the continuing pacification process.

Victory for Tshombe's Congolese National Convention (CONACO) in 122 of the 167 seats available during the polls provided evidence that voters believed he was the best man to take the Congo forward. Despite the electoral results in a number of districts being contested and the elections rerun, when the Congolese parliament opened its doors in September 1965, the CONACO found itself with a large enough majority to win control of the Lower House. Though other parties retained control of the Upper House and therefore provided a political buffer to absorb the strength of Tshombe's ambitions, Kasa-Vubu chose this moment to strike back at a formidable political opponent. Using the powers invested in him by the constitution, the president dismissed Tshombe and appointed Evariste Kimba of the BALUBAKAT. This was bound to anger Tshombe given the tribal rivalry between his Lunda tribe and the Luba. It also brought back the memory of Patrice Lumumba's decision to undermine Tshombe's political authority by appointing Baluba leader Jason Sendwe as his representative in Katanga in July 1960. This decision convinced Tshombe that Katanga would be better off running its own political affairs.

Not without its own constitutional powers, it was inevitable that the Lower House would refuse to accept Kimba's appointment and in the coming days forced through motions which led to the resignation of the government. Once more politically rudderless, to all intents and purposes the Congo had turned back the clocks to September 1960 when Mobutu mounted a *coup d'Etat* and suspended parliament. The difference this time was that Mobutu had no intention of giving Kasa-Vubu and Tshombe the time to resolve their dispute by setting up a college of commissioners in place to act as a temporary executive.[2] Mobutu simply declared himself president and used the Congo's armed forces to make sure there would be no challenge to his authority. Assisted to a certain extent by the United States, he would do so for the next 32 years.

Though it is unclear what role the CIA played in Mobutu's second *coup d'Etat* its political analysts in Langley quickly came to the realisation that Mobutu as president was the best option during a time of political instability. In the absence of any credible alternative, the CIA therefore believe that it should provide Mobutu with support lest there be "even greater political crisis" and the potential for the undermining of US objectives.[3] Continuing to make payments to Mobutu that had started sometime in October 1965, the 303 Committee then approved a number of payments including one totalling $100,000 made sometime after 23 November. This payment may have been used by Mobutu to bribe army officers in order to prevent them from taking what he termed as "unilateral action",[4] but it did not stop his political opponents conspiring to remove him. One such conspiracy that was uncovered at the end of May 1966 involved Everest Kimba, three other former ministers and a number of associates. With the possible collusion of the French and Belgian embassies, they were found to have been plotting a coup d'Etat. The plot was foiled by Congolese army officers who had pretended to be part of the conspiracy.[5] Along with Kimba, Jerome Anany, Alexandre Mahamba and Senator Emmanuel Bamba were hanged in public in Leopoldville on 2 June 1966.

Continuing Financial Support for the Congo

Although $100,000 represented a colossal amount of money in the Congo of the 1960s it was a mere fraction of the approximate $543 million it would eventually spend in an attempt to prop up the fledging country.[6] $349 million of this amount had been used by the Congolese government to spur the economy into some form of action but had yielded meagre returns, and $194 million had been used to provide the Congo with the means of fighting off internal and external threats to the country's security. If a percentage of this sum was used in vain to transform the ANC into a viable combat unit, the CIA's programme of covert tactical support was one of the largest beneficiaries of funds which were provided through the US Military Assistance Program. For those involved in US geostrategic planning, this was money well spent: by November 1965, different threats of varying nature had been more or less nullified. Nevertheless, the ongoing political instability meant that the potential for further civil unrest was never far from the surface.

On the military front the role of the Makasi in the first few months of 1966 was no different than it had been over the previous three years or so: its fleet of aircraft continued to provide invaluable support for ground attacks on rebel positions and its small but highly effective naval force patrolled Congolese waters in the east to discourage the further importation of weapons. Combing their efforts with those of mercenary forces and the ANC, the Makasi had all but put an end to any rebel activity on the eastern front. Indeed, Operation South had gone so well that by June 1966 US Army Chief of Staff General Earle Wheeler felt optimistic enough to submit a report in which he recommended that the extent of the CIA's covert support programme be reduced and its personnel and aircraft be gradually withdrawn. In relative terms, it appeared that the Congo was as peaceful as it had ever been and so it was time to obtain an agreement to replace the CIA force with Congolese personnel.[7] Wheeler's recommendations proved to be slightly premature given the discovery of Kimba's plot and the rumours received by the CIA in early July 1966 that Tshombe was planning a military coup. Apparently, Tshombe planned to use a force of some 200-250 South African and Rhodesian mercenaries already in Katanga.[8] As it turned out, however, the expected revolt against Mobutu's authority did not start in Katanga and neither did it directly involve Tshombe. Instead, it was led by soldiers of the Katangese Baka Regiment in Stanleyville on 22 July 1966. The grievances of the Katangan soldiers were familiar in that they had not been paid for several months and they also coincided with rumours that Prime Minister General Mulamba planned to integrate members of the regiment into other ANC units. With the help of groups of French, Belgian and German mercenaries,[9] the Baka Regiment had hoped to incite others to join them. After suffering several defeats along with tens of casualties, Jean Schramme of the Leopard Battalion was then sent to Stanleyville by Mobutu to negotiate a peaceful outcome.

Jean Schramme's military involvement in the Congo dated back to 1960. (Albert Grandolini Collection)

The Mercenary Revolt of 1967

From the beginning of his tenure as president, Mobutu sought to seal his place as the "Father of the Congolese Nation" at home as well as abroad. The overthrow of Ghanaian leader Kwame Nkrumah in February 1966 had created the place for a new inter-African statesman, and this was a role that Mobutu believed he could fulfil. In a clever move, he sought to improve relations with African nations that had supplied weapons to Congolese rebel movements thus further decreasing their supplies, and in 1967 Mobutu took part in tripartite talks between President Kayibanda of Rwanda and President Micombero of Burundi when tensions emerged between the two. At one fell swoop, Mobutu was therefore able to ensure non-interference in Congolese affairs from its eastern neighbours.

On the home front, Mobutu's commitment to the Africanisation of the Congo could be witnessed through the decision to change the

Mercenaries opposed to Mobutu at the US Consulate building in Bukavu, 1967. (Albert Grandolini Collection)

The Congolese border with Ruanda. Mercenaries including Schramme crossed this border in 1967 after the failed mercenary revolt.

names of Congolese towns and cities: Leopoldville became Kinshasa, Stanleyville became Kisangani, and a whole host of places whose names reflected a former Belgian presence now found themselves "Congolised" and renamed overnight. Their names formalised in the N'Sele Manifesto of 20 May 1967, Mobutu's plan was to create a Congolese national identity and to create a fully independent nation free from western influence. Mobutism was the order of the day.

In order to demonstrate the Congo's desire to move away from its reliance on Belgium in economic matters, in June 1966 Mobutu's government created the Bakajika Law. Giving the Congolese government the right to "retake full and free disposition of all land, forest and mining rights conceded or granted prior to June 30 1960",[10] the intention of the Bakajika Law was to force companies such as Union Minière to pay sufficient dues to the Congolese government. [11] However, as UMHK refused to cede to Mobutu's demands and saw the Bakajika Law as a means of nationalising its activities, given the company's support from foreign interests it was inevitable that sooner or later there would be serious repercussions. As UMHK's European employees left the Congo through the fear of reprisals against them, in early 1967 the economy was gradually grinding to a halt.[12]

While Mobutu struggled to come to terms with the demands of overseeing the Congo's economy, the ghosts of the Congo's political and military past again began to rear up and complicate matters even further. To deal with the political spectre and the threat presented by Katanga, Mobutu's authorities tried the exiled Moïse Tshombe *in absentia* and sentenced him to death in March 1967. Shortly after, Schramme hatched a plot to overthrow Mobutu using a substantial mercenary force and former Katangese Gendarmes. This mercenary revolt gained momentum after Tshombe's kidnapping and imprisonment in early July 1967, and it could very well have resulted in a victory for the mercenary forces had the ANC not have been given air cover by the Makasi. Though forces under the command of Schramme and Denard made rapid gains and controlled parts of Kisangani, Bukavu and Kindu from 15 July 1967, by the first week of August they had been forced to retreat after sustained attacks by B-26s, T-28s and Israeli-trained ANC paratroopers transported into battle by US C-130s. Finally, the mercenaries surrendered and made their way to Rwanda in November 1967. While Schramme would end up dying in Brazil, Denard would go on to take part in a number of other mercenary operations. Most famously, he attempted to invade the Congo from Angola while riding a bicycle. This was shortly after he had been wounded at Kisangani and had forced Cuban exile pilot Panchito Alvarez to fly him to Rhodesia.[13]

As for the CIA's covert forces of Cubans, the 303 Committee had decided to phase out the CIA's maritime programme on 4 November 1966 and was in the process of transferring the responsibility of defending Lake Tanganyika over to the Congolese authorities. The CIA's air programme had been terminated on 31 March 1967 meaning that aircraft and aircrew were now under direct Congolese control. As we have just seen, Mobutu would make full use of their capacity. Like Mobutu, the United States integrated the exiles into its armed forces to serve in one capacity or another. Hundreds would join the regular forces and fight in Vietnam while others became special force operatives and fully-fledged CIA employees. Some were to be found in Nicaragua where they aided the Contras or in Angola where they acted as advisors to UNITA forces led by Jonas Savimbi. In fact, the exiles joined the fight wherever Fidel Castro attempted to spread his ideology. This is the Cuban exiles' lasting legacy and is one which survives today.

Appendix I

Pilot Instructions for Makasi pilots serving in the Congo in the mid-1960s.

20 APRIL 1965
LEOPOLDVILLE

REGULATIONS FOR PILOTS/ CREWMEN

CONTENTS

I. REPORTING TO THE CONGO

1. ARRIVAL

UPON YOUR ARRIVAL AT N'DJILI AIRPORT, LEOPOLDVILLE YOU WILL BE MET BY THE CHIEF PILOT OR HIS DESIGNATED REPRESENTATIVE. THIS INDIVIDUAL WILL EXPIDITE YOUR PASSAGE THRU CUSTOMS AND IMMIGRATIONS AND WILL PROVIDE YOU WITH TEMPORARY LODGING UNTIL A PERMANENT ASSIGNMENT CAN BE MADE FOR YOU WHICH USUALLY IS THE FOLLOWING DAY.

2. CHECK-IN PROCESS

THE DAY FOLLOWING YOUR ARRIVAL YOU WILL REPORT TO THE CHIEF PILOT OR THE ADMINISTRATION OFFICER AT 0800 FOR PROCESSING. YOU WILL BE ASSIGNED QUARTERS DURING YOUR TRAINING IN LEOPOLDVILLE. YOU WILL FILL IN AND COMPLETE PERSONAL INFORMATION PAPERS, ARRANGE FOR SIGNING OF YOUR GOVERNMENT OF TH CONGO CONTRACT AND WILL BE BRIEFED BY THE CHIEF PILOT/ ADMIN OFFICER ON GENERAL INFORMATION, OPERATIONS, PILOT POSITION, ETC. YOU WILL MEET THE CAO AT N'DJILI OPERATIONS AND DRAW FLIGHT AND PERSONAL EQUIPMENT AT WIGMO SUPPLY DEPARTMENT. IN REGARDS TO THIS EQUIPMENT: YOU WILL SIGN FOR AND BE HELD RESPONSIBLE FOR THE CUSTODY OF ALL EQUIPMENT DURING YOUR STAY IN THE CONGO. THIS GEAR WILL BE RETURNED TO WIGMO UPON COMPL TION OF YOUR CONTRACT. ANY EQUIPMENT LOST OR NOT ACCOUNTED FOR WILL BE CHARGED TO YOU AND DEDUCTED FROM YOUR PAY AT A RATE THAT WILL BE TWICE THE COST SINCE THIS EQUIPMENT IS NOT READILY ACCESSABLE IN THE CONGO. IF YOU HAVE ANY QUESTIONS DURING THE CHECK-IN PERIOD CONSULT THE ADMIN OFFICER FIRST AS HE SHOULD BE ABLE TO ANSWER ANY QUESTIONS THAT MIGHT ARISE. THE CHIEF PILOT CAN ALSO BE CONSULTED IF THE ADMIN OFFICER IS IN THE FIELD.

3. GENERAL INFORMATION

NORMALLY YOUR PAY WILL BE DEPOSITED INTO YOUR BANK ABOUT THE 30th OF THE MONTH. FIELD PAY WILL BE DISTRIBUTED BY THE ADMINISTRATION OFFICER ABOUT THE 15th IN CASH AND YOU WILL RECEIPT FOR THIS MONEY. MAIL IS TAKEN CARE OF BY THE ADMIN OFFICER AND IS NORMALLY GOTTEN TO THE FIELD LOCATIONS PROMPTLY. YOUR RETURN ADDRESS IS:

JOSE LOPEZ
BP 2175
LEOPOLDVILLE
REPUBLIQUE DU CONGO

ALL PILOTS ARE CAUTIONED TO USE DESCRETION WHEN WRITING LETTERS OR MAKING LONG DISTANCE PHONE CALLS. OPERATIONAL MATTERS, MISSIONS, TARGET LOCATIONS, TARGET AREAS, DAMAGE, CASUALTIES, ETC, WILL NOT BE DISCUSSED OR DISCLOSED IN LETTERS OR BY PHONE. DO NOT TRY TO MAKE YOURSELF LOOK LIKE A HERO BY WRITING THIS GARBAGE AS IT COULD HAVE ADVERSE AFFECT ON YOUR FAMILY OR YOUR FLYING MATES FAMILIES. PHOTOGRAPHS OF YOU OR YOUR FELLOW PILOTS, THE AIRCRAFT CONCERNED, THE COUNTRY ARE ACCEPTABLE; HOWEVER PICTURES DEALING WITH

WITH STRIKES, MISSIONS OR TARGETS ARE FORBIDDEN. VIOLATION OF THIS REGULATION CAN RESULT IN YOUR BEING SENT HOME. TRANSPORTATION IS NORMALLY PROVIDED FOR BY 2-3 VW BUSES SUPPLIED FROM A MOTOR POOL. THESE BUSES WILL BE RUN ON A SCHEDULE MADE-UP BY THE ADMIN OFFICER AND WILL BE AVAILABLE FOR PILOTS IN TRAINING IN LEO, R AND R PILOTS, PILOTS REQUIRING MEDICAL TREATMENT, ETC; DUE TO THE FLEXIBILITY OF FLIGHT OPERATIONS THERE CANNOT BE A FIXED AND DEFINITE SCHEDULE: BUSES WILL GENERALLY BE UTILIZED FOR TRIPS TO N'DJILI TO MEET SCHEDULED FLIGHTS. PILOTS COMING INTO LEO ON R AND R, FERRY FLIGHTS, MEDICAL OR FOR ANY OTHER AUTHORIZED REASON WILL INFORM THE AO AT HIS STATION SO THAT ARRANGEMENTS CAN BE MADE TO HAVE TRANSPORTATION AWAITING YOUR ARRIVAL AT N'DJILI AIRPORT. IN CASE OF NO TRANSPORTATION CALL WIGMO-6062 AND THEY WILL USUALLY BE ABLE TO GET YOU INTO TOWN. IN THESE INSTANCES DO NOT EXPECT A SPECIAL CAR OR BUS FOR YOURSELF AS WIGMO RUNS A MOTOR POOL FOR THEIR OWN PERSONNEL AND YOU WILL BE EXPECTED TO MEET THEIR SCHEDULE. THE ADMIN OFFICER WILL BE RESPONSIBLE FOR SERVICING AND MAINT. OF THE VEHICLES ASSIGNED TO THE PILOTS. A MEDICAL DOCTOR IS HIRED BY WIGMO AND IS ON DUTY AT THE AIRPORT OFFICES FROM 0900-1200 EACH DAY; HE IS ALSO GENERALLY AT THE FIELD IN THE AFTERNOON; IF YOU HAVE ANY MEDICAL TREATMENT REQUIRED YOU WILL FIRST CONSULT HIM FOR DIAGNOSIS AND TREATMENT. IN CASES OF PILOTS BEING GROUNDED THE DOCTOR WILL ISSUE YOU A GROUNDING CHIT WHICH WILL THEN BE TURNED IN BY YOU TO THE ADMIN OFFICER. DURING OFF-DUTY HOURS OR IN CASE OF EMERGENCY YOU CAN VISIT THE DOCTOR AT WIGMO HOUSE "FOX TROT" OR CALL 9165 AND ASK THAT THE PARTY GET THE DOCTOR FOR YOU. DO NOT HESITATE TO UTILIZE THIS DOCTOR.

-2-

III. PILOT TRAINING---LEOPOLDVILLE

PILOT ASSIGNMENT WILL BE MADE BY TYPE AIRCRAFT BY THE CHIEF PILOT AND CHIEF AIR OFFICER AT LEO. AIRCRAFT ASSIGNMENT WILL BE MADE ACCORDING TO YOUR EXPERIENCE, FLIGHT BACKGROUND AND PRESENT AND ATICIPATED FIELD DETACHMENT NEEDS.

WHEN YOU COMMENCE TRAINING AT LEO YOU WILL BE GIVEN STANDARD OPERATING PROCEEDURES (SOP) AND LOANED A PILOTS HANDBOOK FOR THE TYPE AIRCRAFT ASSIGNED. PRIOR TO FLIGHT TRAINING YOU WILL BE GIVEN A WRITTEN EXAMINATION COVERING THE AIRCRAFT YOU ARE ASSIGNED. EACH DAY A FLIGHT SCHEDULE WILL BE PREPARED BY THE ADMIN OFFICER AND APPROVED BY THE CHIEF PILOT. THIS SCHEDULE WILL BE POSTED AT THE FOLLOWING LOCATIONS:

1. WIGMO BULLITIN BOARD OUTSIDE WIGMO SUPPLY
2. SABENA APT.
3. RIVER HOUSE

IT IS THE PILOTS RESPONSIBILITY TO BE ON TIME FOR FLIGHTS AND THEREFORE SHOULD BE READY FOR FLIGHTS AT LEAST 30 MINUTES PRIOR TAKE-OFF TIME. PILOTS IN TRAINING ARE RESPONSIBLE FOR LOGGING FLIGHT TIME INCLUDING DUAL TIME; FLIGHT LOGS ARE KEPT IN THE WIGMO LOG OFFICE. REGARDING THIS OFFICE, IT IS NOT TO BE USED AS A "READY ROOM" . WE ARE ATTEMPTING TO OBTAIN A SPACE FOR THE PILOTS TO USE TO STORE FLIGHT CLOTHING AND PERSONAL GEAR WHILE FLYING, BUT LIKE ALL THINGS IT TAKES TIME.

YOUR FLIGHT INSTRUCTION AND SYLLABUS WILL BE DEPENDANT UPON YOUR FLIGHT PROGRESS AT LEO. GENERALLY THE FLIGHT INSTRUCTION WILL BE GIVEN BY THE CHIEF PILOT WHEN HE IS IN TOWN; IN HIS ABSENCE THE CHIEF AIR OFFICER OR HIS REPRESENTATIVE WILL CONDUCT FLIGHT TRAINING. THE FIELD ASSIGNMENT WILL BE MADE AFTER YOU FINISH THIS TRAINING. IN CASES WHERE THE PILOT IS NOT CONSIDERED ADEQUATELY QUALIFIED FOR OPERATIONAL FLYING THE PILOT WILL BE GIVEN 30 DAYS NOTICE AND TERMINATED IN ACCORDANCE WITH THE PROVISIONS OF THE GOC CONTRACT.

RETRAINING WILL ALSO BE CONDUCTED FOR PILOTS COMING IN ON R AND R TO ENABLE THIS ORGANIZATION TO BE COMPLETELY STANDARDIZED IN THE FIELD. PILOTS ON R AND R WILL GENERALLY BE SCHEDULED FOR 1 FLIGHT PER DAY DURING THE R AND R PERIOD. A RETRAINING SYLLABUS WILL BE PUBLISHED FOR THIS PURPOSE.

IV. FIELD ORGANIZATION AND TRAINING

AFTER COMPLETION OF TRAINING AT LEO YOU WILL BE ASSIGNED TO ONE OF THE FIELD DETACHMENTS. YOU WILL REPORT TO THE STATION CHIEF PILOTWHO HAS BEEN DESIGNATED AS SUCH BY THE CHIEF PILOT. THE STATION CHIEF PILOT WILL BRIEF YOU ON LOCAL OPERATIONS, CONDITIONS, ETC. THE SCP WILL BE YOUR DIRECT SUPERVISOR AND YOU ARE RESPONSIBLE TO HIM AND WILL RECEIVE INSTRUCTIONS AND ORDERS FROM HIM. THE SCP SHOULD BRIEF YOU ON SOPS FOR THE AREA OF OPERATIONS, RADIO AIDES, GENERAL PREVAILING WEATHER CONDITIONS, TERRAIN, NAVIGATION, OPPOSITION,GROUND FIRE EXPECTED TO BE ENCOUNTERED, ETC. HE WILL ALSO ASSIGN YOU A POSITION IN THE FLIGHT DETACHMENT. THE SCP IS RESPONSIBLE TO THE DETACHMENT AIR OFFICER AND WILL ACCEPT FLIGHTS AND MISSIONS FROM THE AO ONLY. THE AO AND THE SCP SHOULD WORK TOGETHER TO INSURE THAT THERE IS A COMPLETE UNDERSTANDING IN ALL FLIGHT OPERATIONS AND THAT THE SCP AND OTHER PILOTS UNDERSTAND WHAT IS REQUIRED OF THEM ON EACH MISSION. THE AO AND THE SCP HAVE AUTHORITY TO GROUND ANY PILOT FOR DISIPLINARY., FLIGHT OR MEDICAL REASONS;

V. GENERAL AIR OPERATIONS

ALTHOUGH THIS OPERATION COULD BE CONSIDERED A "BUSH WAR" IT IS EVIDENT THAT PILOTS AND PLANES CAN BE LOST. BAD FLYING HABITS AND A NON-PROFESSIONAL APPROACH CAN BE THE CAUSE OF LOSING A PILOT OR AIRCRAFT AND THIS ORGANIZATION CANNOT AFFORD TO LOSE EITHER. THE TACTICAL TRAINING YOU RECEIVE IN LEO HAS BEEN PROVED IN OTHER COMBAT SITUATIONS AND IT HAS BEEN PROVED THAT IF YOU UTILIZE THESE TACTICS THAT YOUR LONGEVITY WILL BE INCREASED. DUE TO THE NATURE OF OPERATIONS THE FLYING CAN BECOME ROUTINE AND A BORE AND THIS IS THE TIME THAT YOU CAN TAKE A FEW ARROWS IN THE CAN.

1; SCHEDULED FLIGHTS

TRAINING, OPERATIONAL, TEST AND FERRY FLIGHTS WILL BE CARRIED OUT AS PER THE SCHEDULED TIME. TARDINESS WILL NOT BE TOLERATED.

2. AIR DISIPLINE

IT IS THE FLIGHT LEADER'S RESOPONSIBILITY TO BRIEF HIS FLIGHT PRIOR TO ANY AND EACH FLIGHT OR MISSION AND THEN DEMAND THAT THESE INSTRUCTIONS BE CARRIED OUT. IN THE PAST BRIEFING HAS BEEN DONE IN THE AIR; MORE LIKE A DISCUSSION. RADIO DISIPLINE HAS BEEN NON-EXISTENT AND TALK BETWEEN PLANES RESEMBLES A RUNNING COMENTARY. THERE IS NO EXCUSE FOR THIS CONTINUAL CHATTER AND IF PROPERLY

AIR DISIPLINE-CONT.

BRIEFED YOU SHOULD BE ABLE TO FLY MOST MISSIONS WITHOUT OPENING UP ON THE AIR. IN THIS MATTER YOU MUST REALIZE THAT MOST OF OUR PLANES ARE OPERATING ON 118.1 AND THAT IN CASES OF EMERGENCY IT COULD BECOME IMPOSSIBLE TOGET IMPORTANT MESSAGES ON THE AIR. IT IS ALSO PROBABLE THAT MOST OF OUR TACTICAL FREQUENCIES ARE BEING MONITERED AND WITH DF EQUIPMENT YOU WOULD BE PIN-POINTED EVERY TIME YOU OPEN UP. PROPER AND ADEQUATE BRIEFING CAN DO AWAY WITH 95% OF THE RADIO CHATTER.

3. FERRY FLIGHTS

THE APPROVED FERRY ROUTES IN THE CONGO ARE LISTED ON THE MAP IN THE CAO OFFICE AT N'DJILI AND YOU ARE EXPECTED TO BE FAMILIAR WITH THESE ROUTES. T-28 FLIGHTS WILL TAKE THE LISALA-COQ-LEO ROUTE WHEN COMING AND GOING AND WILL ALWAYS REPORT INTO STAN ASLONG AS WE ARE OPERATING THERE. B-26 AND C-46 AIRCRAFT WILL NORMALLY OPERATE ON DIRECT ROUTES DURING FERRY; NATURALLY PILOTS MUST CONSIDER WEATHER CONDITIONS, DARKNESS, ETC. BUT IN THE INTEREST OF SAFETY DO NOT ALTER YOUR ROUTE AS IN CASE OF EMERGENCY WE WOULD AT LEAST HAVE A GOOD IDEA AS TO YOUR LOCATION. AIRCRAFT BEING FERRIED TO LEO FOR INSPECTION WILL FLY VFR ONLY.

4. TEST FLIGHTS

TEST FLIGHTS WILL BE CARRIED OUT AFTER EACH INSPECTION AT LEO. PILOTS DEPARTING LEO ON FERRY FLIGHTS SHOULD TEST FLY THE AIRCRAFT THE DAY BEFORE DEPARTURE TO ENSURE THAT THERE ARE NO DISCREPANCIES.

5. TRANSPORT FLIGHTS

THE TRANSPORT SECTION WILL BE UNDER THE CONTROL OF THE CAO AT LEO. HE WILL SCHEDULE ALL TRANSPORT (C-46) FLIGHTS ORIGINATING FROM N'DJILI. IN THE FIELD THESE AIRCRAFT WILL OPERATE UNDER THE AO AND THE AO WILL KEEP LEO ADVISED AS TO UTILIZATION AND LOCATION OF TRANSPORT PLANES. THESE AIRCRAFT WILL OPERATE IN SUPPORT OF OUR OPERATIONS ONLY AND THE AOS IN THE FIELD SHOULD MAKE EVERY EFFORT TO COORDINATE ON FLIGHTS SO THAT MAXIMUM UTILITY CAN BE MADE OF THESE PLANES AND THEIR TRIPS. THE PILOT-IN-COMMAND OR AIRCRAFT COMMANDER IS RESPONSIBLE FOR THE AIRCRAFT AND WILL INSURE THAT IN ALL OPERATIONS THAT SAFETY IS PARAMOUNT. THE PILOT-IN-COMMAND WILL BE REPONSIBLE FOR NOT ONLY THE AIRCRAFT, BUT ALSO THE PASSENGERS AND CARGO ABOARD HIS PLANE. REGARDING PASSENGERS AND CARGO: IN THE PAST IT HAS BEEN FOUND THAT UNAUTHORIZED PASSENGERS AND CARGO HAVE BEEN TRANSPORTED BY OUR AIRCRAFT WHICH SHOWS SOME LAXITY ON THE PART OF THE AO AND THE PILOT-IN-COMMAND.

Appendix II

Extracts from Antonio Soto Vazquez's Contract with Caribbean Marine Aero Corporation (Caramar), in 1963.[1]

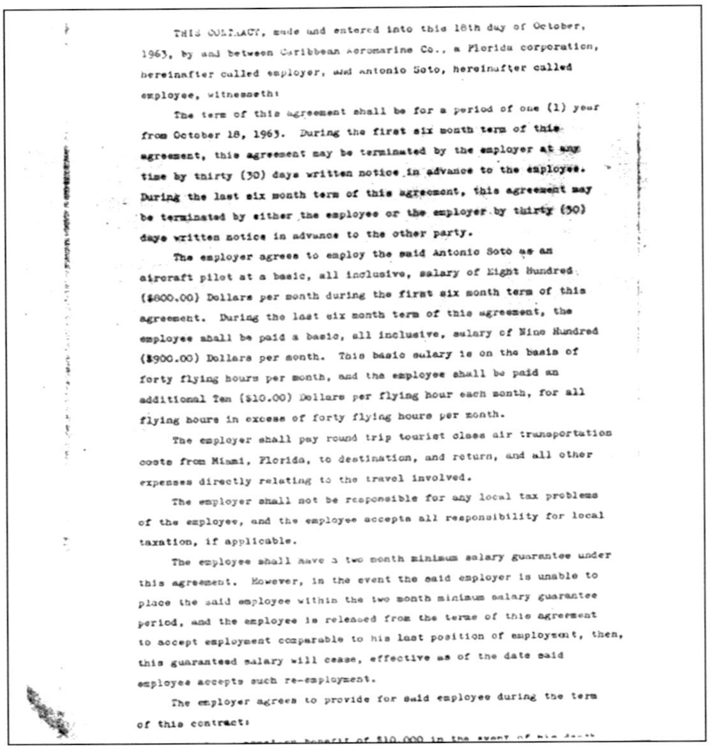

THIS CONTRACT, made and entered into this 18th day of October, 1963, by and between Caribbean Aeromarine Co., a Florida corporation, hereinafter called employer, and Antonio Soto, hereinafter called employee, witnesseth:

The term of this agreement shall be for a period of one (1) year from October 18, 1963. During the first six month term of this agreement, this agreement may be terminated by the employer at any time by thirty (30) days written notice in advance to the employee. During the last six month term of this agreement, this agreement may be terminated by either the employee or the employer by thirty (30) days written notice in advance to the other party.

The employer agrees to employ the said Antonio Soto as an aircraft pilot at a basic, all inclusive, salary of Eight Hundred ($800.00) Dollars per month during the first six month term of this agreement. During the last six month term of this agreement, the employee shall be paid a basic, all inclusive, salary of Nine Hundred ($900.00) Dollars per month. This basic salary is on the basis of forty flying hours per month, and the employee shall be paid an additional Ten ($10.00) Dollars per flying hour each month, for all flying hours in excess of forty flying hours per month.

The employer shall pay round trip tourist class air transportation costs from Miami, Florida, to destination, and return, and all other expenses directly relating to the travel involved.

The employer shall not be responsible for any local tax problems of the employee, and the employee accepts all responsibility for local taxation, if applicable.

The employee shall have a two month minimum salary guarantee under this agreement. However, in the event the said employer is unable to place the said employee within the two month minimum salary guarantee period, and the employee is released from the terms of this agreement to accept employment comparable to his last position of employment, then, this guaranteed salary will cease, effective as of the date said employee accepts such re-employment.

The employer agrees to provide for said employee during the term of this contract:

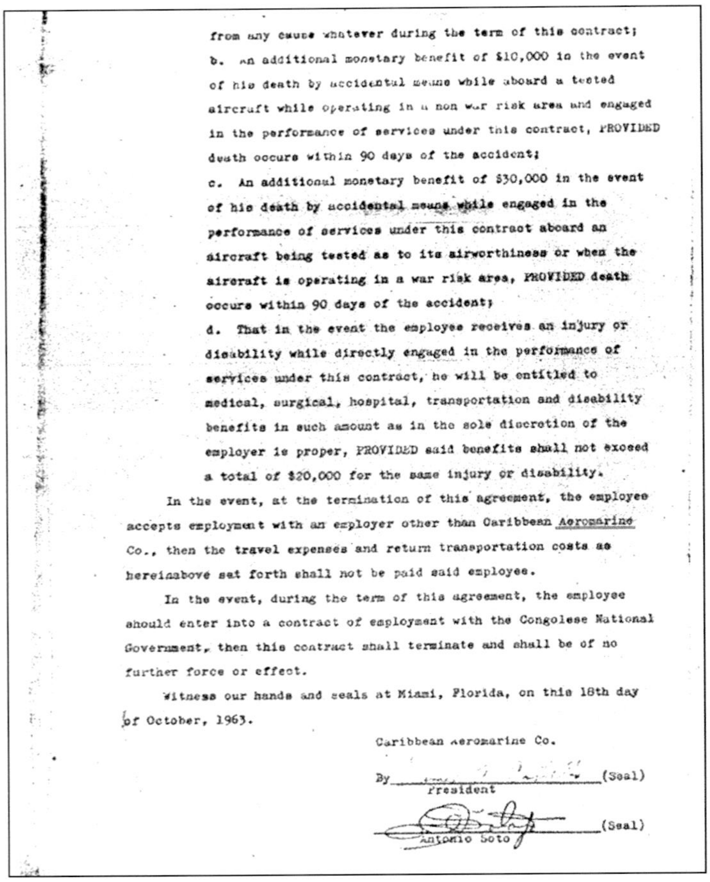

from any cause whatever during the term of this contract;

b. An additional monetary benefit of $10,000 in the event of his death by accidental means while aboard a tested aircraft while operating in a non war risk area and engaged in the performance of services under this contract, PROVIDED death occurs within 90 days of the accident;

c. An additional monetary benefit of $30,000 in the event of his death by accidental means while engaged in the performance of services under this contract aboard an aircraft being tested as to its airworthiness or when the aircraft is operating in a war risk area, PROVIDED death occurs within 90 days of the accident;

d. That in the event the employee receives an injury or disability while directly engaged in the performance of services under this contract, he will be entitled to medical, surgical, hospital, transportation and disability benefits in such amount as in the sole discretion of the employer is proper, PROVIDED said benefits shall not exceed a total of $20,000 for the same injury or disability.

In the event, at the termination of this agreement, the employee accepts employment with an employer other than Caribbean Aeromarine Co., then the travel expenses and return transportation costs as hereinabove set forth shall not be paid said employee.

In the event, during the term of this agreement, the employee should enter into a contract of employment with the Congolese National Government, then this contract shall terminate and shall be of no further force or effect.

Witness our hands and seals at Miami, Florida, on this 18th day of October, 1963.

Caribbean Aeromarine Co.

By ______________ (Seal)
President

______________ (Seal)
Antonio Soto

Appendix III

Cuban Exiles who served in the Congo (Pilots, technicians, administration):

Afont Rodriguez, Tomás ★
Alvarez, Francisco "Panchito" ★
Balboa Alvarado, Jose ★
Baro, Cesar
Bartes, Francisco
Batista Hernandez, Nildo ★
Blanco, Reginaldo
Bernal Fernandez, Gaston
Blazquez del Pozo, Antonio "El Pedrusco"
Bringuier, Jorge
Brito Garcia, Orlando
Cadena, Enrique
Cantillo Huget, Amado ★
Carol Armand, Oscar Alfonso ★
Castellanos Reyes Gavilan, José Manuel "Memel" ★
Castillo Leyva, Rafael "Propela"
Castresana, Elpidio
Cereceda Coira, Castor ★
Chabau, Sosa
Cordo Lugo, Oscar
Cosme Toribo, Luis ★
Cross Quintana, Raul
De La Guardia, Luis
Despagne Perez, Ernesto
Diaz, Manuel
Entriago Telledo, José
Fernandez, Segisberto
Fernandez Ardois-Anduz, Luis ★
Filpes, Claudio
Flaquer Carballal, Frederico ★
Garcia Acosta, Tristan ★
Garcia Fernandez, René ★
Garcia Pujol, Rafael ★
Garcia Tuñon, Juan (KIA, Bunia, Congo, 17 February, 1965)
Ginebra-Groero Perez, Mario (KIA, Albertville, Congo, 1964) ★
Ginebra-Groero Perez, Francisco "Chiqui" ★
Gomez Gomez, Fausto (KIA, Bunia, Congo, 17 December, 1964) ★
Gonzales Molina, Guillermo (1957)
Guiterrez, Alberto "Dr. Kildare"
Hernadez Rojo, Angel Manuel
Hernandez Reyes, Hector "Moropo" ★
Herrera Cabrera, Gonzalo ★

Herrera Perez, Eduardo ★
Intriago, Jorge
Izquierdo Ramirez, Orlando ★
Landazuri, Ramiro
Lopez Dominguez, Angel ★
Luaices Sotelo, César ★
Maza Barrios, Alfredo ★
Mendez Acosta, Santiago
Navarro Rodriguez, Jorge "El Puma" ★
Organvidez Dominguez, Hernan
Padron Sanchez, Cecilio ★
Pedrianes, Angel
Pedroso Amores, Acelo ★
Pellon Blanco, José Leonardo ★
Perez Menendez, José ★
Perez Sordo, Alberto ★
Peron Sosa, Juan C. "Titi"
Peyno Inclan, Ernesto ★
Piedra, Armando
Piqué Fernandez-Coca, Aturo (KIA, Congo) ★
Ponzoa Alvarez, Gustavo ★
Quintero, Jorge "Toto"
Ramos, Mario
Rodriguez Rendueles, Gaston
Rojas Gonzales, Ignacio "Max" ★
Roque, Luis ★
Salas Baro, Antonio ★
Seda Reyes, Leonardo ★
Solis Sariol, Raul ★
Soto Vasquez, Antonio ★
Travesio Pla, René
Tuya, René
Valdez Campaneria, or Companel, Fausto ★
Varela, Joaquin "Jack"
Verdaguer, Guillermo
Whitehouse Inzua, Eduardo ★
Yabor Justiz, Carlos
★ Denotes Bay of Pigs veteran

GROUND FORCES

William "Rip" Robertson, Commanding Officer ★
Lt. Colonel Garza, Arthur (US Army)
"Mitch" (USAF/CIA)
Arguelles, Santiago ★
Benitez, Angel
Calas, Alicio
Fernandez, Alfredo "Calviño"
Fuentes, Felix "Felo"
Garcia, Orlando
Gonzalez Castro, José Angel "El Chino" ★
Hernandez, José "Juan Roque"
Lazo, Guillermo
Martinez, Raimundo
Morales Navrette, Ricardo "El Mono" ★
Perez, Alberto
Rivero, Manuel "El Gallego"
Rodriguez, Jorge
Romero, Andres
Silva Cadebra, Jorge "Fotingo"
Tamayo Cordovi, Juan "El Negro" ★

CUBAN EXILE NAVAL FORCE

SWIFT Boat: *Monty*

Alavarez, Anael
Arroyo, Jorge
Cao, Roberto
Cepero, Serapio
Chavez, Ricardo
Salcedo, Justo "Papa"
Toledo, Felix

Radio/Radar Technician

SWIFT Boat: *Gitana*

Arce, Remigio
Borges, Domingo
Bringas, Generoso
Fernandez, Luis ★
Hernandez, Gumersindo
Ramirez, Pedro
Reyes, Eulogio "Papo"★
Sanchez, Andres
Pichardo, Roberto★

Bibliography

Persons interviewed

Santiago Alvarez (Alpha 66 and Commando L)
Angel Manuel Benitez (Cuban Exile Commando force, Congo)
Reginaldo Blanco (Pilot, Congo)
Frederico Falquer (Pilot, Congo)
Jim Hawes (Central Intelligence Agency, Congo)
Robert Houke (Helicopter pilot, Congo)
David McAllister (Survivor of Kilometre 8, Congo)
Jon Merriman (Son of John Merriman, Intermountain pilot, KIA, Congo)
Peter Mishou (Son of Leighton Mishou, Central Intelligence Agency, Congo)
Nigel Osborne (Member of *Compagnie Internationale*, Congo)
Juan Peron (Pilot, Congo)
Roberto Pichardo (Bay of Pigs and Force Navale Congolaise)
Ignacio Rojas (Pilot Bay of Pigs and Congo)
Eulogio 'Papo' Reyes (Force Navale Congolaise)
Felix Toledo (Force Navale Congolaise)

Governmental Documents and Publications (presented in chronological order where possible)

"Coordination and Policy Approval of Covert Operations", Washington, February 23, 1967, FRUS, *Congo*, 1964-1968, D263.

"Cuban Revolutionary Council: A Concise History", HSCA, Vol. 10, AC 4, CRC, Hist.

"Political situation in the Union of South Africa", ORE 1–49, 31 January 1949, *Central Intelligence Reports*, Intelligence File, President's Secretary's Files: Box 215. HSTL.

Dirección de Inteligencia, "Expediente de Manuel Artime Buesa, Informede Rodrigo Rivas Vega, Delegado del Buró Agrario de Manzanillo", MININT Archives, Manzanillo, 15 June 1959.

"Memorandum from Edmund A. Gullion to J.K. Gustafson Regarding US Policy towards South Africa,", May 17, 1948, *History and Public Policy Program Digital Archive*, National Archives at College Park, 21.79 South Africa.

"Comite Interamericano de Desarrollo Agricola (CIDA), Tenencia de la tierra y desarrollo socio-economico del sector agricola: Guatemala" (Washington, D.C.: Union Panamericana, Secretaria General de la Oraganizacion de los Estados Americanos, 1965).

"Letter from the Ambassador to Guatemala (Schoenfeld) to the Secretary of State's Special Assistant for Intelligence (Armstrong)", Guatemala City, 13 February 1953, FRUS, 1952-1954, *Guatemala*, D34.

"National Intelligence Estimate (NIE-62)", *Present Political Situation in Guatemala and Possible Developments during 1952*, Washington, 11 March, 1952, https://2001-2009.state.gov/r/pa/ho/frus/ike/iv/20208.htm, accessed 8 June 2019.

"Memorandum from the Acting Chief of the Western Hemisphere Division, Central Intelligence Agency ([name not declassified]) to the Deputy Director of Central Intelligence (Helms)", Washington, March 17, 1952, Central Intelligence Agency, Job 79–01025A, Box 7.

"Memorandum by the Executive Secretary of the National Security Council (Lay) to the President", Washington, 5 November 1952, FRUS, 1952-1954, National Security Files, Vol. II, Part 1, D32.

"Memorandum Prepared by the Officer in Charge of West, Central, and East Africa Affairs (Feld), Washington, August 17, 1953", FRUS 1952-1954, Africa and South Asia, vol. XI, part 1.

"Memorandum by the Director, Office of African Affairs (Utter) (to the Deputy Executive Director, Bureau of Near Eastern, South Asian, and African Affairs (Moore)", Washington, September 9, 1953, FRUS 1952-1954, Africa and South Asia, vol. XI, part 1.

"Memorandum for the Record: PBSUCCESS", Washington, September 18, 1953, Central Intelligence Agency, Job 79–01025A, Box 76, Folder 2. Secret.

"Memorandum for Chief of Project, Control of PBSUCCESS Black Flights Through Panama Air Traffic Control", 8 April 1954, https://www.cia.gov/library/readingroom/docs/DOC_0000916573.pdf, accessed 7 June, 2019.

"Memorandum by the Secretary of State to the President", Washington, 24 March 1952, FRUS, 1952-1954, *The American Republics*, Volume IV, D327.

"Dispatch from the Embassy in Cuba to the Department of State", Havana, 10 January 1958, FRUS, Volume VI, Cuba, D2.

"White House Special Staff Note" Washington, 13 January 1959, FRUS, *Cuba*, 1958-1960, Vol.VI, D224.

"Memorandum by the Assistant Secretary of State for Inter-American Affairs' Special Assistant (Hill)", 6 February 1959, FRUS, *Cuba*, 1958-1960, Vol.VI, D.249.

"Despatch from the Embassy in Cuba to the Department of State", Havana, 18 February 1959, FRUS, *Cuba*, 1958-1960, Vol.VI, D.253.

"Despatch from the Embassy in Cuba to the Department of State", Havana, 25 February 1959, FRUS, *Cuba*, D257.

"List of nineteen Cubans in Congo under WIPEGASUS", NARA Record Number: 104-101104-10069, accessed 28 August 2019.

"Maritime Assets", RIF Number 104-10241-10136, maryferrell.org, accessed 19 September 2019.

"Cable: My Joann left Baltimore Port, 1 December A.M.", RIF 104-10077-10244, maryferrell.org, accessed 19 September 2019.

"Contact Report #15, Pass Instructions Re. Procurement of Material Next Meeting", RIF 104-10275-10051, maryferrell.org, accessed 19 September 2019.

"Memorandum from the Assistant Secretary of State for Inter-American Affairs' Special Assistant (Hill) to the Assistant Secretary of State (Rubottom)", Washington, 24 April 1959, FRUS, *Cuba*, D295.

"Paper Prepared by the 5412 Committee", *A Program of Covert Action Against the Castro Regime*, Washington, March 16, 1960, Eisenhower Library, Project "Clean Up" Records, Cuba.

CIA Cable, "Leopoldville to Director", 18 August, 1960, FRUS, *Congo*,1958-1960, Vol. XIV, D421.

CIA Cable, "Dulles to Station Officer", 26 August, 1960, CIA Cable, "Leopoldville to Director", 24 August, FRUS 1958-1960, Vol. XIV, 1960, D429.

"FBI Airtel to Director from SAC", *Sergio Arcacha Smith Black Line File*, New Orleans, December 12, 1960, HSCA (JFK document 012691).

"National Security Action Memorandum No.97: Use of US Fighter Aircraft in the Congo", 19 September 1961, available at https://fas.org/irp/offdocs/nsam-jfk/nsam97.jpg, accessed 19 August 2019.

"John F. Kennedy to Kwame Nkrumah", 2 February 1961, Papers of John F. Kennedy, Presidential Papers, President's Office Files, Countries, *Congo*, General, 1959-1960, https://www.jfklibrary.org/Asset-Viewer/Archives/JFKPOF-114-006.aspx, accessed 17 December 2018.

"Memorandum from Secretary of Defense McNamara to His Special Assistant (Yarmolinsky)", Washington, 5 May 1961, FRUS, 1961-1963, Vol.X, *Cuba*, January 1961-September 1962, D207.

"Memorandum for the Special Group", Washington 5 June 1961, FRUS, *Congo*, D82.

"Memorandum from Secretary of Defense McNamara to President Kennedy", Washington, 13 September 1962, FRUS 1961-1963, *Cuba*, Vol.X, January 1961-September 1962, D426.

"Telegram from the Mission to the United Nations to the Department of State", New York, 24 September 1962, FRUS, *Congo*, Vol.XX, D293.

"Telegram from the Department of State to the Embassy in the Congo, Washington, 25 October 1962", FRUS, 1961-1963, Volume XX, *Congo Crisis*, D318.

"Telegram from the Station in the Congo to the Central Intelligence Agency, Leopoldville", 26 October, 1962, Central Intelligence Agency Files, Job 78–00435R, DDO/ISS Files, Box 1, Folder 12.

Editorial note to, "Telegram from the Station in the Congo to the Central Intelligence Agency, Léopoldville 26 October 1962", FRUS, *Congo*, Vol.XX, D123.

"Telegram 1113 from US Embassy in Leopoldville to Secretary of State" 15 November 1962, Papers of John F. Kennedy, Presidential Papers, NSF, Box 33, Congo: Security, 1962.

"From Chief, WH Division to Chiefs, Certain Stations and Bases: Book Dispatch AMWORLD-Background of Program, Operational Support, Requirements and Procedural Rules", 28 June 1963, CIA Record Number 104-10315-10004, accessed 19 September 2019.

"Letter from the Under Secretary of State for Political Affairs (Harriman) to the Deputy Secretary of Defense (Vance)", Washington, 18 March 1964, FRUS, *Congo*,1964-1968, Vol. XXIII, D161.

"Report Prepared in the Central Intelligence Agency", *Status report on CIA Assistance to the Congolese Air Force*, Washington, 5 May 1964, FRUS, *Congo*,1964-1968, Vol. XXIII, D168.

"Movimento Recuperacion Revolucionario, 1962-1964" Miami, Florida, 18 May 1964, United States Department of Justice, Federal Bureau of Investigation.

"Movimento de Recuperacion Revolucionario", United States National Archives, NARA Record Number 180-10141-10365, accessed 19 September 2019.

"Memorandum for the Record", 26 January, 1965, FRUS, Volume XXIII, *Congo*, D392.

"Memorandum from Harold H. Saunders of the National Security Council Staff to President Johnson", 25 February, 1965, Johnson Library, National Security File, Congo, Vol. XI, Memos & Miscellaneous, 1/65-9/65, Secret.

"Memorandum from Robert W. Kromer of the National Security Council to the President's Special Assistant for National Security Affairs (Bundy)", 26 January, 1965, Johnson Library, National Security File, Country File, Congo, Vol. X, Cables, Memos & Miscellaneous, 12/64, Secret.

"Telegram from the Department of State to the Embassy in the Congo", Washington, 12 April 1965, FRUS, *Congo*, D414.

"Memorandum from the President's Special Assistant for National Security Affairs (Bundy) to President Johnson, 25 August, 1965", Johnson Library, National Security File, Country File, *Congo*, Vol. XI, Memos & Miscellaneous, 1/65-9/65, Secret.

"Memorandum from the Chief of the Africa Division, Directorate of Plans, Central Intelligence Agency (Fields) to the Deputy Director of Plans (Fitzgerald)", Washington, 30 August 1965, FRUS, Congo, 1960-1968, Vol.XIII, D427.

"Memorandum for President Johnson, 29 September 1965", *US Covert Support for Congolese Government on Lake Tanganyika*, National Security Council, Intelligence Files, *Congo*, 1960-1965, Secret; Eyes Only.

"Memorandum for the 303 Committee", FRUS, Volume XXIII, 23 November, 1965, Document 450.

"Information Memorandum from the Deputy Assistant of State for African Affairs (Fredericks) to Secretary of State Rusk", Washington, 31 May 1966, FRUS, *Congo*, D471.

"Memorandum from the Deputy Secretary of Defense's Military Assistant (Greenleaf) to the Deputy Secretary of Defense (Vance)", Washington, 3 June 1966, FRUS, *Congo*, D472.

"Memorandum from the Board of National Estimates to Director of Central Intelligence McCone", Washington, 27 January 1967, FRUS, Congo, D488.

"Mobutu and the Congo", Directorate of Intelligence, Weekly Review, 23 June 1967, p.6, available at https://www.cia.gov/library/readingroom/docs/DOC_0000680536.pdf, accessed 2 October 2019.

"Memorandum from the President's Special Assistant (Rostow) to President Johnson", Washington, 13 July 1967, FRUS, *Congo*, D524.

"Alleged Assassination Plots involving Foreign Leaders" Senate Select Committee, Report No. 94-95 (Washington: US Government Printing Office, 1975), p.92.

"Cobalt: Policy Options for a Strategic Mineral", Special Study, *Congressional Budget Office*, September 1982.

"Revolution in Cuba: Efforts of the United States to Aid in Restoring Political Peace", FRUS, *The American Republics*, Vol.5, pp.370-376.

"2008 Yearbook of Immigration Statistics", United States Department of Homeland Security (Washington, DC, 2008), p.8.

Foreign Relations of the United States, Volume XIII, *Congo, 1960-1968* (Washington: United States Government Printing Office, 2013), introduction, pp.xxxi.

US/UN Laws, Resolutions and Reports

"The National Security Act of 1947-July 26, 1947", Public Law 253, 80th Congress; Chapter 343, 1st Session; S. 758.

United Nations "Resolution 161: The Congo Question", 21 February 1961, available at http://unscr.com/en/resolutions/doc/161, accessesd 19 August 2019.

"Security Council resolution 169 (1961), The Congo Question", available at https://www.refworld.org/docid/3b00f1be4c.html, accessed 18 August 2019.

"United Nations General Assembly, Fifteenth Session, Official Records, 869th Plenary Meeting", New York, 23 September, 1960 (points 94-143).

"National Security Act of 1947", available at https://archive.org/details/nsact1947, accessed 12 July 2019.

Articles Published in Academic Reviews

"A Report by Grayston Lynch of the Central Intelligence Agency, 4 May 1961", National Defense University, Taylor Papers, Box 12, Cuba, *Paramilitary Study*. Secret; Eyes Only.

Hartman L. Butler, Jnr., "Aerospace Fundamentals and Industry Analysis", *Financial Analysts Journal*, Vol.22, No.1, January-February, 1966.

"A Stockpile History", *Managing Materials for a Twenty-first Century Military*, National Research Council, Division on Engineering and Physical Sciences (The National Academies Press, 2008).

Cox, Alfred T., "Civil Air Transport (CAT): A Proprietary Airline, 1946-1955", *Clandestine Services Historical Paper*, No. 87, Volume I of IV (SO Division, April 1969).

Cullather, Nicholas, "Operation PBSUCCESS: The United States and Guatemala, 1952-1954", History Staff, *Center for the Study of Intelligence*, Central Intelligence Agency, Washington, DC, 1994.

Dodenhoff, George H., "The Congo: A Case Study of Mercenary Employment", *Naval College Review*, April 1969.

Dorn, A. Walter, "The UN's First "Air Force": Peacekeepers in Combat, Congo 1960-64", *Journal of Military History*, Vol.77, No.4, October 2013.

Hellström, Leif, "The Instant Air Force: The Creation of the CIA's Air Unit in the Congo, 1962", 3rd Term Paper (C-uppstas), Autumn Term 2005, available at http://sh.diva-portal.org/smash/get/diva2:15224/FULLTEXT01.pdf, p.21, accessed 19 August 2019.

Gleijeses, Piero, "Ships in the Night: The CIA, the White House and the Bay of Pigs", *Journal of Latin American Studies*, Vol. 27, No. 1, February 1995.

Gleijeses, Piero, "Cuba's First Venture in Africa: Algeria, 1961-1965", *Journal of Latin American Studies*, Vol.28, No.1, February 1996.

Hernandez, José M., "The ACU: Transplanting a Cuban Lay Organization to the United States", *US Catholic Historian*, Vol.21, No.1, Recovering the U.S. Hispanic Catholic Heritage, Part Two: Parishes, Organizations, and Latina Leadership (Winter, 2003).

Holbrook, Joseph, "The Catholic Church in Cuba, 1959-1962: The Clash of Ideologies", *International Journal of Cuban Studies*, Vol.2, No.3/4, Autumn/Winter 2010.

Kneitel, Tom, "Inside the CIA's Secret Radio Paradise: Part II", *Popular Communications*, December 1985.

Lemarchand, René, "The Democratic Republic of Congo: From Collapse to Potential Reconstruction", Occasional Paper, Centre of African Studies, University of Copenhagen, September 2001.

Laumann, Dennis, Che Guevara's Visit to Ghana, *Transactions of the Historical Society of Ghana*, New Series, No. 9, 2005.

Mazov, Sergey, "Soviet Aid to the Gizenga Government in the Former Belgian Congo (1960-61) as Reflected in Russian Archives", *Cold War History*, Vol. 7, No. 3, August 2007.

Morgan, John Davis, Jr., "Strategic Materials in World War II", *Bureau of Mines*, 1 December, 1983.

Odom, Thomas P., "Dragon Operations: Hostage Rescues in the Congo, 1964-1965", Leavenworth Papers, Number 14, *Combat Studies Institute*, Fort Leavenworth, Kansas, 1986.

Pfeiffer, Jack B., Official History of the Bay of Pigs Operation, "Vol.III: Evolution of CIA's Anti-Castro Policies, 1959-January 1961", December 1979, available at https://nsarchive2.gwu.edu//NSAEBB/NSAEBB355/bop-vol3.pdf, accessed 9 August 2019.

Sharif, A., "Reference Module", *Materials Science and Materials Engineering*, 2007.

Published sources

Anderson, John Lee, *Che Guevara: A Revolutionary Life* (London: Bantam Press, 1997).

Arboleya, Jesus (translated by Rafael Betancourt), The Cuban Counterrevolution (Ohio: Ohio University Press, 2000).

Attwood, William, *The Reds and the Blacks: A Personal Adventure* (New York: Harper and Row, 1967).

Bamford, James, *Body of Secrets: Anatomy of the Ultra-Secret National Security Agency* (First Anchor Books, 2002).

Bardach, Ann Loiuise, *Without Fidel: A Death Foretold in Miami*, Havana and Washington (New York: Scribner, 2014).

Bonachea, Ramon, and San Martin, Marta, *The Cuban Insurrection, 1952-1959* (Oxford: Transaction Publishers, 1974).

Bonachea, Rolando E. and Valdés, Nelson P. (eds.), *Cuba in Revolution* (New York: Anchor Books, 1972).

Bucheli, Marcelo, *Good dictator, bad dictator: United Fruit Company and Economic Nationalism in Central America in the Twentieth Century* (University of Illinois at Urbana-Champaign, 2006).

Buick, Robert Clayton, *Age of Inquiry* (Bloomington: Xlibris Corporation, 2010).

Burrows, James C., *Cobalt: An Industry Analysis* (Lexington: Lexington Books, 1971).

Byrd, Martha, *Chennault: Giving Wings to the Tiger* (Alabama: University Alabama Press, 2003).

Carrozza, Anthony R., *William D. Pawley: The Extraordinary Life of the Adventurer, Entrepreneur, and Diplomat Who Cofounded the Flying Tigers* (Dulles, Virginia: Potomac Books, Inc., 2012).

Chomsky, Noam, *Hopes and Prospects* (London: Penguin, 2010).

Dreke, Victor, *From Escambray to the Congo: In the Whirlwind of the Cuban Revolution* (Pathfinder Press, 2002).

Dumbrell, John, *President Johnson and Soviet Communism* (Manchester: Manchester University Press, 2012).

Escalante, Fabian, *The Secret War: CIA Covert Operations Against Cuba, 1959*-62 (Melbourne: Ocean Press, 1995).

Eyck, F. Gunther, *L'Expansion Belge sous Léopold Ier (1831-1865): Recueil d'Etudes* (Académie royale des Sciences d'Outre-Mer, Brussels, 1965).

Ferrer, Edward B., *Operation Puma: The Air Battle of the Bay of Pigs* (International Aviation Consultants Inc., 1982).

Foden, Giles, *Mimi and Toutou Go Forth: The Bizarre Battle for Lake Tanganyika* (London: Penguin, 2005).

Fonzi, Gaetan, *The Last Investigation* (New York: Thunder's Mouth Press, 1993).

Ganser, Daniele, *NATO's Secret Armies: Operation GLADIO and Terrorism in Western Europe* (London: Frank Cass, 2005).

George, Edward, *The Cuban Intervention in Angola, 1965-1991: From Che Guevara to Cuito Cuanavale* (New York & London: Frank Cass, 2005).
Gleijeses, Piero, *Shattered Hope: The Guatemalan Revolution and the United States, 1944-1954* (Princeton: Princeton University Press, 1991).
Guevara, Ernesto, *Guerrilla Warfare: A Method* (Peking: Foreign Language Press, 1964).
Guevara, Ernesto, *The African Dream: The Diaries of the Revolutionary War in the Congo* (London: Harvill Press, 2001).
Guevara, Ernesto, *The Che Reader* (Ocean Press, 2005).
Hancock, Larry with Wexler, Stuart, *Shadow Warfare: The History of America's Undeclared Wars* (Counterpoint: Berkeley, 2014).
Hawes, James, and Koenig, Mary Ann, *Cold War Navy Seal: Che Guevara, CIA Black Ops, and My Experience as the First Seal in Africa* (New York: Skyhorse Publishing, 2018).
Hersh, Burton, *The Old Boys: The American Elite and the Origins of the CIA (*Tree Farm Books, 2001).
Hingston, Michael, *Renegade Hero: the true story of RAF pilot Terry Peet and his clandestine mercy flying with the CIA* (Barnsley, UK: Pen and Sword Books Ltd, 2011).
Hinkle, Warren and Turner, William W., *Deadly Secrets: The CIA-Mafia War Against Castro and the Assassination of JFK* (New York: Thunder's Mouth Press, 1993).
Hoare, Mike, *Congo Mercenary* (Colorado: Paladin Press, 2008).
Hoare, Mike, *The Road to Kalamata: A Congo Mercenary's Personal Memoir* (Boulder, Colorado: Paladin Press, 1989).
Howard Hunt, E., *Give Us This Day* (New York: Popular Library Edition, 1973).
Hudson, Andrew, *Congo Unravelled: Military Operations from Independence to the Mercenary Revolt, 1960-1968* (Warwick: Helion & Company, 2012).
Immerman, Richard H., *The CIA in Guatemala: The Foreign Policy of Intervention* (Austin: University of Texas Press, 1982).
Jackson, Julian, *The Popular front in France: Defending Democracy, 1934-1938* (Cambridge, University of Cambridge Press, 1998).
Johnson, Haynes, *The Bay of Pigs: The Leaders' Story of Brigade 2506* (New York: Dell Publishing, 1964).
Kalb, Madeleine G., *The Congo Cables*: The Cold War in Africa – From Eisenhower to Kennedy (London: Macmillan, 1982).
Kellner, Douglas, *Ernesto 'Che' Guevara* (London: Chelsea House Publishers, 1989).
Kisangani, Emizet François, *Historical Dictionary of the Democratic Republic of the Congo* (New York: Rowmand & Littelfield).
La Feber, Walter, *Inevitable Revolutions: The United States in Central America* (Cornell University: Norton, 1993).
Lert, Frédérick, *Wings of the CIA* (Paris: Histoire & Collections, 1998).
Lynch, Grayston L., *Decision for Disaster: The Battle of the Bay of Pigs* (New York: Pocket Books, 1998).
Meriwether, James Hunter, *Proudly We Can be Africans, Black Americans and Africa, 1935-1961* (North Carolina, University of North Carolina Press, 2002).
Meriwether, James Hunter, *The African Connection and the Struggle for Freedom: Africa's Role in American Life* (Los Angeles, University of California, 1995).
Nichols, K.D., *The Road to Trinity* (New York: Morrow, 1987).
Nixon, Richard, *Six Crises* (New York: Doubleday, 1962).
Pérez-Cisneros, Pablo, Donovan, John B., and Koenreich, Jeff, *After the Bay of Pigs: Lives and Liberty on the Line* (Miami: Alexandria Library, 2007).
Pfeiffer, Jack B., *CIA Official History of the Bay of Pigs Invasion: Volume IV, The Taylor Committee Investigation of the Bay of Pigs* (New York: Military Bookshop, 2011).
Robbins, Christopher, *Air America: The Explosive True Story of the CIA's Secret Airline* (London: Cassell Military, 2012).
Rookes, Stephen, *Ripe for Rebellion: Congolese Political and Military Insurgency in the Congo, 1946-1964* (Helion & Company, 2020).
Russo, Peter with Esperian, John H., *Offshore Vegas: How the Mob Brought Revolution to Cuba* (Bloomington: iUniverse, 2007).
Shapiro, Samuel, *Invisible Latin America* (Boston: Beacon Press, 1964).
Smith, Earl E.T., *The Fourth Floor: An Account of the Castro Communist Revolution* (New York: Random House, 1962).
Snyder, D.H., *Stockpiling Strategic Materials: Politics and National Defense* (San Francisco: Chandler Publishing, 1966).
Trento, Joseph J., *Prelude to Terror: Edwin P. Wilson and the Legacy of America's Private Intelligence Network* (New York: Carrol & Graf Publishers, 2005).
Villafaña, Frank, *Cold War in the Congo: The Confrontation of Cuban Military Forces* (New Brunswick: Transaction Publishers, 2012).
Waldron, Lamar, *Watergate: The Hidden History, Nixon, The Mafia, and the CIA* (Counterpoint, 2013).
Weiner, Tim, *Legacy of the Ashes: The History of the CIA* (New York: Doubleday, 2007).
Zeilig, Leo, Renton, David, and Seddon, David, *The Congo: Plunder and Resistance* (London: Zed Books, 2006).
Zoellner, Tom, *Uranium: War, Energy and the Rock that Shaped the World* (New York: Viking Publishers, 2009).

Newspaper Articles (Listed by date of publication)

"US Garrison Duty in China Forecast", *New York Times*, 13 September 1945.
"Tientsin is Joyous in Hailing Marines", *New York Times*, 30 September 1945.
"China Reds Charge US. Active Help to Chiang in Strife", *New York Times*, 5 November 1945.
Paul Hoffman, "Lumumba Group to Get Arms", *New York Times*, 15 December, 1960.
"OAS Expels Cuba After Delegates Stalk Out", *Chicago Daily Tribune*, 15 February 1962.
"Cuba Began Role in Zanzibar in '61: Havana's Part in Revolution Outlined in Washington – Guerrilla Course Cited", *New York Times*, 2 January 1964.
"Soviet Sees Plot by West in Congo; Tells UN Council Tshombe is Puppet of 'Monopolies – Accuses US Banks", *New York Times*, 18 December 1964.
"Guevara Receives Rousing Welcome", *Ghanaian Times*, 16 January 1965.
Tim Weiner, "Samuel Cummings, 71, Trader in Weapons on a Grand Scale", *New York Times*, 5 May 1998.
Mark Fineman and Dolly Mascarenas, "Bay of Pigs: the Secret Death of Pete Ray", *Los Angeles Times*, 15 March 1998.
"Victor Dreke Cruz: Cuba's history man still talks of revolution", *The Independent*, 17 April, 2011.
John Avlon, "A beloved icon in death, in life Kennedy was hated by many", *Daily Telegraph*, 23 November, 2013.

Glenn Garvin, "Anniversary recalls Congo rescue by Miami Cubans", *Miami Herald,* 15 November, 2014.

Tom Archdeacon, "Arch: CIA to award Navy operative highest honor", *Dayton Daily News*, 21 May, 2016.

"Democratic Republic of the Congo's Mineral Resources", *Le Monde Diplomatique*, August 2018.

Documentaries/Motion Pictures

Jihan El Tahri, *Cuba: une odyssée africaine* (Paris: Editions Arte, 2007).

Digital Documents

"6-6 Cuba: Counter Revolutionary Handbook", 10 October 1962-21 January 1963, p.14., available at https://www.jfklibrary.org/asset-viewer/archives/RFKAG/217/RFKAG-217-007, accessed 9 August 2019.

"Chronology of the United Fruit Company", https://www.unitedfruit.org/chron.htm, accessed 8 June 2019.

"The Evolution of the US Intelligence Community-An Historical Overview", available at https://fas.org/irp/offdocs/int022.html, accessed 15 July 2019.

"A Look Back... Gen. William Donovan Heads Office of Strategic Services", https://www.cia.gov/news-information/featured-story-archive/gen.-william-j.-donovan-heads-oss.html, accessed 1 September, 2016.

"Ernesto Guevara's speech at the Afro-Asian Conference in Algeria", 24 February, 1965, The Che Reader, Ocean Press, 2005, available at https://www.marxists.org/archive/guevara/1965/02/24.htm, accessed 3 June 2019.

"Ernesto Guevara speech in Santiago de Cuba, 30 November, 1964", available at http://www.politique-actu.com/dossier/ernesto-guevara-discours-historique-anniversaire/1702290/, accessed 3 June 2018.

"Farewell letter from Che to Fidel Castro" 1 April, 1965, available at https://www.marxists.org/archive/guevara/1965/04/01.htm, accessed 23 June 2018.

"Fidel Castro at the National Press Club" 20 April 1959, available at https://www.loc.gov/rr/record/pressclub/pdf/FidelCastro.pdf, accessed 8 August 2019.

"Garrison Investigation of Kennedy Assassination", available at https://www.archives.gov/files/research/jfk/releases/104-10189-10021.pdf, accessed 12 September 2019.

"Going Critical: Being Strategic with Our Mineral Resources", http://www.usgs.gov/blogs/features/usgs_top_story/going-critical-being-strategic-with-our-mineral-resources/, accessed 17 May, 2019.

"Guatemalan Arms Acquisition", 21 June 1954, p.2., available at https://www.cia.gov/library/readingroom/docs/DOC_0000921490.pdf, accessed 17 July 2019.

"Inspector General's Survey of the Cuban Operation and Associated Documents", 16 February 1962, available at https://nsarchive2.gwu.edu//NSAEBB/NSAEBB341/IGrpt1.pdf, accessed 9 August 2019.

Joe Leeker "Air America at the Bay of Pigs", available at https://www.utdallas.edu/library/specialcollections/hac/cataam/Leeker/history/BayOfPigs.pdf, accessed 15 September, 2019.

Jeswald W. Salacuse, "The National Land Law System of Zaire", A Report to the University of Wisconsin in Land Tenure Center and USAID/Kinshasa, May 1985, http://pdf.usaid.gov/pdf_docs/PNAAT376.pdf, accessed 2 September 2017.

"John F. Kennedy's Inaugural Address", 20 January 1961, available at http://ap.gilderlehrman.org/history-by-era/sixties/resources/john-f-kennedy%E2%80%99s-inaugural-address-1961, accessed 15 August 2019.

"Leopoldville 1957: Battle of the Breweries", available at http://kosubaawate.blogspot.com/2016/01/leopoldville-1957-battle-of-breweries.html, accessed 22 August 2019.

"Non-US Military T-28s", available at http://www.det156sow.com/download/t_28_non_us_military.pdf, accessed 22 August 2019.

"Olga Patricia=Laissez Faire, at https://web.archive.org/web/20120504052446/http://www.offshore-radio.de/fleet/laissez.htm, accessed 19 September 2019.

"Part II, Foreign Service Work and Life: Embassy, Employee, Family", available at https://www.afsa.org/sites/default/files/iuse_country_team_local_staff_role.pdf, accessed 20 September 2019.

"Remarks on Presenting Cuban Invasion Brigade Flag, Orange Bowl, Miami, Florida, 29 December 1962", available at https://www.jfklibrary.org/asset-viewer/archives/JFKPOF/042/JFKPOF-042-014, accessed 12 August 2019.

"Speech of Dr. Fidel Castro at the UN General Assembly, September 1960", available at http://www1.lanic.utexas.edu/project/castro/db/1960/19600926.html, accessed 23 June 2018.

"The Office of Strategic Services: The Forerunner of Today's CIA", https://www.cia.gov/news-information/featured-story-archive/2008-featured-story-archive/office-of-strategic-services.html, accessed 1 September 2016.

"The Beginning of Intelligence Analysis in CIA", https://www.cia.gov/library/center-for-the-study-of-intelligence/csi-publications/csi-studies/studies/vol51no2/the-beginning-of-intelligence-analysis-in-cia.html, accessed 6 June 2017.

"The History Behind the Ukrainian Trident", available at, https://ukraineliving.com/ukrainian-trident/, accessed 12 September 2019.

"Truman Doctrine: President Harry S. Truman's Address before a Joint Session of Congress, March 12, 1947", http://avalon.law.yale.edu/20th_century/trudoc.asp, accessed 6 June 2019.4

"VOA Through the Years", 3 April 2017, https://www.insidevoa.com/a/3794247.html, accessed 7 June 2019.

Conferences

"The Congo Crisis, 1960-1961, A Critical Oral History Conference", The Woodrow Wilson Center for Scholars, 23-24 September 2004.

Doctoral Theses

"216 Documented Victims of Ché Guevara in Cuba: 1957 to 1959" from Armando M. Lago's Ph.D thesis entitled "Cuba: The Human Cost of Social Revolution", available at http://www.cubaarchive.org/downloads/CA08.pdf, accessed 7 August 2019.

Kurt X. Metzmeier, "John F. Kennedy, Ghana and the Volta River project: a study in American Foreign Policy towards neutralist Africa", *Electronic Theses and Dissertations*, Paper 967, https:// doi.org/10.18297/etd/967, accessed 19 June, 2019.

Notes

Chapter 1

1 "The Evolution of the US Intelligence Community-An Historical Overview", available at https://fas.org/irp/offdocs/int022.html, accessed 15 July 2019.

2 "The Evolution of the US Intelligence Community-An Historical Overview".

3 "A Look Back... Gen. William Donovan Heads Office of Strategic Services", https://www.cia.gov/news-information/featured-story-archive/gen.-william-j.-donovan-heads-oss.html, accessed 1 September, 2016.

4 "The Office of Strategic Services: The Forerunner of Today's CIA", https://www.cia.gov/news-information/featured-story-archive/2008-featured-story-archive/office-of-strategic-services.html, accessed 1 September 2016.

5 Tim Weiner, *Legacy of the Ashes: The History of the CIA* (New York: Doubleday, 2007), p.11.

6 "The Beginning of Intelligence Analysis in CIA", https://www.cia.gov/library/center-for-the-study-of-intelligence/csi-publications/csi-studies/studies/vol51no2/the-beginning-of-intelligence-analysis-in-cia.html, accessed 6 June 2017.

7 "Truman Doctrine: President Harry S. Truman's Address before a Joint Session of Congress, March 12, 1947", http://avalon.law.yale.edu/20th_century/trudoc.asp, accessed 6 June 2019.

8 "Truman Doctrine: President Harry S. Truman's Address before a Joint Session of Congress, March 12, 1947".

9 The act also recognised the US Air Force (USAF) as independent from the army.

10 "The National Security Act of 1947-July 26, 1947", Public Law 253, 80th Congress; Chapter 343, 1st Session; S. 758.

11 In regard to these two terms, and in view of their similarity in meaning, it would seem judicious at this point to clarify just which activities are deemed as being 'covert' and those which are deemed as 'clandestine'. While both signify that activities should be hidden from the public eye, covert activities are defined by the US Department of State as being 'operations that are so planned and executed as to conceal the identity of or permit plausible denial by the sponsor'. This was the case in the Congo where surrogate troops carried out the work which, traditionally, would be carried out by regular forces of a given nation/state/sovereign entity. On the other hand, clandestine activities are operations sponsored or conducted by governmental departments or agencies in such a way as to assure secrecy or concealment. See, http://www.dtic.mil/doctrine/dod_dictionary/, accessed 17 December, 2017.

12 For further information on this episode in France's history see, for example, Julian Jackson, *The Popular Front in France: Defending Democracy, 1934-1938* (Cambridge, University of Cambridge Press, 1998).

13 Daniele Ganser, *NATO's Secret Armies: Operation GLADIO and Terrorism in Western Europe* (London: Frank Cass, 2005), pp.87-88.

14 *Paix et Liberté* had branches in several European countries and carried out psychological operations such as printing anti-communist posters, broadcasting anti-communist propaganda on the radio, and organising anti-communist demonstrations. See, Ganser, *NATO's Secret Armies: Operation GLADIO and Terrorism in Western Europe*, p.103.

15 These activities include the organisation of a military coup in Iran in 1953; flying relief supplies to Chinese nationalist forces using CIA front company Civil Air Transport (CAT); the evacuation of thousands of Chinese nationalists to Taiwan using the same means; and flying military supplies to French forces at Dien Bien Phu.

16 "Coordination and Policy Approval of Covert Operations", Washington, February 23, 1967, FRUS, *Congo*, 1964-1968, D263.

17 "VOA Through the Years", 3 April 2017, https://www.insidevoa.com/a/3794247.html, accessed 7 June 2019.

18 "US Garrison Duty in China Forecast", *New York Times*, 13 September 1945.

19 "Tientsin is Joyous in Hailing Marines", *New York Times*, 30 September 1945.

20 "China Reds Charge US. Active Help to Chiang in Strife", *New York Times*, 5 November 1945.

21 Martha Byrd, *Chennault: Giving Wings to the Tiger* (Alabama: University Alabama Press, 2003), p.152.

22 Frederic Lert, *Wings of the CIA* (Paris: Histoire & Collections, 1998), p.36.

23 Alfred T. Cox, "Civil Air Transport (CAT): A Proprietary Airline, 1946-1955", *Clandestine Services Historical Paper*, No. 87, Volume I of IV (SO Division, April 1969), p.4.

24 "Civil Air Transport (CAT): A Proprietary Airline, 1946-1955".

25 Christopher Robbins, *Air America: The Explosive True Story of the CIA's Secret Airline* (London: Cassell Military, 2012), p.36.

26 Tim Weiner, "Samuel Cummings, 71, Trader in Weapons on a Grand Scale", *New York Times*, 5 May 1998.

Chapter 2

1 Noam Chomsky, *Hopes and Prospects* (London: Penguin, 2010), p.37.

2 F. Gunther Eyck, *L'Expansion Belge sous Léopold Ier (1831-1865): Recueil d'Etudes* (Académie royale des Sciences d'Outre-Mer, Brussels, 1965), p.293.

3 "Chronology of the United Fruit Company", https://www.unitedfruit.org/chron.htm, accessed 8 June 2019.

4 Walter La Feber, *Inevitable Revolutions: The United States in Central America* (Cornell University: Norton, 1993), pp.120-121.

5 For a definition of 'spiritual socialism' see Vaneesa Cook, "Bernie Sanders and the Spiritual Case for Socialism", 25 November 2015, accessed 7 June 2019, https://www.dissentmagazine.org/blog/bernie-sanders-spiritual-socialism-debs-wallace.

6 Marcelo Bucheli, "Good dictator, bad dictator: United Fruit Company and Economic Nationalism in Central America in the Twentieth Century" (University of Illinois at Urbana-Champaign, 2006), p.15.

7 For further information on this aspect of UFCO's business activities in Guatemala see, Piero Gleijeses, *Shattered Hope: The Guatemalan Revolution and the United States, 1944-1954* (Princeton: Princeton University Press, 1991), pp.91-94.

8 "Letter from the Ambassador to Guatemala (Schoenfeld) to the Secretary of State's Special Assistant for Intelligence (Armstrong)", Guatemala City, 13 February 1953, FRUS, 1952-1954, *Guatemala*, D34.

9 "Comite Interamericano de Desarrollo Agricola (CIDA), Tenencia de la tierra y desarrollo socio-economico del sector agricola: Guatemala" (Washington, D.C.: Union Panamericana, Secretaria General de la Oraganizacion de los Estados Americanos, 1965), p.41.

10 Nicholas Cullather, "Operation PBSUCCESS: The United States and Guatemala, 1952-1954", History Staff, *Center for the Study of Intelligence*, Central Intelligence Agency, Washington, DC, 1994, p.16.

11 "Operation PBSUCCESS: The United States and Guatemala, 1952-1954", p.21.

12 "National Intelligence Estimate (NIE-62)", *Present Political Situation in Guatemala and Possible Developments during 1952*, Washington, 11 March, 1952, https://2001-2009.state.gov/r/pa/ho/frus/ike/iv/20208.htm, accessed 8 June 2019.

13 "Memorandum from the Acting Chief of the Western Hemisphere Division, Central Intelligence Agency ([name not declassified]) to the Deputy Director of Central Intelligence (Helms)",

Washington, March 17, 1952, Central Intelligence Agency, Job 79–01025A, Box 7.

14 "Memorandum from the Acting Chief of the Western Hemisphere Division, Central Intelligence Agency ([name not declassified]) to the Deputy Director of Central Intelligence (Helms)",

15 Richard H. Immerman, *The CIA in Guatemala: The Foreign Policy of Intervention* (Austin: University of Texas Press, 1982), pp.120-122.

16 "Memorandum for the Record: PBSUCCESS", Washington, September 18, 1953, Central Intelligence Agency, Job 79–01025A, Box 76, Folder 2. Secret.

17 Fabian Escalante, *The Secret War: CIA Covert Operations Against Cuba, 1959-62* (Melbourne: Ocean Press, 1995), p.29.

18 In 1960, the Gibraltar Steamship Company, a CIA front company, established Radio Swan and operated from Swan Island in the Caribbean. From here, it broadcast anti-Castro propaganda in an attempt to discredit the Cuban leader. See, Tom Kneitel, "Inside the CIA's Secret Radio Paradise: Part II", *Popular Communications*, December 1985, pp.18-22.

19 "Operation PBSUCCESS: The United States and Guatemala, 1952-1954", p.46.

20 The '32' campaign, for example, consisted in painting the number 32 on walls. This was in protest at Article 32 of the Guatemalan constitution which banned international political parties.

21 "Memorandum for Chief of Project, Control of PBSUCCESS Black Flights Through Panama Air Traffic Control", 8 April 1954, https://www.cia.gov/library/readingroom/docs/DOC_0000916573.pdf, accessed 7 June, 2019.

22 "Operation PBSUCCESS: The United States and Guatemala, 1952-1954", p.50.

23 Burton Hersh, *The Old Boys: The American Elite and the Origins of the CIA* (Tree Farm Books, 2001), pp.344–346, in Larry Hancock, with Stuart Wexler, *Shadow Warfare: The History of America's Undeclared Wars* (Counterpoint: Berkeley, 2014), p.87.

24 Frank Villafaña, *Cold War in the Congo: The Confrontation of Cuban Military Forces* (New Brunswick: Transaction Publishers, 2012), p.85.

25 "Guatemalan Arms Acquisition", 21 June 1954, p.2., available at https://www.cia.gov/library/readingroom/docs/DOC_0000921490.pdf, accessed 17 July 2019.

26 "Guatemalan Arms Acquisition", p12.

27 "Operation PBSUCCESS: The United States and Guatemala, 1952-1954", p.65.

28 *Shattered Hope: The Guatemalan Revolution and the United States, 1944-1954*, p.390.

29 "Operation PBSUCCESS: The United States and Guatemala, 1952-1954", p.9.

30 "Operation PBSUCCESS: The United States and Guatemala, 1952-1954", p.9.

Chapter 3

1 Peter Russo with John H. Esperian, *Offshore Vegas: How the Mob Brought Revolution to Cuba* (Bloomington, iUniverse, 2007), p.7.

2 "Revolution in Cuba: Efforts of the United States to Aid in Restoring Political Peace", FRUS, *The American Republics*, Vol.5, pp.370-376.

3 "Memorandum by the Secretary of State to the President", Washington, 24 March 1952, FRUS, 1952-1954, *The American Republics*, Volume IV, D327.

4 Rolando E. Bonachea and Nelson P. Valdés (eds.), *Cuba in Revolution* (New York: Anchor Books, 1972), p.72.

5 Ramon Bonachea and Marta San Martin, *The Cuban Insurrection, 1952-1959* (Oxford: Transaction Publishers, 1974), p.11.

6 *Offshore Vegas: How the Mob Brought Revolution to Cuba*, p.16.

7 Samuel Shapiro, *Invisible Latin America* (Boston: Beacon Press, 1964), p.77.

8 Antonio Rafael de la Cova, *The Moncada Attack: Birth of the Cuban Revolution* (University of South Carolina, 2007) p.153.

9 "Dispatch from the Embassy in Cuba to the Department of State", Havana, 10 January 1958, FRUS, Volume VI, Cuba, D2.

10 Earl E.T. Smith, *The Fourth Floor: An Account of the Castro Communist Revolution* (New York: Random House, 1962), p.89.

11 Haynes Johnson, *The Bay of Pigs: The Leaders' Story of Brigade 2506* (New York: Dell Publishing, 1964), p.25.

12 "216 Documented Victims of Ché Guevara in Cuba: 1957 to 1959" from Armando M. Lago's Ph.D thesis entitled "Cuba: The Human Cost of Social Revolution", available at http://www.cubaarchive.org/downloads/CA08.pdf, accessed 7 August 2019.

13 "Despatch from the Embassy in Cuba to the Department of State", Havana, 25 February 1959, FRUS, *Cuba*, D257.

14 Douglas Kellner, *Ernesto 'Che' Guevara* (London: Chelsea House Publishers, 1989), p.112.

15 "Memorandum from the Assistant Secretary of State for Inter-American Affairs' Special Assistant (Hill) to the Assistant Secretary of State (Rubottom)", Washington, 24 April 1959, FRUS, *Cuba*, D295.

16 "Memorandum from the Assistant Secretary of State for Inter-American Affairs' Special Assistant (Hill) to the Assistant Secretary of State (Rubottom)".

17 "Memorandum from the Assistant Secretary of State for Inter-American Affairs' Special Assistant (Hill) to the Assistant Secretary of State (Rubottom)".

18 Joseph Holbrook, "The Catholic Church in Cuba, 1959-1962: The Clash of Ideologies", *International Journal of Cuban Studies*, Vol.2, No.3/4, Autumn/Winter 2010, pp.264-275.

19 *The Cuban Counterrevolution*, pp.48-49.

20 *The Cuban Counterrevolution*, p.59.

21 Joseph Holbrook, "The Catholic Church in Cuba, 1959-1962: The Clash of Ideologies", *International Journal of Cuban Studies*, Vol.2, No.3/4, Autumn/Winter 2010, pp.264-275.

22 José M. Hernandez, "The ACU: Transplanting a Cuban Lay Organization to the United States", *US Catholic Historian*, Vol.21, No.1, Recovering the U.S. Hispanic Catholic Heritage, Part Two: Parishes, Organizations, and Latina Leadership (Winter, 2003), pp.99-114 .

23 "The ACU: Transplanting a Cuban Lay Organization to the United States", p.99.

24 "The ACU: Transplanting a Cuban Lay Organization to the United States", p.101.

25 It still remains unclear why the trident was chosen to represent the MRR. One theory backed by a conversation with MRR co-founder Emilio Martinez in Miami in September 2019 is that Artime was inspired to use it through its use by Ukrainian anti-Communist movements. Found on the Ukrainian coat of arms, the trident represents the Holy Trinity of the Father, the Son, and the Holy Ghost. The link to Ukraine is substantiated by the use of Ukrainian mercenaries in Central America by the CIA. According to Felix Rodriguez, they were used to train exile infiltration teams and were known as *Halcones* or Falcons in Spanish. In turn, the falcon is often used as a representation of the trident. See, "The History Behind the Ukranian Trident", available at, https://ukraineliving.com/ukrainian-trident/, accessed 12 September 2019. Further evidence that supports the theory of the trident-falcon link can be seen in a photo found in the Bay of Pigs Museum in Miami. It depicts a group of men holding a flag on which both the falcon and the MRR appear. This said, the group of men could belong to another exile group known as *Unidad Revolucianario* (UR). Working in conjunction with the MRR, these *Halcones Negros* or Black Falcons carried out missions against Castro from February 1961 onwards. Like the MRR, this group was funded and trained by the CIA.

26 It should be pointed out that these Catholic organisations were not the first counterrevolutionary groups. This honour falls to the *Rosa Blanca* (White Rose) group founded in New York on 28

January 1959 by Batista supporter Rafael Diaz-Balart. Another group was the *Legion Anticomunista*. Based in the Dominican Republic and backed by Rafael Trujillo, this group made an attempt to stir a rebellion in Cuba in August 1959. Its plans to do so were uncovered by Cuban intelligence services, the G-2. Felix Rodriguez, the last Cuban exile to see Che Guevara alive was part of this operation.

27 *The Cuban Counterrevolution*, p.62.

28 *The Bay of Pigs: The Leaders' Story of Brigade 2506*, p.25.

29 Dirección de Inteligencia, "Expediente de Manuel Artime Buesa, Informede Rodrigo Rivas Vega, Delegado del Buró Agrario de Manzanillo", MININT Archives, Manzanillo, 15 June 1959, p.6., in *The Cuban Counterrevolution*, pp.63-64.

30 *The Cuban Counterrevolution*, p.64.

31 *The Bay of Pigs: The Leaders' Story of Brigade 2506*, p.26.

32 *The Bay of Pigs: The Leaders' Story of Brigade 2506*, p.26.

33 "White House Special Staff Note" Washington, 13 January 1959, FRUS, *Cuba*, 1958-1960, Vol.VI, D224.

34 "Memorandum by the Assistant Secretary of State for Inter-American Affairs' Special Assistant (Hill)", 6 February 1959, FRUS, *Cuba*, 1958-1960, Vol.VI, D.249.

35 "Despatch from the Embassy in Cuba to the Department of State", Havana, 18 February 1959, FRUS, *Cuba*, 1958-1960, Vol. VI, D.253.

36 "Fidel Castro at the National Press Club" 20 April 1959, available at https://www.loc.gov/rr/record/pressclub/pdf/FidelCastro.pdf, accessed 8 August 2019.

37 Richard Nixon, *Six Crises* (New York: Doubleday, 1962), p.352 in *The Secret War: CIA Covert Operations against Cuba, 1959-1962*, p.31.

38 Anthony R. Carrozza, *William D. Pawley: The Extraordinary Life of the Adventurer, Entrepreneur, and Diplomat Who Cofounded the Flying Tigers* (Dulles, Virginia: Potomac Books, Inc., 2012), p.24.

39 "2008 Yearbook of Immigration Statistics", United States Department of Homeland Security (Washington, DC, 2008), p.8.

40 Jack B. Pfeiffer, Official History of the Bay of Pigs Operation, "Vol.III: Evolution of CIA's Anti-Castro Policies, 1959-January 1961", December 1979, available at https://nsarchive2.gwu.edu//NSAEBB/NSAEBB355/bop-vol3.pdf, accessed 9 August 2019.

41 "Inspector General's Survey of the Cuban Operation and Associated Documents", 16 February 1962, available at https://nsarchive2.gwu.edu//NSAEBB/NSAEBB341/IGrpt1.pdf, accessed 9 August 2019.

42 "Inspector General's Survey of the Cuban Operation and Associated Documents".

43 "Inspector General's Survey of the Cuban Operation and Associated Documents".

44 Created through Presidential Directive NSC 5412/2, its role was to coordinate covert operations. In June 1964, the group was renamed the 303 Committee after National Security Memorandum No. 303 and, in 1970, it was succeeded by the 40 Committee. In 1976, 40 Committee was replaced by the Operations Advisory Group and, in 1977, Jimmy Carter created the NSC Special Coordination Committee. Under Ronald Reagan, this committee was replaced by the National Security Planning Group.

45 Warren Hinkle and William W. Turner, *Deadly Secrets: The CIA-Mafia War Against Castro and the Assassination of JFK* (New York: Thunder's Mouth Press, 1993), p.42.

46 "Alleged Assassination Plots involving Foreign Leaders" Senate Select Committee Report No. 94-95 (Washington: US Government Printing Office, 1975), p.92.

47 Gaetan Fonzi, *The Last Investigation* (New York: Thunder's Mouth Press, 1993), p.382.

48 Born Frank Fiorini in Norfolk, Virginia in 1924, Sturgis joined in the US Marines in 1942 and served in the Pacific. After leaving the military, Sturgis worked as a police officer and also as the owner-manager of a nightclub in Virginia. In 1956, Sturgis moved to Cuba but also spent time in a number of Latin American countries such as Mexico and Guatemala. Moving in circles which included high-ranking Mafia officials, Sturgis was involved in attempts to assassinate Fidel Castro. In 1963, Sturgis met with Lee Harvey Oswald after the latter had attempted to infiltrate the Anti-Communist Brigade and, along with three other anti-Castro exiles and a former member of the CIA in June 1972, he was to take part in an attempted burglary at the Watergate apartment block in Washington, DC. It is rumoured that Sturgis was also involved in a conspiracy to assassinate President Kennedy. For further biographical information see, http://spartacus-educational.com/JFKsturgis.htm.

49 On 21 October 1958, Lanz and Sturgis took to the skies above Havana and, from a CIA aircraft, dropped thousands of anti-Castro and anti-communist leaflets over the capital.

50 Gray to Don Wilson (Assistant Director, Dwight D. Eisenhower Library), 3 Dec. 1974, p.i (introduction), Gray Papers, box 2, DDEL, quoted in Piero Gleijeses,"Ships in the Night: The CIA, the White House and the Bay of Pigs", *Journal of Latin American Studies*, Vol. 27, No. 1, February 1995, p.4.

51 David Atlee Phillips set up Radio Swan for this purpose.

52 "Paper Prepared by the 5412 Committee", *A Program of Covert Action Against the Castro Regime*, Washington, March 16, 1960, Eisenhower Library, Project "Clean Up" Records, Cuba.

53 *The Bay of Pigs: The Leaders' Story of Brigade 2506*, p.26.

54 This group was originally composed of lawyers, bankers and medical doctors opposed to Batista. The group attempted to overthrow Batista in 1956 and joined Castro's movement in 1958. Its members held important positions in Urrutia's cabinet but resigned as Castro moved further towards Communism. See, "6-6 Cuba: Counter Revolutionary Handbook", 10 October 1962-21 January 1963, p.14., available at https://www.jfklibrary.org/asset-viewer/archives/RFKAG/217/RFKAG-217-007, accessed 9 August 2019. In March 1961, a month before the invasion, the State Department pressured the group into accepting the *Movimento Revolutioniaro del Pueblo* (MRP) into its ranks. See, "FBI Airtel to Director from SAC", *Sergio Arcacha Smith Black Line File*, New Orleans, December 12, 1960, HSCA (JFK document 012691), quoted in "Cuban Revolutionary Council: A Concise History", HSCA, Vol. 10, AC 4, CRC, Hist.

55 The *Rescate Democratico Revolucionario*, or Revolutionary Democratic Rescue (aka, Rescate) was formed in Cuba in February-March 1960. Described as middle-of-the-road in its political alignment, this group was led by Manuel Antonio de Varona. "Emphatically anti-socialist", this group was part of the Cuban Revolutionary Council with Varona as its deputy leader. Varona was also seen as one of the driving forces behind the Bay of Pigs invasion. *6-6 Cuba: Counter Revolutionary Handbook*, *op.cit*, p.98.

56 The Triple A group was linked to the Autenticos and was formed to combat Batista.

57 Ann Loiuise Bardach, *Without Fidel: A Death Foretold in Miami, Havana and Washington* (New York: Scribner, 2014), p.104.

58 *Without Fidel: A Death Foretold in Miami*, p.104.

59 *Inspector General's Survey of the Cuban Operation and Associated Documents*, p.17.

60 *Inspector General's Survey of the Cuban Operation and Associated Documents*, p.17.

61 "A Report by Grayston Lynch of the Central Intelligence Agency, 4 May 1961", National Defense University, Taylor Papers, Box 12, Cuba, *Paramilitary Study*. Secret; Eyes Only. Lynch prepared the report for the investigative committee chaired by General Taylor.

62 "A Report by Grayston Lynch of the Central Intelligence Agency, 4 May 1961".

63 Robert Clayton Buick, *Age of Inquiry* (Bloomington: Xlibris Corporation, 2010), p.31.

64 *Age of Inquiry*, p.31.

65 Mark Fineman and Dolly Mascarenas, "Bay of Pigs: the Secret Death of Pete Ray", *Los Angeles Times*, 15 March 1998.

66 Jack B. Pfeiffer, *CIA Official History of the Bay of Pigs Invasion: Volume IV, The Taylor Committee Investigation of the Bay of Pigs* (New York: Military Bookshop, 2011).

67 *CIA Official History of the Bay of Pigs Invasion: Volume IV, The Taylor Committee Investigation of the Bay of Pigs*, pp.199-202.

68 *CIA Official History of the Bay of Pigs Invasion: Volume IV, The Taylor Committee Investigation of the Bay of Pigs*, pp.199-202.

69 "Taylor Committee Report", p.204.

70 Grayston L. Lynch, *Decision for Disaster: The Battle of the Bay of Pigs* (New York: Pocket Books, 1998).

71 See for example, John Avlon, "A beloved icon in death, in life Kennedy was hated by many", *Daily Telegraph*, 23 November, 2013.

72 Lamar Waldron, *Watergate: The Hidden History, Nixon, The Mafia, and the CIA* (Counterpoint, 2013), p.209.

73 The majority of prisoners were released on 24 December 1962 in exchange for $53 million in food and medical aid for the Castro regime.

74 "Remarks on Presenting Cuban Invasion Brigade Flag, Orange Bowl, Miami, Florida, 29 December 1962", available at https://www.jfklibrary.org/asset-viewer/archives/JFKPOF/042/JFKPOF-042-014, accessed 12 August 2019.

Chapter 4

1 "Memorandum from Edmund A. Gullion to J.K. Gustafson Regarding US Policy towards South Africa,", May 17, 1948, *History and Public Policy Program Digital Archive*, National Archives at College Park, 21.79 South Africa.

2 "Political situation in the Union of South Africa", ORE 1–49, 31 January 1949, *Central Intelligence Reports*, Intelligence File, President's Secretary's Files: Box 215. HSTL.

3 "Political situation in the Union of South Africa".

4 "Memorandum by the Director, Office of African Affairs (Utter) (to the Deputy Executive Director, Bureau of Near Eastern, South Asian, and African Affairs (Moore), Washington, September 9, 1953", FRUS 1952-1954, *Africa and South Asia*, vol. XI, part 1.

5 "Memorandum Prepared by the Officer in Charge of West, Central, and East Africa Affairs (Feld), Washington, August 17, 1953", FRUS 1952-1954, Africa and South Asia, vol. XI, part 1.

6 John Davis Morgan, Jr., "The Domestic Mining Industry of the United States in World War II: A Critical Study of the Economic Mobilization of the Mineral Base of National Power, 1949" in "A Stockpile History", *Managing Materials for a Twenty-first Century Military*, National Research Council, Division on Engineering and Physical Sciences (The National Academies Press, 2008).

7 The U.S. Geological Survey defines 'critical' minerals as those being vital to the economy whereas a 'strategic' mineral is one that is important to the nation's economy but particularly necessary for defence issues. A strategic mineral does not have any replacements and primarily comes from foreign countries. The term implies that the U.S. is reliant on the supply of strategic minerals and that measures need to be taken when necessary to ensure their supply. See, "Going Critical: Being Strategic with Our Mineral Resources", http://www.usgs.gov/blogs/features/usgs_top_story/going-critical-being-strategic-with-our-mineral-resources/, accessed 17 May, 2019.

8 "Going Critical: Being Strategic with Our Mineral Resources", http://www.usgs.gov/blogs/features/usgs_top_story/going-critical-being-strategic-with-our-mineral-resources/, accessed 17 May, 2019.

9 The Japanese invasion of Manchuria and, later, southeast Asia was prompted by its need for rubber, tin, petroleum, rice, and vegetable oils. Italy also invaded Ethiopia in 1936 for similar reasons.

10 D.H. Snyder, *Stockpiling Strategic Materials: Politics and National Defense* (San Francisco: Chandler Publishing, 1966), in "Managing Materials for a Twenty-first Century Military".

11 Between 1942 and 1944, the United States imported up to 100% of metals and minerals such as asbestos, cobalt, diamonds, nickel, palladium, radium, tantalum and zircon. See, John Davis Morgan, Jr., "Strategic Materials in World War II", *Bureau of Mines*, 1 December, 1983, p.2.

12 "Strategic Materials in World War II".

13 "National Security Act of 1947", available at https://archive.org/details/nsact1947, accessed 12 July 2019.

14 "National Security Act of 1947".

15 K. D. Nichols, *The Road to Trinity* (New York: Morrow, 1987), pp.44-47.

16 Tom Zoellner, *Uranium: War, Energy and the Rock that Shaped the World* (New York: Viking Publishers, 2009), https://www.economist.com/media/management/uranium-zoellner-e.pdf, 3, accessed 17 January, 2019.

17 *Uranium: War, Energy and the Rock that Shaped the World*, p.3.

18 D. Klarstrom, "Cobalt Alloys: Alloying and Thermomechanical Processing", in A. Sharif, "Reference Module", *Materials Science and Materials Engineering*, 2007.

19 "Memorandum by the Executive Secretary of the National Security Council (Lay) to the President", Washington, 5 November 1952, FRUS, 1952-1954, National Security Files, Vol. II, Part 1, D32.

20 "Memorandum by the Executive Secretary of the National Security Council (Lay) to the President",

21 Hartman L. Butler, Jnr., "Aerospace Fundamentals and Industry Analysis", Financial Analysts Journal 22, No.1, January-February, 1966.

22 A transonic turbo jet fighter manufactured by North American Aviation.

23 A turbojet fighter manufactured by Republic Aviation.

24 A single-seat jet fighter manufactured by McDonnell Aircraft.

25 A high-altitude strategic bomber manufactured by Boeing.

26 A supersonic jet fighter manufactured by North American Aviation.

27 An interceptor aircraft manufactured by Convair.

28 James C. Burrows, *Cobalt: An Industry Analysis* (Lexington: Lexington Books, 1971), p.60.

29 "Cobalt: Policy Options for a Strategic Mineral", Special Study, Congressional Budget Office, September 1982.

30 "Cobalt: Policy Options for a Strategic Mineral".

31 "Democratic Republic of the Congo's Mineral Resources", *Le Monde Diplomatique*, August 2018.

32 "John F. Kennedy's Inaugural Address", 20 January 1961, available at http://ap.gilderlehrman.org/history-by-era/sixties/resources/john-f-kennedy%E2%80%99s-inaugural-address-1961, accessed 15 August 2019.

33 The Republic of the Congo became the Democratic Republic of the Congo (DRC) in 1964.

34 "John F. Kennedy's Inaugural Address", 20 January 1961.

35 Foreign Relations of the United States, Volume XIII, *Congo, 1960-1968* (Washington: United States Government Printing Office, 2013), introduction, pp.xxxi.

36 CIA Cable, "Leopoldville to Director", 18 August, 1960, FRUS, *Congo*,1958-1960, Vol. XIV, D421.

37 "Alleged Assassination Plots", p.18.

38 Weiner, *Legacy of the Ashes: A History of the CIA* (Anchor, 2012), p.162.

39 "Leopoldville to Director", 18 August, 1960.

40 A number of works contradict these perceptions of Lumumba. Although not entirely at ease with Lumumba's political leanings they saluted his stand against what was considered as continuing Belgian exploitation of the Congo. Lumumba's struggle for Congolese unity and his refusal to accept independence with "strings attached" made him somewhat of a martyr and a even a 'saviour' of Africa in the eyes of some. See, James Hunter Meriwether, *Proudly We Can be Africans, Black Americans and Africa, 1935-1961* (North Carolina, University of North Carolina Press,

2002), p.233. For further analysis of how black Americans related to Africa's fight for independence see, James Hunter Meriwether, *The African Connection and the Struggle for Freedom: Africa's Role in American Life* (Los Angeles: University of California, 1995).

41 CIA Cable, "Dulles to Station Officer", 26 August, 1960, CIA Cable, "Leopoldville to Director", 24 August, FRUS 1958-1960, Vol. XIV, 1960, D429.

42 Madeleine G. Kalb, *The Congo Cables*: The Cold War in Africa – From Eisenhower to Kennedy (London: Macmillan, 1982), p.102.

43 "United Nations General Assembly, Fifteenth Session, Official Records, 869th Plenary Meeting", New York, 23 September, 1960 (points 94-143).

44 Paul Hoffman, "Lumumba Group to Get Arms", *New York Times*, 15 December, 1960.

45 This would have been around 2,000-6,000 Congolese francs. See, "Transcript of the talk between Deputy of Foreign Minister of the USSR V. V. Kuznetsov and Minister of Education and Arts of the Republic of Congo, Pierre Mulele, 8 March 1961", as quoted in Sergey Mazov, "Soviet Aid to the Gizenga Government in the Former Belgian Congo (1960-61) as Reflected in Russian Archives", *Cold War History*, Vol. 7, No. 3, August 2007, p.433.

46 "The Congo Crisis, 1960-1961, A Critical Oral History Conference", The Woodrow Wilson Center for Scholars, 23-24 September 2004, p.38.

47 "John F. Kennedy to Kwame Nkrumah", 2 February 1961, Papers of John F. Kennedy, Presidential Papers, President's Office Files, Countries, Congo, General, 1959-1960, https://www.jfklibrary.org/Asset-Viewer/Archives/JFKPOF-114-006.aspx, accessed 17 December 2018.

48 "John F. Kennedy to Kwame Nkrumah", 2 February 1961.

49 Kurt X. Metzmeier, "John F. Kennedy, Ghana and the Volta River project: a study in American Foreign Policy towards neutralist Africa", *Electronic Theses and Dissertations*, Paper 967, https:// doi.org/10.18297/etd/967, accessed 19 June, 2019.

50 *The Congo Cables*, p.201.

51 *The Congo Cables*, p.201.

52 See footnotes to "Memorandum for the Special Group, Washington 5 June 1961", FRUS, *Congo*, D82.

53 "Memorandum for the Special Group, Washington 5 June 1961".

54 "Memorandum for the Special Group, Washington 5 June 1961".

55 Andrew Hudson, *The Congo Unravelled: Military Operations from Independence to the Mercenary Revolt, 1960-1968* (Warwick: Helion & Company, 2012), p.27.

56 United Nations "Resolution 161: The Congo Question", 21 February 1961, available at http://unscr.com/en/resolutions/doc/161, accessesd 19 August 2019.

57 A. Walter Dorn, "The UN's First "Air Force": Peacekeepers in Combat, Congo 1960-64", *Journal of Military History*, Vol.77, No.4, October 2013.

58 "Security Council resolution 169 (1961), The Congo Question", available at https://www.refworld.org/docid/3b00f1be4c.html, accessed 18 August 2019.

59 "National Security Action Memorandum No.97: Use of US Fighter Aircraft in the Congo", 19 September 1961, available at https://fas.org/irp/offdocs/nsam-jfk/nsam97.jpg, accessed 19 August 2019.

60 *Congo Cables*, p.315, in "The UN's First "Air Force": Peacekeepers in Combat, Congo 1960-64".

61 "Bomb Supply on Way," *New York Times*, 2 January 1962, p.2, in "The UN's First "Air Force": Peacekeepers in Combat, Congo 1960-64".

62 Leif Hellström, "The Instant Air Force: The Creation of the CIA's Air Unit in the Congo, 1962", 3rd Term Paper (C-uppstas), Autumn Term 2005, available at http://sh.diva-portal.org/smash/get/diva2:15224/FULLTEXT01.pdf, p.21, accessed 19 August 2019.

63 "Telegram from the Department of State to the Embassy in the Congo, Washington, 25 October 1962", FRUS, 1961-1963, Volume XX, *Congo Crisis*, D318.

Editorial note to, "Telegram from the Station in the Congo to the Central Intelligence Agency, Léopoldville 26 October 1962", FRUS, *Congo*, Vol.XX, D123.

64 "Telegram from the Mission to the United Nations to the Department of State", New York, 24 September 1962, FRUS, *Congo*, Vol.XX, D293.

65 "Telegram from the Mission to the United Nations to the Department of State".

Chapter 5

1 "Telegram from the Station in the Congo to the Central Intelligence Agency, Leopoldville", 26 October, 1962, Central Intelligence Agency Files, Job 78–00435R, DDO/ISS Files, Box 1, Folder 12.

2 "Editorial Note", FRUS, *Congo*, 1960-1968, Vol.XXIII, D124.

3 "Editorial Note", FRUS, *Congo*, 1960-1968, Vol.XXIII, D124.

4 "Telegram 1113 from US Embassy in Leopoldville to Secretary of State" 15 November 1962, Papers of John F. Kennedy, Presidential Papers, NSF, Box 33, Congo: Security, 1962.

5 *Cold War in the Congo: The Confrontation of Cuban Military Forces, 1960-1967*, p.37. See also, "Garrison Investigation of Kennedy Assassination", available at https://www.archives.gov/files/research/jfk/releases/104-10189-10021.pdf, accessed 12 September 2019.

6 *Cold War in the Congo: The Confrontation of Cuban Military Forces, 1960-1967*, p.37.

7 Another was the Double-Chek Corporation. Supposedly set up by wealthy Cubans and Miami lawyer Alex Carlson, and operating under the cover of a New York insurance firm, Double-Chek gave bi-weekly payments of $225 to all widows and dependents of men killed at the Bay of Pigs. First payments were received in July 1961. Personal correspondence with Janet Joy Ray, 20 July 2017.

8 *Cold War in the Congo: The Confrontation of Cuban Military Forces, 1960-1967*, p.37.

9 The existence of Soto's second one-year contract indicates that recruitment for the Congo mission began sometime around mid-October 1962. Soto also trained on Bell helicopters from 27 March-15 April 1965. He completed 50 hours of training and one of his instructors was Alexander V. Declippel. See, CIA file on Antonio Soto Vazquez, available at https://www.maryferrell.org/showDoc.html?docId=147905&relPageId=21, accessed 22 August 2019. Antonio Soto was born in Mariano, Havana on 20 August 1934.

10 The six T-6s sent to the Congo were Harvard Mark 4 Canadian-built models. See, Michael Hingston, *Renegade Hero: the true story of RAF pilot Terry Peet and his clandestine mercy flying with the CIA* (Barnsley, UK: Pen and Sword Books Ltd, 2011), p.94.

11 *Cold War in the Congo*, p.69.

12 Mike Hoare, *The Road to Kalamata: A Congo Mercenary's Personal Memoir* (Boulder: Colorado: Paladin Press, 1989), p.19.

13 *Renegade Hero*, p.125.

14 *Air America: The explosive true story of the CIA's secret airline,* p.89.

15 "Leopoldville 1957: Battle of the Breweries", available at http://kosubaawate.blogspot.com/2016/01/leopoldville-1957-battle-of-breweries.html, accessed 22 August 2019.

16 Cosme commanded a B-26 codenamed "Linda One" at the Bay of Pigs.

17 Maza was the navigator on "Linda Three" at the Bay of Pigs.

18 Mario Ginebra was the commander of this CIA unit. He was born in Camaguey, Cuba on 26 July 1933.

19 Rafael Garcia was the navigator on "Gorilla One" at the Bay of Pigs.

20 Nildo Batista was the navigator on "Linda One".

21 Solís was the co-pilot of a C-46 numbered "855" at the Bay of Pigs. This aircraft dropped paratroopers close to the San Blas

junction north of Playa Girón. See, Joe Leeker "Air America at the Bay of Pigs", available at https://www.utdallas.edu/library/specialcollections/hac/cataam/Leeker/history/BayOfPigs.pdf, p.31.

22 Luaices was the captain of a C-46 numbered "788" at the Bay of Pigs. See, "Air America at the Bay of Pigs", p.31.

23 Joaquin Vieytes Varela was born in Havana on 17 February 1933. He was married with one child.

24 See https://www.cia.gov/library/readingroom/docs/DOC_0000141186.pdf, accessed 19 August 2019.

25 Francisco Ginebra Groero was the gunner on a C-54 codenamed "Falcon One" at the Bay of Pigs. See Edward B. Ferrer, *Operation Puma: The Air Battle of the Bay of Pigs* (International Aviation Consultants Inc., 1982), p.207.

26 "Letter from the Under Secretary of State for Political Affairs (Harriman) to the Deputy Secretary of Defense (Vance)", Washington, 18 March 1964, FRUS, *Congo*,1964-1968, Vol. XXIII, D161.

27 "Letter from the Under Secretary of State for Political Affairs (Harriman) to the Deputy Secretary of Defense (Vance)".

28 "Report Prepared in the Central Intelligence Agency", *Status report on CIA Assistance to the Congolese Air Force*, Washington, 5 May 1964, FRUS, *Congo*,1964-1968, Vol. XXIII, D168.

29 "Report Prepared in the Central Intelligence Agency".

30 "Air America at the Bay of Pigs", p.34.

31 Adapted from "Non-US Military T-28s", available at http://www.det156sow.com/download/t_28_non_us_military.pdf, accessed 22 August 2019.

32 *Renegade Hero*, p.92.

33 *Wings of the CIA*, pp.242-244.

34 Cereceda captained a C-54 codenamed "Falcon Three" at the Bay of Pigs. See, "Air America at the Bay of Pigs", p.32.

35 Except for five B-26Ks, the CIA drew four older, non-overhauled B-26Bs from USAF's stocks, for deployment in the Congo. All were in poor condition and one has never left Okinawa, while another crashed at RAF Khormaksar, outside Aden, during delivery flight. Of the two that eventually reached the Congo, one was used as a source of spares, while the other – serial number 44-35890 – was rarely flown: if, then for reconnaissance purposes, earning itself the ironic nick-name 'U-3' (in allusion to the famous Lockheed U-2, operated in another CIA-run operation at the same time).

36 Stephen Rookes, *Ripe for Rebellion: Congolese Political and Military Insurgency in the Congo, 1946-1964* (Warwick: Helion & Company, 2020).

37 Due to their sometimes arbitrary nature, a certain degree of caution should be taken when looking for any hidden meaning in the CIA's cryptonyms. However, we can speculate that the commando operation was given codenamed Pegasus for the following reason. In Greek mythology, Pegasus is mounted by Bellerophon in order to defeat the Chimera. The latter being usually depicted as a lion, we can wonder if there is, indeed, a reference to the Simba (lions). Pegasus is also one of the offspring of Poseidon. We will remind ourselves that Poseidon used a three-pronged fork to defeat his enemies and that this symbol was used by the MRR.

38 "List of nineteen Cubans in Congo under WIPEGASUS", NARA Record Number: 104-101104-10069, accessed 28 August 2019.

39 Glenn Garvin, "Anniversary recalls Congo rescue by Miami Cubans", *Miami Herald,* 15 November, 2014.

40 Correspondence with David McAllister, 29 August, 2017.

Chapter 6

1 "Soviet Sees Plot by West in Congo; Tells UN Council Tshombe is Puppet of 'Monopolies – Accuses US Banks", *New York Times*, 18 December 1964.

2 William Attwood, *The Reds and the Blacks: A Personal Adventure* (New York: Harper and Row, 1967), p.218.

3 Reed, *111 Days in Stanleyville* (London: Collins, 1966), pp.269-270.

4 Leo Zeilig, David Renton, and David Seddon, *The Congo: Plunder and Resistance* (London: Zed Books, 2006), p.106.

5 "Speech of Dr. Fidel Castro at the UN General Assembly, September 1960", available at http://www1.lanic.utexas.edu/project/castro/db/1960/19600926.html, accessed 23 June 2018.

6 Piero Gleijeses, "Cuba's First Venture in Africa: Algeria, 1961-1965,*Journal of Latin American Studies*, 1996, p.160.

7 *The Congo: Plunder and Resistance*, p.106.

8 "Cuba Began Role in Zanzibar in '61: Havana's Part in Revolution Outlined in Washington – Guerilla Course Cited", *New York Times*, 2 January 1964.

9 John Lee Anderson, *Che Guevara: A Revolutionary Life* (London: Bantam Press, 1997).

10 *Che Guevara: A Revolutionary Life*, p.615.

11 "Ernesto Guevara speech in Santiago de Cuba, 30 November, 1964", available at http://www.politique-actu.com/dossier/ernesto-guevara-discours-historique-anniversaire/1702290/, accessed 3 June 2018.

12 "Ernesto Guevara speech in Santiago de Cuba, 30 November, 1964".

13 "Ernesto Guevara's speech of 11 December, 1964 at the 19th Assembly of the United Nations in New York", in *The Che Reader*, Ocean Press, 2005.

14 "Ernesto Guevara's speech of 11 December, 1964 at the 19th Assembly of the United Nations in New York".

15 Cuba had been formally expelled from the OAS on 14 February, 1962. See, "OAS Expels Cuba After Delegates Stalk Out", *Chicago Daily Tribune*, 15 February 1962.

16 John Dumbrell, *President Johnson and Soviet Communism* (Manchester: Manchester University Press, 2012), p.146.

17 *Che Guevara: A Revolutionary Life*, p.619.

18 See "Letter from Roberto Gonzales Gomez, 7 July 1994", in Piero Gleijeses, "Cuba's First Venture in Africa: Algeria, 1961-1965",*Journal of Latin American Studies*, Vol.28, No.1, February 1996, p.161.

19 "Guevara Receives Rousing Welcome", *Ghanaian Times*, 16 January 1965, in Dennis Laumann, Che Guevara's Visit to Ghana, *Transactions of the Historical Society of Ghana*, New Series, No. 9, 2005, pp.61-74.

"Guevara Receives Rousing Welcome", p.61.

20 "Guevara Receives Rousing Welcome", p.61.

21 According to British historian Richard Gott, for many years the *Guardian's* correspondent in Latin America, and an historian who met Guevara in Cuba in 1963, Massamba-Débat had asked Guevara to provide Cuban military assistance to Pierre Mulele. See Richard Gott's introduction to Ernesto "Che" Guevara, *The African Dream: The Diaries of the Revolutionary War in the Congo* (London: Harvill Press, 2001).

22 It was during meetings with the latter that Guevara promised support for the MPLA through the provision of military advisors who would operate from the Angolan enclave of Cabinda. It was the beginning of Cuban intervention in Angola which would last for over two decades. For Gleijeses a detailed account of Cuba's involvement in Angola, see Piero Gleijeses, *Conflicting Missions: Havana, Washington, and Africa, 1959-1976* (North Carolina: North Carolina University Press, 2003).

23 "Ernesto Guevara's speech at the Afro-Asian Conference in Algeria", 24 February, 1965, The Che Reader, Ocean Press, 2005, available at https://www.marxists.org/archive/guevara/1965/02/24.htm, accessed 3 June 2019.

24 "Ernesto Guevara's speech at the Afro-Asian Conference in Algeria".

25 "Ernesto Guevara's speech at the Afro-Asian Conference in Algeria".

26 Anderson, *Che Guevara: A Revolutionary Life*, p.625.

27 "Ernesto Guevara's speech at the Afro-Asian Conference in Algeria".

28 Edward George, *The Cuban Intervention in Angola, 1965-1991: From Che Guevara to Cuito Cuanavale* (New York & London, Frank Cass, 2005), p.25.

29 Anderson, *Che Guevara: A Revolutionary Life*, p.627.

30 Anderson, *Che Guevara: A Revolutionary Life*, p.627.

31 "Memorandum from Robert W. Kromer of the National Security Council to the President's Special Assistant for National Security Affairs (Bundy)", 26 January, 1965, Johnson Library, National Security File, Country File, Congo, Vol. X, Cables, Memos & Miscellaneous, 12/64, Secret.

32 "Memorandum from Robert W. Kromer of the National Security Council to the President's Special Assistant for National Security Affairs (Bundy)".

33 "Memorandum from Harold H. Saunders of the National Security Council Staff to President Johnson", 25 February, 1965, Johnson Library, National Security File, Congo, Vol. XI, Memos & Miscellaneous, 1/65-9/65, Secret.

34 "Memorandum from Harold H. Saunders of the National Security Council Staff to President Johnson".

35 "Memorandum from Harold H. Saunders of the National Security Council Staff to President Johnson".

36 "Memorandum for the Record", 26 January, 1965, FRUS, Volume XXIII, *Congo*, D392.

37 George H. Dodenhoff, "The Congo: A Case Study of Mercenary Employment", *Naval College Review*, April 1969, p.61.

38 Clines was a highly-decorated veteran of the Korean War, Clines was involved in covert operations in Cuba between 1961-1962, and had worked with Ted Shackley, David Atlee Phillips, and David Morales at the CIA's JM/WAVE in Miami. According to Trento, Clines also had close ties to Nicaragua's President Somoza, and it was the friendship between the two which had enabled the CIA to train anti-Castro Cubans for the Bay of Pigs invasion. Later, when a revolt threatened Somoza's regime, anti-Castro Cubans were used to put it down. See, Joseph J. Trento, *Prelude to Terror: Edwin P. Wilson and the Legacy of America's Private Intelligence Network* (New York: Carrol & Graf Publishers, 2005), p.134.

39 A pseudonym used by James Hawes and Mary Ann Koenig, see *Cold War Navy Seal: Che Guevara, CIA Black Ops, and My Experience as the First Seal in Africa* (New York: Skyhorse Publishing, 2018). It is possible that 'Jordy McKay' is the 'Jaques Noel' referred to by Hoare in *Congo Mercenary*, p.240. Hoare speaks of Noel being assigned to G3 (operations) in Léopoldville, and tells of how Noel outlined the tactical picture in the Fizi-Baraka pocket. The G3 section of military staff is responsible for operations and training. Equally, it is possible that Hoare, too, has used a pseudonym to protect the identity of the person in question.

40 *Cold War Navy Seal: Che Guevara, CIA Black Ops, and My Experience as the First Seal in Africa*, p.22.

41 Andrew Hudson states that these boats were Chris Craft P boats. See, *Congo Unraveled: Military Operations from Independence to the Mercenary Revolt, 1960-1968*, p.55.

42 Mike Hoare, *Congo Mercenary* (Colorado: Paladin Press, 2008), p.239.

43 *Congo Mercenary*, p.239.

44 *Congo Mercenary*, p.240.

45 James Bamford, *Body of Secrets: Anatomy of the Ultra-Secret National Security Agency* (First Anchor Books, 2002), pp.159-160.

46 *The African Dream: The Diaries of the Revolutionary War in the Congo*, pp.5-7.

47 *The African Dream: The Diaries of the Revolutionary War in the Congo*, p.8.

48 Nasser told Guevara that he should not become directly involved in the Congo conflict. In Nasser's view, if Guevara thought he could be like "Tarzan, a white man among blacks, leading and protecting them", he was wrong. See, *Che Guevara: A Revolutionary Life*, p.623.

49 *Che Guevara: A Revolutionary Life*, p.622.

50 Dreke had fought alongside Guevara most notably in the battle to take control of Santa Clara on 31 December, 1958. Two years later, and after three days of fighting, he was captured by members of Brigade 2506 at the Bay of Pigs, only to be released at the end of the failed invasion. See, "Victor Dreke Cruz: Cuba's history man still talks of revolution", *The Independent*, 17 April, 2011.

51 Edward George, *The Cuban Intervention in Angola, 1965-1991: From Che Guevara to Cuito Cuanavale* (London: Routledge, 2012), p.25.

52 According to *Che Guevara: A Revolutionary Life*, p.639, Castro had already informed Alexander Alexiev, the Soviet Ambassador to Cuba, of the mission. Castro swore Alexiev to secrecy and asked him not to communicate this information to the Kremlin but, as George notes in *The Cuban Intervention in Angola, 1965-1991: From Che Guevara to Cuito Cuanavale* , p.308, Castro would have been in little doubt that the ambassador would do so.

53 Jihan El Tahri, *Cuba: une odyssée africaine* (Paris: Editions Arte), 28.27 – 29.00.

54 *Cuba: une odyssée africaine*, 28.27 – 29.00.

55 "Farewell letter from Che to Fidel Castro" 1 April, 1965, available at https://www.marxists.org/archive/guevara/1965/04/01.htm, accessed 23 June 2018.

56 *African Dream*, p.10.

57 *The Cuban Intervention in Angola, 1965-1991: From Che Guevara to Cuito Cuanavale*, p.26.

58 Asymmetric warfare is warfare between forces of different sizes and different capabilities. Ostensibly smaller or weaker military forces will use unconventional tactics to overcome what is perceived as a larger or stronger force. An irregular form of warfare, 'asymmetric warfare' can be used to describe guerilla warfare or insurgencies.

59 Ernesto Che Guevara, *Guerilla Warfare: A Method* (Peking: Foreign Language Press, 1964).

60 *Guerilla Warfare: A Method*, pp.9-10.

61 *Guerilla Warfare: A Method*, p.16.

62 *Guerilla Warfare: A Method*, p.26.

63 The Rwandans in question were members of the Bafulero tribe. In 1965, this tribe which had settled in the South Kivu region of the Congo and which supported Mulele was opposed to Tshombe as a result of ANC reprisals. Taking advantage of the anger of the Bafulero, the CNL offered its support in the Bafulero's tribal conflict with another Rwandan tribe residing in the Congo, the Banyamulenge. See, Thomas Odom, "Dragon Operations: Hostage Rescues in the Congo, 1964-1965", Leavenworth Papers, Number 14, *Combat Studies Institute*, Fort Leavenworth, Kansas, 1986, p.7, and René Lemarchand, "The Democratic Republic of Congo: From Collapse to Potential Reconstruction", Occasional Paper, Centre of African Studies, University of Copenhagen, September 2001, p.57.

64 "The Democratic Republic of Congo: From Collapse to Potential Reconstruction", p.22.

65 Victor Dreke, *From Escambray to the Congo: In the Whirlwind of the Cuban Revolution* (Pathfinder Press, 2002), p.141.

66 *African* Dream, p.18.

67 *African Dream*, p.43.

68 *African Dream*, pp.25-28.

69 *African Dream*, p.68.

70 *African Dream*, pp.33-34.

71 Pablo Pérez-Cisneros, John B. Donovan and Jeff Koenreich, *After the Bay of Pigs: Lives and Liberty on the Line* (Miami: Alexandria Library, 2007), pp.216-226.

72 E. Howard Hunt, *Give Us This Day* (New York: Popular Library Edition, 1973), p.221.

73 This was normal procedure in the absence of background checks.

74 "Memorandum from Secretary of Defense McNamara to President Kennedy", Washington, 13 September 1962, FRUS 1961-1963, *Cuba*, Vol.X, January 1961-September 1962, D426.

75 "Memorandum from Secretary of Defense McNamara to President Kennedy", D246.

76 "Memorandum from Secretary of Defense McNamara to His Special Assistant (Yarmolinsky)", Washington, 5 May 1961, FRUS, 1961-1963, Vol.X, *Cuba*, January 1961-September 1962, D207.

77 Interview with Felix Rodriguez, 8 September 2019.

78 "Movimento de Recuperacion Revolucionario", United States National Archives, NARA Record Number 180-10141-10366, accessed 19 September 2019.

79 "From Chief, WH Division to Chiefs, Certain Stations and Bases: Book Dispatch AMWORLD-Background of Program, Operational Support, Requirements and Procedural Rules", 28 June 1963, CIA Record Number 104-10315-10004, accessed 19 September 2019.

80 "Maritime Assets", RIF Number 104-10241-10136, maryferrell.org, accessed 19 September 2019.

81 The *Olga Patricia* was originally known as the USS *Deal*. Built in 1944 and acquired by the US Navy in 1947, it saw service in the Korean War where it was used to carry American dead back to the United States. Entering civilian service and renamed the *Laissez Faire* in 1966, it was then anchored off the coast of Essex in the United Kingdom and used as a base for pirate radio stations. See, "Olga Patricia=Laissez Faire, at https://web.archive.org/web/20120504052446/http://www.offshore-radio.de/fleet/laissez.htm, accessed 19 September 2019.

82 The cryptonym AMRUM provides an interesting insight into how operations, organisations and personalities came to be codenamed. Indeed, AMRUM refers to José Pepin Bosch, the director of Bacardi's operations outside Cuba after Fidel Castro exiled the family and seized the company's properties in 1960. Bosch was a friend of Augusto Valdes Miranda, an exile in charge of Operation Pepe in 1962. Operation Pepe was another attempt by the MRR to stir up rebellion in the mountains of the Sierra Maestra.

83 "Maritime Assets".

84 "Maritime Assets".

85 "Cable: My Joann left Baltimore Port, 1 December A.M.", RIF 104-10077-10244, maryferrell.org, accessed 19 September 2019.

86 Helga Silva, "Profile of Manuel Artime", *Miami News*, 2 July 1977.

87 "Contact Report #15, Pass Instructions Re. Procurement of Material Next Meeting", RIF 104-10275-10051, maryferrell.org, accessed 19 September 2019.

88 "Movimento Recuperacion Revolucionario, 1962-1964" Miami, Florida, 18 May 1964, United States Department of Justice, Federal Bureau of Investigation. Documents obtained through request made under Freedom of Information-Privacy Acts Section of the FBI, 13 November 1984.

89 "Movimento de Recuperacion Revolucionario", United States National Archives, NARA Record Number 180-10141-10365, accessed 19 September 2019.

90 "Movimento de Recuperacion Revolucionario".

91 "Memorandum from the President's Special Assistant for National Security Affairs (Bundy) to President Johnson, 25 August, 1965", Johnson Library, National Security File, Country File, *Congo*, Vol. XI, Memos & Miscellaneous, 1/65-9/65, Secret, available at https://history.state.gov/historicaldocuments/frus1964-68v23/d426, accessed 20 September 2019.

92 "Memorandum for President Johnson, 29 September 1965", *US Covert Support for Congolese Government on Lake Tanganyika*, National Security Council, Intelligence Files, *Congo*, 1960-1965, Secret; Eyes Only.

93 "Memorandum for President Johnson, 29 September 1965".

94 "Memorandum for President Johnson, 29 September 1965".

95 "Memorandum for President Johnson, 29 September 1965".

96 According to Shawn Dorman, "The country team meeting represents a regular occasion for the sharing of information among sections and agencies, and an opportunity to coordinate activities. It is where the ambassador can give instructions, share new priorities, request input or feedback, and be briefed on what is going on in the country and throughout the mission." See "Part II, Foreign Service Work and Life: Embassy, Employee, Family", available at https://www.afsa.org/sites/default/files/iuse_country_team_local_staff_role.pdf, accessed 20 September 2019.

97 The Patrol Craft Fast (PCF) or Swift Boat. Conceived by the Naval Advisory Group, Military Assistance Command, Vietnam (NAVADGRP MACV), this was an aluminium boat made by Sewart Seacraft of Berwick, Louisiana used for patrols along the coastal and interior waterways of Vietnam.

98 "Memorandum from the Chief of the Africa Division, Directorate of Plans, Central Intelligence Agency (Fields) to the Deputy Director of Plans (Fitzgerald)", Washington, 30 August 1965, FRUS, Congo, 1960-1968, Vol.XIII, D427.

99 *Cold War, Navy Seal: My Story of Che Guevara, War in the Congo, and the Communist Threat in Africa*, p.30-31.

100 Now Pinal Airpark.

101 Possibly a pseudonym.

102 *Cold War, Navy Seal: My Story of Che Guevara, War in the Congo, and the Communist Threat in Africa*, p.35.

103 *Cold War, Navy Seal: My Story of Che Guevara, War in the Congo, and the Communist Threat in Africa*, p.36.

104 *Prelude to Terror: Edwin Wilson and the Legacy of America's Private Intelligence Networks* p.134.

105 Giles Foden, *Mimi and Toutou Go Forth: The Bizarre Battle for Lake Tanganyika* (London: Penguin, 2005), pp.241-245.

106 *Cold War in the Congo: The Confrontation of Cuban Military Forces, 1960-1967*, p.149.

107 *Cold War in the Congo: The Confrontation of Cuban Military Forces, 1960-1967*, p.149.

108 *Cold War, Navy Seal*, p.57.

109 Alvarez was accused of plotting terrorist activities against Fidel Castro in 2005 and served two and a half years in prison.

110 Born in Colón in Cuba's Matanzas Province in 1933, Reyes joined the MRR in 1960. After arriving in Miami in August, 1961, Reyes was to take part in several covert missions on the Cuban mainland in 1963 and 1964 alongside fellow crew members, Generoso Bringas, Serapio Cepedo. A quiet man in his early 80s when interviewed, the reaction of fellow Exiles to his death in 2017 was testament to the esteem in which this man was held. Many of the operations in which Reyes was to take part are yet to be revealed. 'Papo' passed away in 2017.

111 Interviews carried out in Miami, 24 October 2015.

112 Cold War, Navy Seal, p.72.

113 Tom Archdeacon, "Arch: CIA to award Navy operative highest honor", *Dayton Daily News*, 21 May, 2016.

114 Interview with Felix Toledo.

115 *African Dream*, p.192.

116 *African Dream*, p.200.

Chapter 7

1 "Telegram from the Department of State to the Embassy in the Congo", Washington, 12 April 1965, FRUS, *Congo*, D414.

2 Emizet François Kisangani, *Historical Dictionary of the Democratic Republic of the Congo* (New York: Rowmand & Littelfield), p.166.

3 "Telegram from the Station in the Congo to the Central Intelligence Agency".

4 "Memorandum for the 303 Committee", FRUS, Volume XXIII, 23 November, 1965, Document 450.

5 "Information Memorandum from the Deputy Assistant of State for African Affairs (Fredericks) to Secretary of State Rusk", Washington, 31 May 1966, FRUS, *Congo*, D471.

6 "Memorandum from the President's Special Assistant (Rostow) to President Johnson", Washington, 13 July 1967, FRUS, *Congo*, D524.

7 "Memorandum from the Deputy Secretary of Defense's Military Assistant (Greenleaf) to the Deputy Secretary of Defense (Vance)", Washington, 3 June 1966, FRUS, *Congo*, D472.

8 "Memorandum from Edward Hamilton of the National Security Council Staff to the President's Special Assistant (Rostow)".

9 The mercenaries included Belgium's Major Wauthier, France's Lieutenant Gouault and Germany's Commandant Wilhem.

10 Jeswald W. Salacuse, "The National Land Law System of Zaire", A Report to the University of Wisconsin in Land Tenure Center and USAID/Kinshasa, May 1985, http://pdf.usaid.gov/pdf_docs/PNAAT376.pdf, accessed 2 September 2017.

11 "Mobutu and the Congo", Directorate of Intelligence, Weekly Review, 23 June 1967, p.6, available at https://www.cia.gov/library/readingroom/docs/DOC_0000680536.pdf, accessed 2 October 2019.

12 "Memorandum from the Board of National Estimates to Director of Central Intelligence McCone", Washington, 27 January 1967, FRUS, Congo, D488.

13 *Cold War in the Congo*, p.183.

Appendix II

1 Source: As noted on document.

About the Author

Originally from Exeter in Devon, Dr. Stephen Rookes has spent more than half his life living and working in France. He gained his PhD from the University of Toulouse Jean-Jaurès and specialises in the history of the Congo, Cuban exiles and the use of mercenaries in conflict. Rookes is Associate Professor at the Ecole de l'Air (French Air Force Academy) in Salon-de-Provence, and this is his second book for Helion's @War series.